COHERENCE AND VERIFICATION IN ETHICS

RALPH D. ELLIS, PH.D
Associate Professor of Philosophy
Clark-Atlanta University

UNIVERSITY
PRESS OF
AMERICA

Lanham • New York • London

Copyright © 1992 by
University Press of America®, Inc.
4720 Boston Way
Lanham, Maryland 20706

3 Henrietta Street
London WC2E 8LU England

All rights reserved
Printed in the United States of America
British Cataloging in Publication Information Available

Library of Congress Cataloging-in-Publication Data

Ellis, Ralph D.
Coherence and verification in ethics / Ralph D. Ellis.
p. cm.
Includes bibliographical references and index.
1. Ethics. I. Title.
BJ1012.E37   1991   170—dc20   91-22406 CIP

ISBN 0-8191-8410-1 (hardback, alk. paper)
ISBN 0-8191-8411-X (paperback, alk. paper)

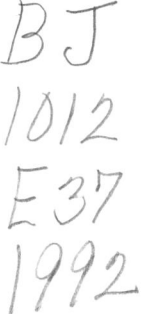

 The paper used in this publication meets the minimum requirements of American National Standard for Information Sciences—Permanence of Paper for Printed Library Materials, ANSI Z39.48–1984.

TABLE OF CONTENTS

PART I---THE VERIFICATION PROBLEM IN ETHICS ... 1

CHAPTER ONE---INTUITIONS AND EMOTIONS ... 1

1. Logical Positivism ... 5
   - (a) The received doctrines: Emotivism and prescriptivism ... 5
   - (b) Modified positivism in combination with a coherence theory of verification ... 11
   - (c) The inadequacies of positivism ... 13

2. Phenomenology ... 17
   - (a) The received doctrine: Phenomenological reduction through imaginative variation ... 17
   - (b) Phenomenological intuitionism ... 20
   - (c) Phenomenological anthropologism ... 23

CHAPTER TWO---COHERENTISM AND IS-OUGHT RELATIONS ... 33

1. Comparative Coherentism and Factual Adequacy ... 35
   - (a) Can an 'ought' contradict an 'is'? ... 38
   - (b) Complications in the coherence criteria ... 44
   - (c) Must there be any value? ... 52

2. The Elimination of Nihilism ... 59
   - (a) A brief review of criticisms of Gewirth ... 59
   - (b) The sense in which the value of consciousness is undeniable ... 62

3. Cumulative Summary and Transition ... 71

PART II---METAETHICAL IMPLICATIONS OF PSYCHOLOGICAL FACTS ... 77

CHAPTER THREE---FIRST FACT: THE MOTIVATION TO BE MORAL ... 77

1. The Problem of Egoism ... 79
   - (a) Inadequacy of received solutions ... 81
   - (b) Toward a workable solution ... 90

2. The Motivation for Altruism ... 92
   - (a) Consciousness must avoid stasis ... 92
   - (b) Consciousness requires symbolization and thus intersubjectivity ... 99
   - (c) Universalized altruism as the motivation to seek moral truth ... 103

TABLE OF CONTENTS

CHAPTER FOUR---SECOND FACT: THE ETIOLOGY OF PERSONALITY ... 109

1. Psychological Determinism ... 112
   (a) Toward a relevant definition ... 114
   (b) The argument ... 116

2. Ethical Implications ... 122
   (a) Compatibilism and the word 'can' ... 122
   (b) To the real ethical matters: the concept of 'ought' ... 127
   (c) The concept of 'desert' ... 130
   (d) The concept of 'responsibility' ... 135

PART III---ELIMINATIONS AND COMPARISONS OF THEORIES ... 145

CHAPTER FIVE---ETHICAL QUESTIONS WITH DEFINITE RESOLUTIONS ... 145

1. Definitions ... 146
   (a) Problems in defining ethical terms ... 146
   (b) Adequately comprehensive definitions of key terms ... 155

2. Qualitative Value Questions ... 162
   (a) Individual values ... 173
   (b) Aggregate value ... 174

3. Questions About the Source of Values ... 181

CHAPTER SIX---ETHICAL QUESTIONS REQUIRING COMPARATIVE-COHERENCE RESOLUTIONS ... 187

1. The Inevitability of Moral Conflict ... 188

2. The Mathematicization of Value ... 196

3. The Problem of the Value of Future Possible Conscious Beings ... 205

4. The Mathematical Commensurability of the Values of Use Value Maximization and Deontic Fairness ... 208

5. The Theoretical Incompleteness of the System ... 218

6. Quantitative Questions About Duties and Oughts ... 219

7. Conclusion ... 227

APPENDIX ... 231

FOREWORD

This book is meant both as an original theory of the justification of ethical beliefs and as a textbook in theoretical ethics. The method proposed is especially suited to serve this dual purpose because it is a coherence method which involves comparing various kinds of ethical theories with each other to see which ones come off better with respect to such criteria as consistency, parsimony, eschewal of ad hoc hypotheses, and adequacy to facts, especially psychological facts---in short, with respect to the 'comparative coherence' of theories.

Teachers using the book at relatively introductory levels or for non-philosophy majors may wish to have students skip section 1 of Chapter Two, which is a somewhat technical defense against objections to the method of comparative coherentism. For professional philosophers, graduate students and advanced undergraduates, on the other hand, this may well be the most interesting section.

I am indebted to the editors of *The Southern Journal of Philosophy, Journal of Value Inquiry* and *Philosophical Inquiry* for allowing me to use portions of some previously published materials in more or less revised forms. I must also express gratitude to the friends and colleagues who contributed to the development of these ideas by means of their arguments and criticisms at various times and places. Most of the worthwhile aspects of the book are attributable primarily to them.

INTRODUCTION

Imagine a ship hopelessly lost at sea, wandering aimlessly, as far from its destination as from its starting point. To make matters worse, it finds itself surrounded on all sides by huge, sharp rocks waiting to smash its hull. Suddenly on the distant horizon, the captain spots the two legendary figures of Charybdis and Scylla. Imagine what a mixture of feelings this sight will provoke. On the one hand, the course between Charybdis and Scylla is a treacherous one, fraught with deadly perils. On the other hand, the fear of navigating such a pernicious course will be more than counteracted by the assurance that at least the captain now knows where we are. This knowledge means above all that, if only we can avoid being sucked into the whirlpools of Charybdis or devoured by the venomous Scylla, we can at last chart a course through what we now know to be the Straits of Messina and sail to our ultimate destination. We no longer must wander aimlessly.

This situation is precisely analogous to the one in which ethical theory finds itself in the late twentieth century. We wander aimlessly lost in a vast sea which we cannot identify or locate on our epistemological maps. Surrounding us on all sides are the sharp rocks of ethical relativisms, attempts to reduce moral values to emotional whims, a plethora of mutually-contradictory theories whose only epistemological basis is a claim to 'coherence' which they all share equally, and---the most razor-sharp reefs of all---positivist epistemologies that insist we can clarify statements but not confirm their truth. In their desperation, many of our crew are seduced by mirages masquerading as 'moral intuitions.'

Now add to this desolate scene the menacing Charybdis and Scylla toward which (I shall argue) we are drifting, and which we ultimately cannot avoid confronting. The Charybdis is the terrible whirlpool (some would say cesspool) of psychological determinism which, as soon as it sees the brash and inflammatory slogan emblazoned on our hull---'OUGHT IMPLIES CAN' ---threatens to swallow whole the vessel of ethics, subsequently to spew forth its material pieces bereft of the all-too-human crew. We shudder and cringe in hopes that we can avoid confronting this Charybdis directly, because we suspect that, if and to the extent that determinism is true, it is a waste of time to tell people that they ought to do anything, since it has already been predetermined that they are either going to do it or not do it; nor would it seem right to hold them responsible for their moral violations. (To add insult to injury, determinism also threatens to rob us of two of the foremost pleasures of the moral seafaring life---flogging our crew-mates for their faults, and riding the foretop of self-righteousness. But the possible sacrifice of these pleasures must become a matter of stoic indifference in the context of the crisis at hand.)

The Scylla we face is a two-headed monster consisting of the 'is-ought' dilemma and the closely related question, 'Why be moral?' Both these questions threaten to devour all moral oughts, leaving in their place only the dead skeletons of egoistic oughts. Then moral philosophy will no longer be moral philosophy, but only a sophisticated way to calculate how to get what one wants---a kind of amateur empirical psychology. It seems impossible to avoid one of these mythic perils without venturing dangerously close to the other. If we deny determinism, then we can develop a 'formalistic' moral theory that emphasizes blame, guilt, and the responsibility of the individual. Then we might be able to say, with Kant,

> When someone who delights in annoying and vexing peace-loving folk receives at last a right good beating,...everyone approves of it and considers it as good in itself *even if nothing further results from it;* nay, even he who gets the beating must acknowledge in his reason, that justice has been done to him, because he sees the proportion between welfare and well-doing....[1](Italics added.)

The problem is that, because of the 'is-ought' dilemma, we cannot demonstrate that any such ethical system is *true and thus binding.* Kant's attempt in this direction was no more adequate than is Gewirth's, as will be discussed in due course.[2] Thus such systems also do not answer the question 'Why be moral?' On the other hand, if we avoid Scylla and succeed in deriving an 'ought' from an 'is', we do so only by corrupting the 'ought' into an 'is'---i.e., a psychological preference or emotional whim. This is the worst problem confronting 'non-formal' or 'material' theories of value such as Scheler's, as well as utilitarianism and emotivism.[3] Moreover, if ethics consists only of telling people that they ought to do whatever they are motivated to do, then we are essentially driven back into the whirlpools of determinism, since we are then only telling people to do what they were going to do anyway.

Yet the captain of a lost ship should welcome the sight of these two monsters, for they are the landmarks that help us plot our course and figure out where we are. In fact, it is lucky that the Charybdis and Scylla stand so close together. For the closer together they stand, the closer we come to being able to choose a unique course between them. Previously, the possibilities were infinite, and for that very reason we had absolutely no indication in which direction lay the correct ethical theory. Thus there was no more reason to believe in one theory than another. But now that the possibilities have suddenly become so limited, we can immediately eliminate all directions of thought that would head us on a collision course with the Charybdis awaiting all those theories that cannot reconcile themselves to determinism in one way or another, or with the Scylla poised to devour all those theories which claim that we should seek X because it is human nature to seek X, i.e., which would reduce 'ought' to 'is'. After eliminating this vast array of possibilities, we no longer have nearly such a problem in choosing from among a vast diversity of theories; the problem is to discover whether *even one* course can be charted through these treacherous straits.

The purpose of this book is to outline the conditions for the possibility of charting such a course toward a new and (what cannot be overemphasized) *demonstrable* system of metaethics---and to make some headway in the charting process itself. To summarize in advance some of the crucial points (the details of the arguments, of course, must await the body of the text): The first condition for the possibility of a demonstrably true ethical theory (i.e., demonstrable even with a certain degree of probability) is that human nature must be constituted in such a way that people are to some extent motivated to do whatever turns out to be morally right prior to the specific determination of what *is* right in the given circumstances. I.e., it cannot be that we are by nature motivated to go to Mecca, while at the same time it happens, coincidentally, that going to Mecca is right. In this case, it would become a waste of time to tell people that they ought to go to Mecca, since they are going there anyway. Worse still would be if we say that going to Mecca is right *because* we are by nature motivated to do so. In this case, ethics becomes merely a sophisticated calculation of how to get what one wants. Rather, we must be motivated to do whatever we decide is right and be prepared to either go to Mecca or stay home, depending on which is right; and this preference for doing-what-is-right-whatever-it-is must outweigh any preference we might have for going to Mecca or staying home based on reasons unrelated to our desire to do what is right. Only in this way can people be motivated to do what is right without the determination of what is right being grounded in emotional whims, and thus becoming trivialized by telling people that they ought to do what they were going to do anyway.

It does no good, for example, to say that we ought to empathize with our fellow man, and thus act in the ways prescribed by this empathy, based on the argument that fellow-feeling (or love, sympathy, identification or any other altruistic emotion) is part of human nature. Then we are merely describing human nature rather than prescribing what human nature should strive to become. But at the same time, we shall find that it is a condition for the possibility of ethics that each individual must have a motive to cultivate an empathy with all human beings, which then gives us a reason to be moral and makes moral action psychologically possible. No harm is done if this motive itself is prudential. For then, when we demonstrate to people that they ought to go to Mecca because it is morally right (objectively), they are motivated to do it out of a desire to do what is morally right (not out of a desire to go to Mecca per se); whereas, if we had demonstrated that they ought to stay home, then they would have been equally motivated to stay home because of the same desire to do what is morally right. We shall find that, fortunately, there is an authentic human motivation to do what is right, grounded in the need on consciousness' part to empathize with the abstract idea of 'conscious being' per se (not just with certain selected individuals); that, moreover, there is a (technically, prudential) reason for people to develop this empathic feeling to a greater extent than it has been so far; and that, if human nature were not constituted along these lines, no meaningful moral theory would be possible, because no solution to the problem of egoism could ever be united with a demonstrably true and binding moral theory.

When we say that people *could* not act morally if there were no authentic motivation to do what is right (though this motivation does not dictate what *is* right), and that in the absence of this motivation there could be no meaningful moral theory, we assume that there is some sense in which 'ought implies can.' Of the many ways in which this statement can be interpreted, we shall find that some are true and others are false. But one sense in which the statement must definitely be true, even if determinism is true and even if there is no compatibility between determinism and free will, is that what people are going to do cannot have been already predetermined *in such a way* that our demonstrating to a person on the basis of legitimate reasoning what she ought to do (or her demonstrating it to herself) has no power to affect what she is going to do since the latter has already been predetermined. It is not necessary either that determinism be false or that compatibilism be true in order for the 'ought implies can' in this sense to be accommodated. It is only necessary that the behavior not be predetermined *in such a way* that the truth about what should be done would be incapable of affecting the person's decision as to what she will do. The crucial thing is that the person *can* do what we tell her she ought to *if* we tell her she ought to, whereas she might not have done it if we had not told her she ought to. To put the same point in more individualistic terms, what is crucial is that the person *can* do what she ought to *if* she correctly discovers the truth about what she ought to do, whereas she might not have done it if she had not correctly discovered the truth about what she ought to do. Whether one does or does not believe in determinism or a compatibilism between determinism and freedom, of course, will affect one's thinking on such issues as guilt, blame, individual responsibility, desert, and other moral concepts.

Notice that we have just assumed that one's opinion on the questions of determinism and compatibilism (which, in the relevant sense, are *factual* opinions) will definitely affect one's *normative* opinion as to which ethical theory is the correct one. It is in this sense that the

INTRODUCTION

Charybdis of determinism is not only an obstacle, but also a welcome landmark that can help us chart our course. If we can reach factual conclusions on such issues as determinism and compatibilism, we thereby circumscribe and delimit our normative conclusions. So, in a very roundabout way, if we can string together enough such 'is' statements, they may well imply a system of 'oughts' after all, by increasingly narrowing the range of 'ought' systems that can possibly be true. They may at least narrow the range of such possible systems so that we are not left with an unmanageable array of theories all of which are equally coherent and thus equally likely to be true. Instead, we will be left with a small number of possible theories which can then be compared on the basis of their coherence in order to decide which one is most likely to be most nearly correct. Moreover, if some specific normative judgments are agreed to or implied by *all* ethical theories which are coherent and do not contradict factual truths, then these specific normative judgments must be regarded as true (if, that is, there are any true normative judgments at all, which also must be considered). This method of using 'ises' to guide us in charting a course toward the most viable possible system of 'oughts' is what I shall call the 'comparative coherence' strategy in ethical epistemology. The term 'coherence', however, must be defined a little differently from the way others have defined it. It must be defined in such a way that a 'coherent' theory is more likely to be true than a less coherent theory.

Granted, there would be little epistemological satisfaction in comparing different possible theories with each other if it is just as possible that they could all be mere pipe-dreams. To overcome this problem, it will be necessary to definitively overcome ethical nihilism, the possibility that there is nothing that one particularly ought to do, or that all 'ought' statements are meaningless. To eliminate this possibility, we must establish beyond reasonable doubt that at least one thing definitely has value, and that any attempt to deny that this thing has value must be false. Without attempting to oversimplify the argument in order to preliminarily summarize it in this introduction, perhaps the reader will allow me to do no more than hint at my conclusion at this point. The thing that can be definitely demonstrated to have value is the existence of conscious beings. The reader will immediately suspect some trick here ---perhaps that, like so many practitioners of the naturalistic fallacy, I am going to show that conscious existence has subjective or prudential value and then by equivocating pretend that I have demonstrated that it has objective and moral value. This objection will be considered in due course when the argument is developed. But once the conclusion that consciousness has value has been demonstrated, ethical nihilism can be rejected, although at that point ethical *egoism* will not yet have been rejected. Ethical nihilism is the view that there is nothing that one particularly ought to do. Ethical egoism holds that there is something one ought to do, namely whatever is in one's own self-interest.

As soon as ethical nihilism is rejected, we must then choose among all possible non-nihilistic theories by first eliminating those which conflict with facts (for example, they may imply a 'can' of which agents by their nature are incapable), and then choosing from the remaining theories the one that is most likely to be true because it is the most coherent. The reason coherence counts as a consideration which tends to increase the probability of a theory is essentially the same as in natural science. The probability that a unified theory with few initial postulates can accommodate a vast diversity of data *without being true* is smaller than the probability that a disunified theory with many initial postulates (functioning as ad hoc hypotheses) can accommodate the same diversity of data without being true. Therefore, all else being equal, the unified theory with few initial postulates is more likely to be true than the disunified theory with many initial postulates. It would be an oversimplification, however, to assume that we must completely embrace a theory simply because it is slightly more probable than the nearest rival theory. The situation becomes very complicated in this regard. For example, if there are N possible theories, then to accept a theory because it is only slightly more coherent than the nearest rival may mean accepting a theory whose probability is only slightly greater than 1/N, which is considerably less than the approximately (N-1)/N probability that this same theory is false. Thus we would be accepting a theory that is more likely to be false than true. It is for this kind of reason that any ethical theory which hopes to be demonstrable (and thus binding) must begin by establishing the truth---not merely the coherence---of at least one postulate beyond reasonable doubt. This consideration underscores the importance of demonstrating beyond reasonable doubt the value of conscious beings just mentioned, which requires no coherence comparisons or probability assessments to ground its truth. It is also the main reason we are likely to end up with a hybrid theory, containing a plurality of intrinsic values whose relative priority is ranked proportionally to (among other variables) the probability with which we know that the goods in question do indeed have value.

In short, the comparison of the probability of coherent theories must be saved as a last resort procedure. The first resort is to establish definitely that something (i.e., the existence of consciousness) has value, on which all minimally coherent theories must end up agreeing. The next step is to eliminate the problems of egoism by means of a phenomenological and logical analysis of the nature of conscious beings as such, without at the same time reducing all moral judgments by definition to egoistic ones. The third step is to eliminate all ethical theories not consistent with the facts about consciousness which will be discovered in this moral-psychological analysis. At this stage, the range of possibly correct theories will have been narrowed to the point where the disagreements between the remaining ones are minimal. And it is these remaining minimal disagreements that should in the end be entrusted to comparative-probability analyses, which are similar to what many metaethical theorists now think of as 'coherence criteria.'

An indispensable prerequisite for fulfilling any of these promises is obviously to lay as careful as possible a groundwork with regard to the epistemology of ethical beliefs. The two chapters of Part I will attempt to establish a general scheme for the accomplishment of this crucial task.

NOTES

[1] Immanuel Kant, *Critique of Practical Reason,* L.W. Beck trans. (New York: Bobbs-Merril, 1956), 40.

[2] See Chapter Two, section 2, and Chapter Five, section 2.

[3] See Chapter One, section 1 and section 2(c), and Chapter Three.

PART I

THE VERIFICATION PROBLEM IN ETHICS

CHAPTER ONE

INTUITIONS AND EMOTIONS

The early twentieth century trend toward 'analytic' philosophy, in the strictly positivistic sense, assumed that the essential purpose of philosophy was to clarify terminology and concepts. With regard to the natural sciences, this assumption meant that philosophy was not to discover scientific truths, but to leave that up to the scientists themselves through empirical methods. (The correct empirical methods, of course, had already been provided by philosophy in the form of the hypothetico-deductive method and the a priori assumptions of statistical reasoning. How these assumptions in turn were grounded was something of a mystery, but fortunately is not our immediate concern here.) In the realm of moral theory, however, it was not clear to whom the discovery of truth was to be left, or what method they were to use. So it might seem in retrospect to have been somewhat short-sighted for some analytic moral philosophers, such as R. M. Hare in his early work,[1] to have assumed that ordinary people somehow already knew the essential truth about ethics, and that the job of philosophy was simply to clarify their terminology for them. After all, what method were ordinary people to use to discover this truth, if not philosophy itself? It now seems inevitable that the analytic movement in ethics should have ended up where A. J. Ayer originally wanted it to end up---believing that, at bottom, there is no ethical truth to be found, that moral 'beliefs' are not really beliefs at all but only emotions masquerading as beliefs, and that the philosopher's job is simply to get people to acknowledge this fact.[2] Perhaps unfortunately, it might seem now that a generation of American philosophy teachers were somewhat successful in this endeavor, as Allan Bloom recently lamented.[3]

Now that the analytic movement has run its course, it is fairly easy to see that, if ordinary people did already know the truth about ethics, then there would be little need for moral philosophy, just as there would have been little need for the French Revolution or the American civil rights movement. No amount of mere clarification of terms or concepts will make people agree in the content and substance of their supposed 'moral intuitions' or 'considered moral judgments.' Yet if the persistence of this disagreement is interpreted to mean that moral beliefs are in their essence only confused emotions, then again there is no need for moral philosophy, for then there is no such thing as morality, as distinguished from a purely self-interested analysis of what one 'really' wants in life. The inquiry becomes a descriptive rather than a normative one.

A further development of the method of mere clarification of terms and concepts is to bring the individual's moral beliefs into 'reflective equilibrium,' so that any self-contradictions entailed by them can be eliminated.[4] But, although a non-self-contradictory belief is of course more likely to be correct than a self-contradictory one, this method still provides little epistemological basis for the beliefs in question, nor does it promise to resolve basic moral disputes. Those who clearly and self-consistently believe that the earth is flat will still fundamentally disagree with those who clearly and self-consistently believe that it is some other shape.[5] The proponent of reflective equilibrium will object that, if a flat-earther checks the implications of her belief against *all* her experiences, some of these implications do end up contradicting each other. But, strictly speaking, the implications of the belief do not contradict *each other;* they contradict scientific evidence that is empirically perceived. The problem is that ethical theory offers no analog for empirically-perceived scientific evidence. Rather, it offers only the often-equivocated term 'moral experience,' which is not analogous to scientific evidence at all, or at least has not been demonstrated to be analogous. For 'moral experience' seems to function in this context as a euphemism for either 'moral intuition' or 'emotional preference.' And anyone who has studied European history knows that beliefs that present themselves as moral intuitions are at least as often as not absurd prejudices whose popularity is no less incredible to us in retrospect than is their content. Even within a relatively homogeneous philosophical community, different people's intuitions, whether reduced to reflective equilibrium or not, utterly contradict each other on the most crucial issues. The need is obvious for some independent epistemological principle against which the validity of these 'intuitions' can be measured.

We must therefore return to the fundamental dilemma of moral epistemology. If ethical beliefs cannot be proven purely analytically (not even Gewirth can claim such an accomplishment, as we shall see), nor can such beliefs be empirically validated, then it seems that either they have no genuine truth value and are mere emotions, or we must ultimately depend on intuitions to reveal their truth. But to elevate moral intuitions (even within reflective equilibrium) into the fundamental source of moral truth is like trying to get light out of a black hole: It instantly cancels whatever effort we make in its behalf by indiscriminately sucking in the most mutually contradictory of 'truths'. On the other hand, if ethical beliefs were mere emotions, then all actions would be equally legitimate. Nor would there be much point in advising people as to what they 'ought' to do even in a prudential sense because, by definition in this case, people 'ought' to do whatever they want to do. It is not that the emotions have no place in moral deliberation. In fact, we shall see that their role is crucial. Intuitions too have their practical function in ethical inquiry, just as the intuition of a geometrical truth may be useful even before it is proven. But the claim that I intuit the truth of a theorem cannot be accepted as proof of the theorem when there are others who intuit that it is false.

Thus the notion that philosophy's purpose is merely to clarify the moral language that people use becomes absurd. J. J. C. Smart forcefully expressed the same point many years ago:

> I wish to repudiate at the outset that milk and water approach which describes itself sometimes as 'investigating what is implicit in the common moral consciousness' and sometimes as 'investigating how people ordinarily talk about morality.' We have only to read the newspaper correspondence about capital punishment or about what should be done with Formosa to realize that the common moral consciousness is in part made up of superstitious elements, of morally bad elements, and of logically confused elements...."The obligation to obey a rule," says Nowell-Smith (*Ethics*, p. 239), "does not, *in the opinion of ordinary men,*" (my italics), "rest on the beneficial consequences of obeying it in a particular case." What does this prove? Surely it is more than likely that ordinary men are confused here. Philosophers should be able to examine the question more rationally.[6]

My position will not be quite as cynical as Smart's. It is not that ordinary people have no knowledge of moral truth, but rather that the knowledge they do have is gained---either directly or indirectly, either formally or informally, and either consciously or in the backs of their minds---through philosophizing of one kind or another. So, just as a professional physicist would never defer to 'the ordinary physical consciousness,' though it is true that ordinary people do have some knowledge of physics, there would seem to be no good reason why philosophers should be constrained by the common moral consciousness. To be sure, there are ordinary individuals who have had philosophical insights which no philosopher would be likely to have unless led to it by the experiences of a peculiar life history which no philosopher may happen to share, just as there are Eskimos who can discern shades of white indistinguishable to most physicists. But it is precisely because such insights tend to arise from the *uniqueness* of an individual's situation in life that philosophers need to pay attention to them (the moral viewpoint of the homeless for example), not because they represent *common* moral opinions. Indeed, in an enlightened age when it is virtually inconceivable that a U.S.

presidential candidate with a Black running mate could have any hope of winning the election, one might almost regard too close an agreement with the 'common moral consciousness' as a sure sign that a philosophical theory of ethics has hit far off target.

If there is any such thing as truth in ethics, then it is obviously among the hardest of truths to come by, for, after thousands of years of intense inquiry by intelligent people, little agreement has been reached even as to whether there is any truth. And what little truth does seem tenuously supportable through rigorous argument spreads very slowly among the majority of people and institutions, for a variety of reasons which need not be discussed here. Humankind as a whole has probably made some progress in its thinking about some moral issues (racism, for example) since climbing down from the trees, and will probably make more progress if we continue to survive. But there seems at this point to be little that ethical theorists can gain by allowing ourselves to be either guided by or limited to the kinds of conclusions consistent with 'the common moral consciousness,' though that consciousness can and sometimes does understand them. It does not understand them, I shall argue, through some mystical intuition, but through the reason that is present in everyone, though we often choose not to use it. The question of the relationship between the emotions and moral deliberation, nonetheless, is an important and complex one which we shall have to consider in some detail later.

The important point at this juncture is to come to terms with the fact that both logical positivism and intuitionism in its various forms (ranging from naive to sophisticated) are inadequate as epistemological foundations for ethics. Furthermore, we must admit to ourselves that within the category of 'intuitionist' approaches must be included many philosophies which would rebel against the label, such as John Rawls' version of 'reflective equilibrium'---which requires that we assume at the outset that whatever is preferable to the person in the 'original position' is the same as what is morally preferable[7]---and most types of phenomenological approaches. Those phenomenological approaches which cannot be reduced ultimately to some form of intuitionism[8] tend to fall into the contrary difficulty: Essentially, they elevate mere emotional preferences on the part of consciousness to the status of moral values, thus eliminating any possible distinction between ethical theory and merely descriptive anthropology.[9]

It might not be too much of an overstatement, in fact, to say that ethical theory presently lacks any satisfactory epistemological basis whatever, unless one accepts the arguments of Gewirth or Searle to the effect that moral skepticism and ethical egoism are logically self-contradictory. But we shall see that most well-informed critics have with good reason rejected these arguments as well. The job of ethical epistemology is more difficult now than it must have seemed in earlier centuries, largely because those earlier philosophers did not really take seriously the possibility of ethical nihilism, though they sometimes pretended to. Kant, for example, assumed as a 'practical necessity' that life must have some meaning, and therefore that there must be some moral values.[10] His task then was only to *choose* among the various possible theories of moral value. It is much easier to choose among possible theories than to demonstrate that one or another theory is true. But citizens of contemporary culture seem ready enough to accept the notion that life has no ultimate moral significance, and then attempt to drown the resulting sorrow in egoistic hedonism. Even if this attempt ultimately is also doomed to failure, at least it does not demand an intellectual effort. But to reject out of hand all merely hedonistic or prudential systems simply because they are 'merely' hedonistic or prudential can no longer constitute an acceptable a priori assumption. Too many thinkers have now taken seriously the possibility that there may be no legitimate non-hedonistic values and have shown that the purely hedonistic and prudential options may not really be as repugnant as Kant thought. In any event, the fact that a proposition is emotionally repugnant is not an adequate reason to deem it false.

In these first two chapters, I shall argue that, if the only epistemological options available were (1) logical positivism as traditionally practiced, or (2) the phenomenological method as used by Hartmann and Scheler, or (3) intuitionism in its various forms, or (4) coherentism as currently conceived, or (5) the attempt to logically derive 'ought' from 'is' (what is now sometimes called 'rationalism' in ethics), no one of these options would be capable of bearing the burden of an adequate epistemological basis for ethics. However, each of these approaches, when used in the right way and given its proper place in the overall fabric of ethical epistemology, has an important and necessary contribution to make within a unified scheme for verifying ethical beliefs. Given the high stakes involved, it is worth the trouble to review some of the crucial weaknesses of these schools (some of which, after all, are still quite fashionable) so that we can salvage their strengths to be fitted into a more adequate epistemological framework.

1. *Logical Positivism*

   (a) The received doctrines: Emotivism and prescriptivism

   The traditional logical positivist approach to ethics begins with the basic insight that one main reason for the difficulty of verifying ethical statements is that ethical principles are not matters of fact. The rightness or wrongness of an action, or the desirability or undesirability of a state of affairs, can never be determined by any empirical observation or scientific measurement. If I throw a stone through a window, someone can measure the weight of the stone, the angle at which it hits, the money value of the damage done, and so forth; yet none of these measurements alone can reveal whether or not I should have thrown the stone. Empirical observation reveals what has happened in a given case, not whether it should have happened.

It is true that a few attempts have been made to define moral rightness in such a way that it could be revealed through observation,[11] but these attempts are now generally rejected, and with good reason. At first glance, Mill seems to define a moral term, 'desirable', in such a way that what is good, and therefore what is right, can be learned through empirical observation of what people actually desire.[12]

But the more thoroughly we analyse his argument, the more we realize that it is really just a coherent moral system based on a fundamental intuition. Mill thought the only reasonable way to define 'desirable' must be to observe what people actually desire, just as the only way to define 'enjoyable' is to discover what people in fact enjoy, and the only way to define 'lovable' is to find out what people in fact love. But this reasoning is based on a mere play of words, an accident of the English language, as Moore points out.[13] Choosing a different example of the suffix '-able' exposes the weakness of the argument. Obviously, it would be absurd to define 'edible' to mean 'whatever anyone in fact eats,' for people clearly sometimes eat things which are not edible. Similarly, people may desire things which are not 'desirable' in the moral sense. It may be that whether something is desirable in the moral sense depends not on whether people desire it, but rather on whether they should desire it. This, however, cannot be determined through any empirical observation, even if whether people do in fact desire it can be.

This objection, of course, does not disallow Mill from using the word 'desirable' to mean whatever he wants it to mean. To dispute over the 'true' meaning of such a word is as silly as if a German and an Englishman were to dispute as to whether the word 'am' *really* means 'on the,' as it does in German, or whether it is a case of the verb 'to be,' as in English. 'Am' simply means one thing to one group of people and another thing to another group, and it is meaningless to say that one group's definition is correct and the other's incorrect. The point is that other moral philosophers can and do use the word 'desirable' to mean something other than 'in fact desired.' By trying to deprive them of this usage, Mill would like to sweep under the rug many of the questions which are generally regarded as the most important questions of ethics---questions such as 'If the majority *desire* to enslave a minority, is it therefore morally right for them to do so?' Empirical observation cannot answer such questions, just as an empirical survey which reveals whether most people favor abortion cannot finally answer the ethical questions as to whether and in what cases people have rights and obligations with respect to abortion, and thus, ultimately, whether any given individual ought to opt for it.

If ethical statements cannot be demonstrated empirically, it also appears unlikely that any ethical statement will ever be provable through pure logic alone. Some philosophers, at least under certain interpretations, have tried to do so, but without much success. To prove an ethical statement logically would mean to prove that its opposite is self-contradictory. For example, in order to prove that lying is wrong by means of

INTUITION AND EMOTIONS

logic alone, we would have to prove that the statement 'lying is sometimes permissable' is logically self-contradictory, as Kant tried to do under certain interpretations.[14] Actually, Kant only wanted to show that one would be committed to a self-contradiction if one were to assert that one is *willing* for people to tell lies. Even so, strictly speaking, there is no such self-contradiction involved in saying 'Lying is sometimes permissible' even if I do not like being lied to. It is always possible for someone to say, without contradiction, 'Whenever I feel that I have a good reason to lie, I shall do so, and I am willing for anyone else to lie to me as well, if he pleases.' Such a statement might be odd, coming from someone who does not like being lied to, but it is not self-contradictory, and it is conceivable that someone who does not like being lied to might say such a thing. For example, the odds that one will be lied to on any given occasion if everyone lies whenever they feel like it may be outweighed by the advantage to be gained from a particular lie. And, as has often been pointed out,[15] telling lies a certain percentage of the time when it is greatly to one's advantage does not completely undermine one's own credibility or the institution of truth-telling in general. Moreover, it is impossible to defend, by means of deductive reasoning alone, the thesis that I ought to act in the ways in which I would be willing for others to act, as Kant himself grants by admitting that ethics cannot be grounded in theoretical reason. One must first assume that life would be meaningless without a universalizable moral law according to which rational beings can determine their own actions through reason.

A number of critics have made fundamentally similar points with regard to Gewirth's 'is-ought' derivation. Kai Nielsen's criticism, notably, is almost identical to the one just mentioned in connection with Kant's proof that lying is impermissible.[16] It is not self-contradictory for a Mafioso, he says, to grant that it is not morally wrong for others to try to murder him, although he does not want them to do so, and will try to prevent them from doing so, and believes that he will probably successfully prevent them from doing so. Later, I shall argue that there is an important insight at the core of Gewirth's argument after all, but that Gewirth has undermined his own insight by trying to make it bear the burden of ethical principles which it cannot by itself support. Moreover, Gewirth does not technically see himself as logically proving an 'ought.' What he thinks he has proven is that each agent is 'dialectically' committed to *claiming* certain rights and therefore to be consistent must respect the same rights for others. Strictly speaking, even this argument fails, primarily because at best it commits the agent to respecting others' 'rights' to certain goods only in the crucially equivocal sense that *it would be good* for them (i.e., in a prudential sense) if they were to have those goods, all else being equal. But the fact that I must admit that *it would be good* for those involved if I were to, say, contribute 50% of my salary to the March of Dimes, does not imply that the March of Dimes has a 'right' to 50% of my salary, even in a prima facie sense. I shall discuss this issue in more detail at a crucial point in the next chapter. For now, the important point is that Gewirth's argument does not show that any normative claim can be strictly proven by means of logic alone. For, given the applicability of Moore's open question argument to any prudential valuational claim, Gewirth cannot strictly prove that there is any particular *moral* valuational claim whose denial would be self-contradictory. Even if the case is stated merely in terms of 'prima facie' prudential values, it cannot be deductively provable that one is *constrained or has a duty* to act in accordance with such prudential values whose value is a value 'for others.' To prove this requires proving rights and duties. But, although it may be good---and even a good necessary to people's agency---for the millions of starving masses around the world to have a substantial part of my paycheck, and even though it might be prima facie a good thing if I were to give it to them, this does not logically prove that they have a *right* to confiscate that portion of my paycheck, nor that I must on pain of self-contradiction grant that they have such a right. They may in fact have such a right after all, but this right, if it exists, cannot be proven purely through deductive logic. Moreover, even if prima facie rights could be proven logically, the rule according to which prima facie rights become *actual* rights cannot be proven deductively, especially in cases of conflict. Thus no *actual* right, and in general no actual normative claim, can be deductively proven. Other defenses of Gewirth could be raised and answered, but let's save those for the fuller discussion of Gewirth in the next chapter. For I do believe that there is a core of truth to be salvaged here, but which cannot be proven through deductive logic.

If Gewirth fails to deductively prove 'ought' from 'is', then certainly so does Searle.[17] In all these attempts, as Hudson points out, the main problem seems to be a hidden equivocation.[18] In Searle's case, the equivocation is similar to Mill's and is also vulnerable to the open question. MacIntyre, in his discussion of the 'is-ought' problem, observes that there have been some cultures in which the word 'ought' means 'owe', so that to say that I borrowed money from someone would in such cultures imply that I 'owe' the money and therefore 'ought' to pay it back, just as Searle would have it.[19] Yet anyone will agree that there is another sense of 'ought' in which the question can be asked whether I ought to do what I 'ought' in the sense of 'owe'---i.e., whether, the accepted rules of the society notwithstanding, I ought to repay what I owe. And in this other sense, Searle's 'is' still does not imply the 'ought'. A Humean utilitarian might grant such inference, but only after having denied the *meaningfulness* of many entire ethical theories, such as Kant's, which discuss the possibility of an 'ought' not derivable from an 'is'. Furthermore, if there is a non-prudential sense of ought, and if some of its possible uses contradict the oughts of prudence, then the question will arise whether I should obey the conventional ought, the prudential ought, or the non-prudential ought. To base the answer to this question (which will be an 'ought') on an 'is', simply because an 'is' can ground a conventional or prudential 'ought', would obviously beg the question. Thus it would seem that even a naturalistic ethical theorist must admit that, if this question has any meaning at all, any acceptable answer must posit an 'ought' which is not derivable from an 'is'.

If ethical statements can be neither empirically nor logically demonstrated, then perhaps the original motivation for emotivist and prescriptivist directions in positivistic philosophy is just as tempting as it ever was. Given the inadequacy of intuitionism, it would seem reasonable to conclude that the only way to verify any statement must be either empirically or logically. So, if the only way to know what a statement means is to know what one would have to do in order to verify the statement, i.e., if one accepts a verification criterion for meaning, then the verification criterion becomes an *empiricist* criterion. And if one accepts an empiricist criterion for meaning, then it only makes sense to deny that ethical statements are literally meaningful at all, as did A. J. Ayer.[20]

According to the empiricist criterion, a statement can have descriptive meaning (that is, meaning as a possible description of some objective reality) only if some conceivable experience could in principle lend empirical support either to the presumption that the statement is true or to the presumption that it is not true. According to Ayer's criterion, for example, a sentence is meaningful if and only if the speaker can specify ways in which, at least theoretically, the truth of the statement could be supported by means of some possible empirical test or observation procedure. Thus the statement 'The moon is made of green cheese' is meaningful as a descriptive statement (although one that happens to be false) because it would be theoretically possible to go to the moon and perform certain tests in order to determine its chemical composition. The reader or listener knows in principle just what would have to be done in order to find out whether the statement is true or not and therefore knows what the statement means. 'The absolute is perfect,' on the other hand, is not literally meaningful by this criterion because the listener has no idea what would have to be done in order to determine the truth or falsity of the statement. This, then, is how we know whether statements mean something or are meaningless (in the sense of literal meaning). It is worthwhile noting, at this point, that Ayer originally wanted all statements which were to qualify as meaningful to be susceptible, at least in principle, of complete empirical verification. But his empiricist colleagues persuaded him to loosen the criterion so that a statement could be meaningful if only some conceivable empirical test would be relevant in *supporting the probability* that the statement might be true, rather than completely verifying it. This modification was introduced in order to allow the meaningfulness of scientific *theories,* which cannot---even in principle---be completely verified by any finite set of observations.[21]

Still other versions of the empiricist criterion have been proposed. For instance, C. G. Hempel has proposed that a statement should be considered meaningful if and only if it is 'translatable into a specified empiricist language.'[22] The outcome of the rivalry among these various empiricist criteria would depend largely on how rigid one wishes to be in prohibiting statements from being considered meaningful if they cannot (even in principle) be verified through empirical observation. Such rivalries become a serious embarrassment to the general program of positivism, as we shall discuss in a moment.

For those who buy any version of the empiricist criterion for meaning, it would appear reasonable to infer that there are only four types of statements: (1) *descriptive* statements, which attempt to describe states of affairs and therefore are capable of being true or false; (2) *emotive* statements, which may sometimes be true or false, but only in the trivial sense that they either do or do not adequately describe the speaker's emotions; (3) *prescriptive* statements, which do not describe states of affairs at all but rather express the speaker's intention or command that the listener do something, such as 'Close the door!' or 'Tell the truth!'; (4) *tautologies,* which, because they are true by definition, merely proclaim the speaker's intention to use words with a certain specified meaning and to remain consistent in this usage. Now, if it is true that ethical statements cannot be demonstrated either empirically or logically, and if one rejects ethical intuitions, and if one accepts an empiricist criterion for meaning, then it is very tempting to conclude, as did many early positivists, that ethical statements are of types (2), (3), and---to the extent that terms must be defined and clarified---(4), but are never of type (1). They may express emotions and/or make commands, but are not capable of being true or false, do not describe objective states of affairs, and cannot be verified or falsified. They therefore lack meaning in the sense of 'literal meaning' required by the empiricist criteria for meaning.

Within this influential school of positivists---who, one must remember, dominated English-speaking philosophy until quite recently---there is a subdivision where ethics is concerned. Some positivists of this strict bent say that the meaning of every prescriptive statement is really the same as the meaning of some corresponding emotive statement. Thus, 'Close the door!' would become equivalent with 'I (or we) *want* you to close the door.' Ayer himself is of this latter opinion. But whether ethical statements are prescriptive or emotive or both, the implication of the empiricist criterion for meaning will clearly be that any argument concerning whether ethical statements are *true* or not is a meaningless argument. We can, according to positivism of such a strict type, analyse the emotive or prescriptive meaning of such statements; one can also construct an ethical system whose essential purpose is to translate all traditional ethical expressions, such as 'Murder is wrong,' into emotive expressions, such as 'I don't like murder,' or into prescriptive statements, such as 'Don't murder people!' Or one can insist that everyone always remain consistent and intellectually honest in the (emotional and prescriptive) meanings which are attributed to ethical statements. In this sense, there can even be a kind of 'logic' which can govern the use of ethical expressions. Anyone who got caught changing the definitions of her emotive or prescriptive terms in the middle of an argument, for example, would be accused of the fallacy of equivocation, just as though she had said something that was literally meaningful. Or anyone who said at one time, 'I don't like murder' and at another time 'I do like murder' would have to explain how the two situations were different, on pain of being accused of contradicting herself.

But, in spite of the possibility of such a 'logic', ethical statements would still lack objective truth value and therefore would not be verifiable. For prescriptivism, value judgments remain completely groundless. For emotivism, they are grounded in arbitrary emotional whims. In either case, if we accept the empiricist criterion for meaning and follow the logic just outlined, the ship of ethics sinks in a sea of nihilism.

But perhaps it is possible to escape this consequence by either loosening the empiricist criterion, or by using some other verification criterion. Let's consider this possibility.

(b) Modified positivism in combination with a coherence theory of verification

Even if we accept a verification criterion for meaning, the possibility may remain that the original positivists may have been hasty in inferring that ethical statements are literally or descriptively meaningless. For the empiricist criterion in its later modifications (motivated primarily by the need to include scientific theories as meaningful) does not require that statements be completely or absolutely verifiable in order to have descriptive meaning---only that *some evidence* can conceivably be brought to bear which could convince us that the theory is more likely to be true than false or vice versa. If we were to further broaden the criterion so as to accept other kinds of evidence than empirical evidence ---for example, the kind of 'evidence' that stems from a theory's being more unified, simpler, or less laden with ad hoc hypotheses than other possible answers to the same questions---then ethical theories might conceivably qualify as meaningtul even by some more or less loose verification criterion for meaning. Or we might be able to prove ethical theories by somehow empirically or logically disproving half of a disjunctive syllogism, as mathematicians do in proofs by 'mathematical induction.' We might then want to explore the possibility that ethical postulates might be (not completely provable, but) demonstrated to be *more credible*, at least, than all possible opposing ethical postulates, and therefore descriptively or literally meaningful even in terms of a broadened verification criterion for meaning.

This possibility would become especially attractive if one should also happen to accept a 'coherence' model of verification such as the one proposed by Rescher.[23] Ethical epistemologists like Geoffrey Sayre-McCord and Michael DePaul have explored such possibilities in considerable detail, and have taken them beyond the limitations of any verification criterion for meaning.[24] But even within these limitations, it can be argued that few if any statements can be demonstrated by means of rigorous deductive logic which remains free of any premises except those which are absolutely unquestionable, nor can any scientific theory be known with a great deal of certainty: This, the coherence theorist points out, does not mean that all theories are equally probable or equally believable. It means rather that a theory should be accepted if it is demonstrably better than all the other theories in the same field by virtue of its capacity to explain, entail, or render intelligible a large, coherent body of information, without getting caught up in self-contradictions or inconsistencies, and without having to make continual ad hoc hypotheses. If a theory can do this better than any of the other available theories, it deserves to be regarded as having some probability, at least, of being true, or of being closer to the truth than the other theories. If it does it better than *any other possible* theory (a very hypothetical situation), then it has in effect been demonstrated to be unequivocally true---assuming, that is, that one or another of the possible theories must be true. In the case of ethics, of course, there is the possibility that no ethical theory whatever is true. Ethics itself may be a grand delusion. In this case, however, the coherence theorist might maintain that the question simply becomes whether or not the most plausible of all ethical theories is more plausible than the thesis that no ethical theories whatever are true. But the very fact that there are coherence criteria by which to decide what theory is most plausible, and whether this theory is more plausible than no theory whatever, could be interpreted as showing that the ethical theories under consideration conform to a *kind* of verifiability criterion for meaning, although not a strictly empiricistic one, and not as strict a one as the empiricists originally had in mind.

Later we shall see that, although such a coherence approach, or something very much like it, is presently the cutting edge of moral epistemology, it is still drastically inadequate, primarily because there are too many equally or approximately equally coherent theories, and because the coherence approach by itself provides no way to eliminate the possibility that there are no true ethical theories or statements. But first, there are two important points that need to be made about verification criteria in moral epistemology. The first point is that, whether or not the verification criteria are tempered by a coherence method, there are good reasons for *rejecting* the verification criteria for meaning themselves. The other point is that there is another entire school of epistemology which both rejects verification criteria for meaning *and* offers another way of verifying statements (once we do know what they mean) besides logic and empirical evidence. Namely, phenomenologists offer phenomenological reflection on one's own consciousness, within an elaborate methodological apparatus, as a way of getting at what the states of consciousness are 'about'. In the realm of moral theory, this method promises to reveal what our moral beliefs and/or feelings (which are states of consciousness) are about. Not only do non-phenomenologists tend to underestimate the contributions of phenomenologists to ethical theory; they also frequently rely on a loose and informal kind of self-reflective knowledge at crucial points in their own work (which is essentially the same thing that phenomenologists are trying to do in a more rigorous and systematic way) without seeming to acknowledge the fact.

First, let's look at some important criticisms of the positivist type of epistemology per se, which highlight the need for phenomenology, especially in moral epistemology, either as an alternative or as a compliment to the positivist/coherentist programs that have dominated English-speaking philosophy.

(c) The inadequacies of positivism

Phenomenologists and others criticize the epistemological basis of logical positivism in several important respects. Perhaps the most frequent criticism is that positivism offers a method of verification which is in principle incapable of discovering anything about the consciousness of man.[25] Human thoughts and feelings are not capable of being observed empirically (at least not through the scientific method), because, precisely *as* conscious events, they must be conceived as functions of the *subject* of experience rather than as *objects* of experience. No matter how many objective tests a psychologist may devise to measure my heart-rate, my adrenal secretion, my responses to ink-blot tests, etc., she can never correlate these objective measurements with states of consciousness unless she first understands the states of consciousness which are to be measured.[26] Thoughts and feelings cannot be directly measured; most empiricists readily admit this fact, responding that the inability to study subjective phenomena directly is simply the price we must pay for the objective rigor of the scientific method.

But, according to the phenomenologists, the inability to study man as a conscious being is not a small shortcoming. For not only does it blind us to the meaning of ethical, social and psychological concepts. It also is a fundamental epistemological weakness in relation to *any* subject matter to which the positivist approach is applied. This is the case, the phenomenologist believes, because by blinding itself to the *subject* of experience, positivism thereby renders itself incapable, in many instances, of determining the difference between the object as it appears to the subject of experience, and the object as it really is. The scientific method, it is true, ideally allows us to do this by allowing different experimentors to replicate the same experiment while achieving the same results, thus demonstrating that the object appears no different (at least in the relevant respects) to different observers. But phenomenology maintains that even in the case of scientific knowledge, errors creep in because the entire community of scientists bring *the same* presuppositions with them to the experience. An entire society may have unexamined presuppositions.[27] Man himself, by his very nature and essence, may necessarily be equipped with modes of experiencing which distort reality as it is perceived.[28] The paradox of the concept of infinity is an example. Here the phenomenologists borrow from the thinking of Kant. It seems inconceivable to the human mind that space and time could be infinite, for then an infinite amount of time would already have elapsed, which seems impossible. But time and space cannot be finite either, for in that case there would have to be a time 'before' which there was not time and a place 'beyond' which there is no place. But the very word 'beyond' indicates that there is an emptiness of some sort on the other side of the limit, which can be conceived only as empty space. The concept of space simply boggles the human mind, as does *any* concept involving infinity. This example shows that the subject's modes of experiencing do contribute to the appearance of things in serious and fundamental ways. Einstein's practical success in dealing with space and time relations was due largely to the fact that he was able to go beyond the ordinary preconceptions about space and time which are fundamental to the human experience, although it remains now for philosophers to make ontological sense out of what he accomplished.

More to the point, phenomenology asserts that the positivists are fundamentally unable to understand the meaning of ethical and other human-related concepts for the simple reason that their epistemological position makes it impossible for them to study the subject of experience (man as a conscious entity), but only allows them to study *objects* which can be unambiguously perceived as objects. Phenomenology's approach to studying these human-related phenomena will be discussed in the next section. Meanwhile, we ought to consider the phenomenologists' criticisms of the empiricist criteria for meaning.

Phenomenologists begin by pointing out that the logical positivists disagree among themselves as to what the empiricist criteria for meaning should be.[29] Critics of Ayer's position, such as Hempel (mentioned in (a) above), have forced him into revisions, which still seem to them inadequate. Rival empiricist criteria have been proposed, notably Hempel's 'translatability into a specified empiricist language' criterion, thus causing dissension and controversy among those empiricists who still feel that a clear-cut criterion for meaning is desirable, but cannot agree on one. These developments, according to phenomenology, not only tend to raise doubts as to whether there can be a consistent empiricist criterion for meaning, but they also seem to suggest that something goes on behind the scenes---something unmentioned by the thinker who proposes one or another criterion, which allows her to choose among the various possible criteria.

The suspicion is that the positivist already knows, before she even formulates her criteria, what kinds of statements she wishes to regard as meaningful; she then devises a criterion which allows her to rule out precisely those classes of statements she wishes to regard as meaningless. Hempel, for example, wants to regard general concepts involved in scientific theories as meaningful, whereas Ayer does not. This is an important point because, unless the positivists can agree on a clear-cut criterion for meaning, then their claim that ethical terms have only emotive rather than descriptive meaning becomes dubious.

There are other criticisms of the empiricist criteria. Paul Marhenke points out that we must first know the meaning of a statement before we can even determine what methods might be used to verify the statement.

Thus, although all verifiable statements are meaningful, it does not follow that all meaningful statements must be verifiable---let alone empirically verifiable.[30] A related criticism is that the empiricist criterion itself is not an empirically or logically verifiable statement and therefore it does not conform to its own criterion for meaning.

Some criticisms are very technical in nature, and are of interest to us in the present context not so much on their own merits, but because the kinds of moves the positivists make to *get around* the objections expose a hidden agenda and a basic circularity at the very root of the whole idea of empiricist and verifiability criteria for meaning. Hempel's criticisms of Ayer's verifiability criterion show that such a criterion would rule out all statements of universal form (thus all general laws), since statements of this type cannot be verified even in principle by any finite set of observational data. Perhaps such observational data could be held to increase the probability of the truth of the statement in some sense, but this sense is also quite problematic. Spence's theory of anxiety, for instance, predicts statistically significant relationships involving eyelid conditioning and scores on the Manifest Anxiety Scale and other measures of 'anxiety'.[31] Yet no amount of verification of these predicted test implications can really establish that the connection between 'anxiety' and eyelid conditioning functions the way Spence claims; nor for this reason can it establish conclusively that the construct 'anxiety', as defined by Spence, is a meaningful one.

The verifiability criterion is thus overly restrictive, according to Hempel, because it cannot account for the meaning of theoretical constructs. But there are also respects in which the criterion is too inclusive of obvious nonsense. For example, Hempel insists that Ayer's criterion fails to rule out any disjunction one of whose alternatives is meaningless; this failure makes the criterion too inclusive if the other alternative is not meaningful. Hempel also argues that the criterion would render the denial of an existential statement meaningless, since the denial of an existential statement is a universal, and Hempel has already shown that the criterion cannot allow meaning to universals.[32] Thus, since a statement can be neither true nor false unless it is meaningful, we would have to give up the logical claim that if a statement is true, then its denial must be false---which would be absurd. Hempel also gives similar arguments to these to refute the possibility of a *falsifiability* criterion.[33]

Hempel's conclusion is that no strict verifiability or falsifiability criterion can be adequate, because it can never succeed in allowing certain classes of statements that we know are meaningful while at the same time excluding other classes of statements that we know are meaningless. So the situation can be summarized this way: We find Ayer offering a criterion for empirical meaning. Hempel rejects the criterion, offering instead his own. Meanwhile, Ayer modifies his criterion (in the second edition of *Language, Truth and Logic* and in several subsequent papers)[34] in an attempt to avoid the implications for which Hempel and other have criticized him. So the original notion of an empiricist criterion for meaning has been modified in several mutually exclusive directions, and we must either choose among them or reject them all.

Regardless of how this debate is ultimately resolved, the remarkable thing is that such a debate can even take place within analytic philosophy of the logical-positivist genre. Indeed, someone might maintain that the revisions and modifications just discussed are of a merely formal nature, involving trivial and peripheral exceptions to Ayer's original rule. But the point of interest for our purposes is the very fact that the notion of an empiricist or verifiability criterion must be modified and qualified at all in order to make it include or exclude the kinds of statements one or another empiricist thinker does or does not wish to regard as meaningful. The necessity for any such qualification suggests that those who construct empiricist criteria first decide what kinds of sentences they would like to regard as significant, and then, after this fact, construct criteria to which these kinds of sentences conform. How inclusive or exclusive the criterion should be has already been decided upon before the criterion is proposed; subsequent revisions of the criterion are proposed primarily on the basis of whether the original criterion succeeded in including all those classes of statements which the author in question had wished to regard as meaningful. Thus there must be some sense in which we already know what kinds of sentences are and are not meaningful before we can even decide among various possible criteria for meaning. Although such a criterion---the criterion of verifiability, for example---may be a helpful test for seeing whether we really know (more or less) what we mean by a sentence, our knowing how to verify the sentence does not tell us what it means.

The very fact that a variety of different kinds of criteria can be proposed suggests a general problem in the whole notion of criteria for meaning. Implicitly or explicitly, there must be a criterion for choosing among the various possible criteria. In this sense, a criterion must be reflexive; it must openly show the author's *reasons* for selecting his criterion and no other. The criterion must in this sense ground its own reasons for being preferable to other possible criteria. If a criterion, A, claims preferability over another criterion, B, for reason A^1, then it implicitly asserts that A^1 is a more basic criterion than itself. A^1 then becomes the real criterion, and A is reduced to the status of a rule for the application of A^1---and this rule is presumably derivative from A^1. If we wish to find a truly 'reflexive' criterion for meaning, in this respect, we must find a criterion, A, which need not appeal to any A^1, but which contains its own reasons for being preferable to B, C, D, etc., within the statement of A itself.

Authors who propose empiricist criteria for meaning seem in fact to continually appeal to the reader's *intuitive sense* that certain kinds of words and sentences cannot reasonably be excluded from the class of meaningful ones. Hempel, for example, appeals to the scientist's sense that scientific theories are meaningful, even though these theories have difficulty conforming to Ayer's criterion. We also find Ayer endeavoring to allow meaning to forms of statement generally believed to be meaningful. For instance, he says at one point, "This criterion seems liberal enough. In contrast to the principle of conclusive verifiability, it clearly does not deny significance to general propositions or to propositions about the past."[35] Analytic philosophers also seem to appeal to the reader's intuitive sense that certain kinds of expression are simply too slippery to pin down, and therefore should not be used on pain of introducing havoc and confusion into discussions. For example, much of the appeal of Ayer's original proposal was that it excluded vague metaphysical words like 'the Absolute' and 'the Real,' which are notorious sources of philosophical confusion and pseudoproblematic debate.[36]

But, if we are going to appeal to the reader's intuitive sense of what sorts of statements our criterion should and should not include, then we may as well candidly recognize the reader's intuitive sense as the criterion at the outset. In this way, we could avoid the necessity for appealing to an implicit criterion by which to decide among criteria. The real problem in this regard, of course, is that some people may 'intuit' that sentences are meaningful which others can hear only as vague and indefinite. Phenomenology, however, provides a safeguard against such vagueness by insisting on an elaborate and rigorous method of excluding unclear meanings---the first and most important function of the 'phenomenological reduction.'

The next section will examine the phenomenological approach to epistemology, especially as it relates to the justification of ethical beliefs. It would be lucky if phenomenology could offer better justifications for these beliefs than can positivism. Unfortunately, we shall find that, although phenomenology is an excellent vehicle for studying moral *psychology,* and for clarifying the *meaning* of moral experiences, all of its attempts to establish the *truth or validity* of moral beliefs have so far reduced ultimately to comparatively sophisticated forms of either intuitionism or emotivism. But neither intuitionism nor emotivism alone can be an adequate epistemological basis for the truth or validity of moral beliefs. On the other hand, certain phenomenological data will turn out to have an absolutely indispensable role in the larger edifice of moral epistemology, even though they are not sufficient by themselves.

2. *Phenomenology*

(a) The received doctrine: Phenomenological reduction through imaginative variation

Even as the ship drifts inexorably into the Strait, a mutiny is in progress. Some crew members want to toss overboard the analytic compass and replace it with a fancy European model---with one or another version of a phenomenological or hermeneutic one. It is difficult to summarize the epistemological approach of phenomenology, primarily because its practitioners disagree with each other on certain very fundamental points. For Husserl, the closest we can come to knowing reality as it 'really is,' by contrast to the way it merely 'appears', is to experience phenomena as they genuinely present themselves to us as subjects, to be clear about which phenomena correspond to which subjective experiences, to separate our presuppositions *about* a given phenomenon from the phenomenon itself, and to understand how much of the experience and which aspects of it are attributable to the subject rather than to the object of the experience.[37] The authentic experience is the experience of the phenomenon as divorced from any unwarranted presuppositions one might have about it, and with the ability to separate the objective *(noematic)* aspects of the experience from the subjective *(noetic)* aspects. But Husserl never aspires to know quasi-Kantian 'things in themselves', 'noumena', or 'the reality behind appearances.' Heidegger, on the other hand, emphasizes that man is born out of the world rather than into it, and is a part of the 'really real.' Thus when man experiences the phenomenal world, he is experiencing the real effect that real beings have on himself, another real being, and thus can know and understand the nature of Being in general.[38] But, within the diversity of phenomenological approaches, it is possible to discover an epistemological program whose important features are shared.

For all phenomenologists, the important thing is to determine how much of the appearance of phenomena is attributable to inappropriate prejudices and preconceptions which the subject brings with him to the experience. It is then possible to devise a method for getting rid of the distorting elements of the subject's presuppositions. I shall speak here in Husserlian terms, but approximately the same points can be translated into the language of other phenomenologists as well.

The phenomenological reduction is a technique designed to authenticate experiences by getting rid of the presuppositions consciousness naturally attaches to its experiences. Husserl calls this conglomerate of presuppositions the 'natural attitude.' Accustomed to perceiving the world as a spacio-temporal manifold of material objects and relationships among material objects with which we are familiar and which we can predict, we forget that the whole subjective apparatus we bring to experience accounts for half of the appearance of the perceived object. The natural attitude also includes more generally a characteristically human inability to own up to the fogginess of our conceptual blind spots, and often a tendency to deceive ourselves. Consciousness in the natural attitude fails to take account of the fact that these subjective contributions to the appearance of an object effectually function as presuppositions about the object. We must purposely and deliberately set about to bracket them out. This problem is as important for objects of thought, whether abstract or of particulars, as it is for objects of perception.

According to Husserl, we can gradually eliminate from our experience of an object all items of supposed information which come from our legacy of past experience rather than from the appearance of the object itself. For

INTUITIONS AND EMOTIONS

example, in our experience of the concept of 'moral wrongness' as applied to some particular action, we can set aside whatever presuppositions we may already have formed about moral wrongness in general, concentrating instead on just those things that can be learned by observing the way the object affects us experientially---on our experience, not of the abstract concept 'moral wrongness,' but rather of the moral wrongness of this particular action, divorced from all preconceptions. All other negative feelings we might also happen to have about the action must be carefully separated out, so that we do not confuse the aspects of the object which correspond with these other negative feelings with the aspects that we experience as 'morally wrong.'

For practical purposes, the easiest way to accomplish this phenomenological reduction is to use 'imaginative variation.'[39] Suppose the 'morally wrong' action in question is a terrorist killing, for example. We 'imaginatively vary' every possible aspect of the action, noting in each case how our subjective reaction to it would change. If we vary the action in our imaginations in such a way that, instead of, say, an Arab killing an innocent American citizen, we imagine Harry Truman dropping the atomic bomb on millions of innocent Japanese citizens, while reflecting on the fact that we may not consider Truman's action as instantiating the same degree of moral repugnance, then we can eliminate 'the killing of innocent civilians per se' as a candidate for the 'morally wrong' aspect of the experience. We may then ask whether it would make a difference whether war has been declared, imagining American soldiers killing in the undeclared Viet Nam war, while reflecting on the fact that we do not experience these killings as morally repugnant in the same way as the action of the Arab terrorist. The more aspects of the experience we vary in our imaginations, the more we can eliminate irrelevant aspects of the experience which have nothing to do with the 'moral wrongness' we experience. Ultimately, we hope to phenomenologically 'reduce' the experience so that we know exactly which aspect of the object corresponds to which aspect of our subjective reaction. This, however, does not yet demonstrate that our experience of 'moral wrongness' is an experience of a reality which exists *independently of our consciousness of it.* It simply serves to rid our experience of the presuppositions involved in the natural attitude, so that the phenomenon is not colored by elements that do not belong to it.

This procedure, once accomplished, serves to delineate authentic from inauthentic experiences of *meaning.* An authentic experience of meaning is one where some meaning is still experienced even after the phenomenological reduction has been performed. Through the rigorous exclusion of presuppositions of all kinds from our concept of the object of our experience, we discover what *we really mean* by the concept. It is entirely conceivable that, after excluding all kinds of presuppositions---theoretical, cultural, historical, psychological, etc.---we may find that there is nothing left of the experience of the meaning, in which case we must admit that the original concept, once reduced, is shown to be a meaningless one. At other times, we find that we really do mean something by our concept, as thus purified, and we now have a concept which authentically characterizes our experience of the object. In this way, we can eliminate the errors which creep into our experience because of tacit or unconscious presuppositions.

Setting aside objections that may arise against what has been said so far, let's continue directly to the next and more interesting question. Once we know what we mean by 'This action is morally wrong,' how do we know whether the statement is *true* or not? How do we even know whether it is the kind of statement that can *be* true or false, as opposed to a description of our emotional reaction to the instance of terrorist or political killing in question?

As far as ethical beliefs are concerned, there seem to be two different methods of trying to establish their truth or validity. The first is to insist that the phenomenological notion of 'intentionality' implies that every subjective experience has an objective correlate. I.e., it assumes that every state of consciousness is the consciousness of *something other than* the consciousness itself. It 'intends' an object beyond itself. Once a moral experience has been phenomenologically reduced, then, whatever subjective 'residuum' remains must have an objective correlate. And this objective correlate, since it has been divorced from all non-moral emotions (including those resulting from my own egoistic involvement), must represent an objective moral principle which any two rational observers would see in the same way if they, too, were to perform the reduction. In effect, this procedure becomes a form of intuitionism, and the phenomenological reduction becomes analogous to the 'thought experiments' which standard intuitionists like Moore, Ross and Prichard thought could reveal what 'any reasonable man' would intuit as the truth about morality. Nicolai Hartmann seems to use the phenomenological method in this way.[40]

The second type of phenomenological approach to verifying the truth about ethics is best exemplified by Max Scheler,[41] and also by Heidegger (at least in the opinion of those who think that Heidegger's thinking has normative implications at all).[42] In Scheler's view, what the phenomenological reduction reveals is not the intuition of a set of abstract ethical truths, but rather a set of concrete facts about the nature of man. The fact that people feel that they intuit moral principles results from the fact that it is the nature of man to empathize with his fellow man.

The next two sections will discuss both these approaches in turn.

(b) Phenomenological intuitionism

Once we have clarified the meaning of a moral experience as described above, the question arises whether the moral principle which appears as the now-reduced object of the experience is an objective truth. According to the intuitionistic type of phenomenologist, we can find this out by means of further phenomenological analysis of our experience. We know that our experience of the phenomenon 'rightness' or 'wrongness' is an experience *of something*---otherwise, after bracketing out all the presuppositions that had previously been indoctrinated into us, there would be nothing left of our moral experience. We would have no subjective moral reaction to the event whatever---only egoistic reactions, insofar that the action affected us personally, or reactions of surprise, interest, and other non-moral emotions. But we can tell the difference between these kinds of emotions and the moral emotions simply by observing them phenomenologically; so, if we know that we have purposely disregarded all these non-moral emotional reactions, and have succeeded in bracketing all preconceived notions about the type of action in question, yet still feel that there is something 'wrong' about it, then there must be some *real phenomenon*---moral value, moral rightness, or something of that nature---which is the object of our experiential reaction. We can then analyse the experiential reaction further to discover exactly which features of the action strike us as morally repugnant, and what this 'moral repugnance' consists of aside from our mere emotional reaction. At the end of such an analysis, the phenomenological intuitionist says, we can compare these features with corresponding features of other actions which also produce in us the experienced meaning 'morally wrong,' finally reaching an understanding of the essence which all of the 'morally wrong' features have in common with each other. This, then, would in truth be what 'moral wrongness' really is.[43]

Notice how much more sophisticated this kind of procedure is than are non-phenomenological types of intuitionism. For it attempts to answer the primary objection against intuitionisms in general. This primary objection, as discussed earlier, is simply that, although people may believe that they directly intuit the truth about morality, different people's intuitions often contradict each other. Traditional (i.e., non-phenomenological) intuitionists try to get around this objection by insisting that the differences in different people's apparent 'intuitions' are caused by personal or emotional involvement with the issue at hand. A logical way to resolve a given dispute between two emotionally-involved parties, they say, is to bring in a disinterested third party who is rational and well-informed about the issues but who has no personal stake in the outcome of the decision. By an extension of this common-sense procedure to cover the basic and most fundamental ethical principles themselves, they suggest that we simply ask ourselves to imagine how we would prefer to see the issue resolved *if* we ourselves had absolutely nothing to gain or lose in the outcome, and if we had no emotional involvement with it of any kind (except for the purely disinterested and thus moral 'preference' for seeing a morally good or right outcome). Hence the familiar 'thought experiments' in which we ask ourselves how 'any reasonable man' would feel about various options in moral situations.[44]

But this traditional intuitionist response does not work. Those who perform the thought experiments, instead of reaching agreement in their intuitions, seem to become more clear as to where their fundamental disagreements lie. For example, Moore thinks that *any* reasonable, disinterested person would intuit the same as any other the ideal utilitarian principle of 'beneficence'---the principle that the right action is always, at least prima facie, the one that produces the most good consequences for the most people; and that the other prima facie values which might conflict with this one must be balanced against it in terms of other types of desirable consequences, such as distributive justice, which Moore regards as one of many types of goods or benefits which it would be desirable to promote.

Now the very fact that Ross, who is also an intuitionist (and is presumably a 'reasonable man') specifically disagrees with Moore on the principle of beneficence, even after having read Moore's book, should adequately refute the claim that all reasonable men intuitively agree on this principle. Ross says in this regard, "If the only duty is to produce the maximum of good, the question who is to have the good...should make no difference to my having a duty to produce the good. But we are all in fact sure that it makes a vast difference."[45]

The question remains, however: Is the relative priority ordering of the general welfare (which Ross calls 'the maximum of good') on the one hand, and fairness on the other ('the question who is to have the good') really intuited in the same way by all reasonable and disinterested reflectors? Obviously not, since philosophers who consciously see themselves as trying to get at their basic intuitions often fail to agree on these issues. An interesting case in point is Ross' claim that "We should not in general consider it justifiable...to steal from one in order to give alms to another."[46] But, obviously, a large number of people who have made Robin Hood into a folk hero over the years could never agree with Ross' intuition on this point, nor, obviously, would most socialists.

Phenomenological intuitionism tries to improve on this situation. The problem with traditional intuitionisms, they believe, is that they have not systematically used the phenomenological reduction to eliminate the non-moral biases and prejudices that distort or contaminate the authentic experience of the moral phenomena (i.e., objectively true principles) in their purity. Ross, for example, has forgotten to imaginatively vary aspects of the concept of property ownership that he unconsciously presupposes due to his cultural and class origins, a culture and class in which people neither question the sanctity of private property nor distinguish between the right to keep moderate amounts of property and the right to keep amounts so huge that one's keeping them may affect others' lives in grotesque ways.[47]

But can it really be as easy as that? What if there are still aspects of the experience that we have forgotten to vary? What if our imaginations are limited? And, given that it is always possible that there may still be necessary variations that we have not yet thought of, how can we know that at the end of all the variations there will be any 'phenomenological residuum' left? More important still, what if the 'phenomenological residuum' is not an objective moral truth, but only the object of a mere *emotion* which human beings by their very nature must universally tend to feel (as Scheler believes)?

Merleau-Ponty, a critic from within phenomenology itself, expresses the problem most simply.[48] A complete phenomenological reduction, he says, is in actual practice impossible. We can never know for sure that we have succeeded in ridding our experience of all unwarranted presuppositions. And if we cannot know this, then we also cannot know that the experience which remains after our reduction is complete is anything more than a prejudice in its own right.[49] It may, as Amedeo Giorgi believes, bring us a little closer to the truth,[50] but we can never know *how* close, or what the final truth will be---even to the extent of knowing whether it will end up being an objectivistic moral system, or an emotivism. The procedure thus remains a dissatisfying answer to the problem of the validation of ethical theories, since it might well leave us with a theory that is completely untrue, as Georg Lukacs has strongly suggested.[51] Lukacs insists that even the most thorough phenomenological analysis of the concept 'devil' can never reveal whether any devil actually exists. To learn this, we must go outside the brackets of the phenomenological reduction.

We shall see later, however, that some such technique must be counted as a consideration which may reveal, within the larger strategy of coherentism, that one moral theory is preferable to another. When it comes to *comparing* one theory with another, the fact that one stands up under phenomenological reductions which would be sufficient to demolish a rival theory must be taken as evidence that the one theory is preferable, at least, to the other.

(c) Phenomenological anthropologism

Another phenomenological approach to the verification of ethical beliefs is to use the phenomenological method to analyse the nature of human consciousness in general, and then to show from this analysis that in order to be *fully and authentically* conscious, an individual must act in such a way as to benefit others on a systematic basis. For example, such theorists may conclude in their analysis of the structure of consciousness that a human being needs to be able to have empathic feelings toward not only some but all other people in order to achieve the level of consciousness she desires.

Thus, rather than analysing the 'essence of moral goodness' or the 'essence of moral rightness,' this type of phenomenology begins by analysing the 'essence of being human,' and then tries to show that in order to be human by such a definition, a person must do things which are moral. It therefore argues that the inevitable penalty of an immoral life is that the immoral person is less fully conscious, less fully aware of her own feelings, and less fully alive as a consequence, than the person who is concerned about others. This type of phenomenological theory is often called 'existential' phenomenology, since it takes as its starting point the analysis of human existence.

The classic theorist of this type, although he wrote before the term 'existentialism' became fashionable among phenomenologists, is Max Scheler, a contemporary of Husserl. For Scheler, ethics is only one part of a broader project which he calls 'philosophical anthropology,' the study of the essential nature of man by means of the phenomenological method.[52] ('Existentialists' of the popular Sartrean variety, of course, are fond of insisting that man has no essence. If this view is taken as the definition of existentialism, then Scheler clearly is not an 'existentialist.' But debates over who is and is not an 'existentialist' often become as silly as the debate over the meaning of the word 'am' mentioned earlier.)

After criticizing 'formalism' in ethics and explaining his concept of phenomenology,[53] Scheler begins his line of reasoning sounding very similar to the intuitionistic phenomenologists described above. The techniques described there are necessary but not sufficient for Scheler's approach. Thus he begins by reflecting on the 'moral experience,' then applies the phenomenological reduction in order to 'bracket out' all the theoretical presuppositions which we might inadvertently have brought with us to the experience. But, in the phenomenological residuum Scheler finds here, the emphasis is on the moral experience as one among many types of *emotional* experiences.[54] The trick then is to keep it from being confused with other emotions that are felt in relation to the same object but are not moral emotions, and to keep the object of the moral emotions from being confused with other objects that might be lumped together with it in one's emotional life. For example, someone may react to an Arab terrorist killing in a way that is contaminated by the fact that the perpetrator is on the opposite side of the ideological fence from those whom we might term 'freedom fighters' rather than terrorists.

As a result of this procedure (I shall skip the details), Scheler thinks that he has found that a certain kind of *sympathy* is the basis of all moral experience. It is from this basic feeling of sympathy for others that all moral principles must be derived. Unlike Hume, however, Scheler does not explain sympathy on the basis of ultimately hedonistic needs, such as the need for security (Hume seemed to think something on the order that people automatically empathize with others because of a feeling of not wanting to believe that we live in a cutthroat, amoral world in which injustice is likely to befall anyone at any time; such radical insecurity Hume thought to be more anxiety-arousing than anything else in human experience).[55] On the contrary, Scheler believes that sympathy with each other is a basic feature of human beings, that is, an essential component of what it means to be a human being. The basis for this belief seems to be essentially that, without an underlying empathy, people would not be able to learn to understand each other's feelings and the meaning of each others' discourse. Since we do, the basic underlying empathy must be there. It is not derivative from egoistic motives, but is equiprimordial with them or even precedes them in the genetic constitution of each individual's emotional makeup. The empathy, then, which is a basic feature of human existence, motivates moral emotions, the essence of which is sympathy with others. It then follows that our sympathy with others will motivate us to help them and also want to see justice done to them.

As descriptive anthropology and prudential wisdom, Scheler's work obviously has a great deal to offer. But its shortcomings as the basis for a *normative* endeavor become obvious as soon as we take a step back and look at the overall structure of Scheler's reasoning in relation to the larger framework of human knowledge in general. Anyone who wants to construe Scheler's analysis as a normative scheme whose values are not completely based on rbitrary emotional whims (and thus completely nihilistic from any objective viewpoint) must assume somehow that, because the nature of man *is* that he feels such-and-such sentiment, then the nature of man *should* be that he feels such-and-such sentiment (sympathy or any other natural feeling). Scheler's theory is ultimately prescriptively impotent for the same reason as Hume's. If the reason we act morally is that we have a natural feeling of sympathy, then what reason can Scheler offer to show that we *ought* to have this feeling if we lack it, or if we have lost it somehow? What reason can he offer to show that we ought to have the feeling of sympathy to any greater *extent* than we already do? Granted, there are prudential reasons to act in accordance with this feeling if it is an essential part of our emotional makeup. We refuse to do so on pain of losing our consciousness and our humanity, as will be discussed further in Part Two. And, if it were not possible to have a genuinely normative system, the prudential wisdom embodied here would by no means be a waste of time. But, in its ultimate foundations, what the theory is really saying is either (1) 'It is in the nature of man that he desires to act according to emotion X; therefore he ought to do so'; or (2) 'It is in the nature of man that he desires to act according to emotion X; therefore, if he does not do so, he is inauthentic and not truly human; however, if he does not consciously believe that he *wants* to be authentic or truly human, I cannot say that it is objectively true that he ought to---only that he is mistaken about *what he really wants.*'

I emphasize 'what he really wants' here because, if (2) is really the reasoning involved, then Scheler's system is an *emotivism* whose normative element is purely prudential and is no different in principle from the (purely prudential) normative element in Ayer's theory. It is only the non-normative part of his thinking whose substantive conclusions differ from Ayer's---i.e., the descriptive anthropology. Ultimately, both philosophers tell me that I ought to do whatever is in my self-interest. They simply have different interpretations of what it means for something to be in my self-interest, with Scheler holding that what I really want is to empathize with other people. Both are forms of egoism. Scheler's egoism is different only in that it tells me that, if I really knew what I want, I would realize that there is no true *conflict* between my interests and those of others with whom I empathize, once I balance my own personality and needs in the right way. But, for anyone who takes the Ring of Gyges seriously, this assumption is far-fetched. Even if people realize that their own self-interest entails acting altruistically a good percentage of the time, can anyone believe that there would not still be some conflicts between one individual and another? Of course, there is altruism in our nature because of the need for empathy, and this altruism will reduce the amount of conflict in the world. But there will still be some instances of conflict. And, in those instances, I need a technically *non-egoistic, non-prudential* normative theory to tell me that I ought to sacrifice some of my own self-interest or modify my life so as to take others' interests into account to an even greater extent, when the situation calls for it, than the need for empathy would naturally motivate me to do, especially if I have taken no particular effort in cultivating this empathy beyond the average level, which apparently does not preclude people from remaining quite indifferent to each others' suffering. The force of this objection should be especially obvious in the context of a socio-political situation in which one of the things necessary for the actualization of one's full potential for humanness, in Scheler's sense, is to compete for the resources necessary for this accomplishment.

There are, of course, other criticisms of Scheler's theory. But they all become insignificant compared with this one.

It is too early at this point to explain what I believe must be viewed as the positive, indeed indispensable, value of phenomenological data and methods within the total project of moral theory. This value will begin to become evident toward the end of the next chapter, and will not be fully obvious until Chapter Three. By then, we shall also have begun to see the positive value of analytic philosophy, coherentism, and rationalistic 'is-ought' derivations, which have also been criticized here, provided that each of them is kept to its proper function. The sail of an ethical-epistemological seafaring vessel cannot do the work of the rudder, nor the hull that of the compass. There are still other pieces that must be fit into place, as the next chapter will show.

NOTES

[1] R. M. Hare, *The Language of Morals* (London: Oxford University Press, 1952); also, to a great extent, *Freedom and Reason* (London: Oxford, 1963).

[2] A. J. Ayer, *Language, Truth and Logic* (London: Gollantz, 1946); "On the Analysis of Moral Judgments," *Philosophical Essays* (New York: St. Martin's Press, 1965), 321-249.

[3]Allan Bloom, *The Closing of the American Mind* (New York: Simon & Schuster, 1987), esp. 25-46 and 377-380.

[4]Although this method was popularized by John Rawls, *A Theory of Justice* (Cambridge: Harvard University Press, 1971), it is also used by many non-Rawlsians, as Michael DePaul points out in "Reflective Equilibrium and Foundationalism," *American Philosophical Quarterly* 23 (1986), 59-69. The method has been criticized by a number of authors, including Gilbert Harman, "Moral Explanations of Moral Facts---Can Moral Claims Be Tested Against Moral Reality?" *Southern Journal of Philosophy* 24 (1986); Geoffrey Sayre-McCord, "Coherence and Models for Moral Theorizing," *Pacific Philosophical Quarterly* 66 (1985), 170-90; Tibor Machan, "Social Contract As a Basis of Norms: A Critique," *Journal of Liberal Studies* 7 (1983), 141-46; Wojciech Sadurski, "Contractarianism and Intuition: On the Role of Social Contract Arguments in Theories of Justice," *Australasian Journal of Philosophy* 61 (1983), 321-47; David Schaefer, *Justice or Tyranny? A Critique of John Rawls' "Theory of Justice"* Port Washington: Kennikat Press, 1979); and many others, some of whom will be discussed below.

[5]For example, the moral systems of G. E. Moore, J. J. C. Smart, and W. D. Ross all seem quite self-consistent, yet are mutually contradictory. For the same reason, as we shall see more fully in Chapter Six, there are an infinite number of self-consistent conceptions of what kind of social contract would be chosen by a rational reflector in a Rawlsian original position (notwithstanding Rawls' insistence that 'maximin' is the only decision principle such a reflector could choose).

[6]J. J. C. Smart, "Extreme and Restricted Utilitarianism,"*Philosophical Quarterly* 6 (1956), 244.

[7]For example, James Sterba, *The Demands of Justice* (Notre Dame: University of Notre Dame Press, 1980), deduces much more conservative political and social implications from the original position concept than would Rawls himself, whereas David Schweickart, "Should Rawls Be a Socialist?" *Social Theory and Practice* 4 (1978), 1-27, pushes the same concept to the exact opposite extreme, just to cite two examples. David Kaye, "Playing Games With Justice," *Social Theory and Practice* 6 (1980), 33-52, shows that a person in the original position might with equal rationality choose any of a very wide variety of possible decision principles.

[8]E.g., the system of Nicolai Hartmann, *Ethics* (New York: Macmillan, 1932) is essentially a form of intuitionism, as we shall see in section 2 of this chapter. Other intuitionistic types of phenomenological ethics would seem to include Eberhard Grisebach, *Gegenwart eine kritische Ethic* (Halle: Niemeyer, 1928); Simon Blackburn, "Errors and the Phenomenology of Value," in Ted Honderich, ed., *Morality and Objectivity* (London: Routledge and Kegan Paul, 1985), 1-22; and, judging from recently transcribed materials at the Husserl Archives, Husserl himself

seems to have leaned in this direction, though this interpretation will doubtlessly be debated when these materials are published.

[9]E.g., Max Scheler, *The Nature of Sympathy*, W. Stark, ed. (Hamden: Archon, 1970). The criticism that Scheler's approach is descriptive rather than prescriptive can be found in Theodore Steinbuchel, *Die philosophiche Grudlegung der Katholischen Sittenlehre* (Dusseldorf: Patmos, 1947), in Otto Bollnow, *Neue Geborgenheit* (Stuttgart: Kohlhammer, 1960), in Quentin Lauer, *Phenomenology* (New York: Harper, 1965), 165, and in William Werkmeister, *Theories of Ethics* (Lincoln: Johnsen, 1961), 269. Both Scheler's and Hartmann's approaches will be discussed further in section 2 of this chapter.

[10]E.g., Kant says in *Critique of Practical Reason*, L.W. Beck, ed. (New York: Bobbs-Merrill, 1956), 72 [70], "Ask yourself whether...if one belonged to such an order of things that anyone would allow himself to deceive when he thought it to his advantage, or felt justified in shortening his life as soon as he was thoroughly weary of it, or looked with complete indifference on the need of others, would he assent of his own will to being a member of such an order of things?"

[11]If Moore's 'open question argument' (which we shall discuss in Chapter Five here) is not sufficient to undermine such 'definist' strategies, many other criticisms of this type of strategy are. See William Frankena, *Ethics* (Englewood Cliffs: Prentice-Hall, 1963), 80ff; R. B. Perry, *Realms of Value* (Cambridge: Harvard, 1954), 107, 109; F. C. Sharp, *Ethics* (New York: Century, 1928), 410-11.

[12]J. S. Mill, *Utilitarianism* (New York: Dutton, 1931), 32-33.

[13]G. E. Moore, *Principia Ethica* (Cambridge: Cambridge University Press, 1956), 67.

[14]Certainly, the passages in *Critique of Practical Reason*, 27 [28], and *Foundations of the Metaphysics of Morals*, L.W. Beck, Ed. (New York: Bobbs-Merrill, 1959), 18-19, seem quite clearly to assert that to will lying as a universal maxim would be strictly self-contradictory.

[15]Smart (see note 6); A.K. Stout, "But Suppose Everyone Did the Same,"*Australasian Journal of Philosophy* 32 (1954), 1-29.

[16]Kai Nielsen, "Against Ethical Rationalism," Edward Regis, Jr., ed.,*Gewirth's Ethical Rationalism* (Chicago: University of Chicago Press, 1984), 59-83.

[17]J. R. Searle, "How To Derive 'Ought' From 'Is'," *Philosophical Review* 73 (1964), 43-58.

[18]W. H. Hudson, *Modern Moral Philosophy* (Garden City: Anchor, 1970).

[19]Alasdair MacIntyre, "'Ought'," in *Against the Self-Images of the Age* (New York: Schocken Books, 1971), 136-56.

[20]See note 2.

[21]Ayer, *Language, Truth and Logic*, second edition (New York: Dover, 1950); *Thinking and Meaning* (London: H.K. Lewis, 1947); *Philosophical Essays* (see note 2); *The Concept of a Person and Other Essays* (New York: St. Martin's Press, 1963). See especially *Language, Truth and Logic*, second ed., 33-39.

[22]C. G. Hempel, "Problems and Changes in the Empiricist Criterion of Meaning," in Ernest Nagel, ed., *Meaning and Knowledge* (New York: Harcourt, 1965), 16-27.

[23]Nicolas Rescher, *The Coherence Theory of Truth* (Washington: University Press of America, 1982).

[24]See note 4. Both Sayre-McCord and DePaul rely extensively on the work of Norman Daniels, "Wide Reflective Equilibrium and Theory Acceptance in Ethics," *Journal of Philosophy* 76 (1979), 256-282; "Reflective Equilibrium and Archimedian Points," *Canadian Journal of Philosophy* 10 (1980), 83-103; "Some Methods of Ethics and Linguistics," *Philosophical Studies* 37 (1980), 21-36.

[25]See R. D. Ellis, "Phenomenological Psychology and the Empirical Observation of Consciousness," *International Philosophical Quarterly* 23 (1983), 191-204, for a discussion of such criticisms. An especially good source for presentations of this aspect of phenomenology is Amadeo Giorgi, ed., *Duquesne Studies in Phenomenological Psychology* (Pittsburgh: Duquesne University Press, 1971).

[26]See Ellis (note 25).

[27]E.g., Martin Heidegger, *What Is a Thing?* (Chicago: Henry Regnery, 1967). Included in that volume is an "Analysis" by Eugene Gendlin which especially emphasizes this type of point, as do most of Gendlin's other works, such as *Experiencing and the Creation of Meaning* (Ontario: Collier-Macmillan, 1962).

[28]This point is of course emphasized by Husserl's discussions of the 'natural attitude' in most of his mature works, such as *Ideas* (London: Collier, 1962), Chapter 3, and is made especially vivid by Jacob Needleman, *Being in the World: Selected Papers of Ludwig Binswanger* (New York: Harper, 1968).

[29]R. D. Ellis, "Phenomenology and the Empiricist Criteria for Meaning," *Philosophy Today* 24 (1980), 146-52, discusses this point in somewhat more detail.

[30] Paul Marhenke, "The Criterion of Significance," *Proceedings and Addresses of the American Philosophical Association* 23 (1950).

[31] J. T. Spence and K. W. Spence, "Anxiety and Strength of U.C.S. as Determinants of Amount of Eyelid Conditioning," *Journal of Experimental Psychology* 42 (1951), 183-88.

[32] Hempel (see note 22), 18-20.

[33] Hempel, 20-21.

[34] Ayer (see notes 2 and 21).

[35] Ayer, *Language, Truth and Logic,* 2nd ed., 39.

[36] This attitude can be seen in all the works of A. C. Danto, N. Rescher, and many other contemporary analytic thinkers.

[37] Perhaps the clearest exposition of this point is in Edmund Husserl, *Ideas* (see note 28). It is especially brought out in Marvin Farber, "The Ideal of a Presuppositionless Philosophy," in Joseph Kockelmans, ed., *Phenomenology* (Garden City: Doubleday, 1967), 37-57.

[38] Martin Heidegger, *Being and Time* (New York: Harper & Row, 1962).

[39] Husserl, *Ideas* (note 28), section 23. Husserl explains imaginative variation in considerably more detail in *Phanomenologische Psychologie* (Den Haag: Nijhoff, 1962).

[40] Hartmann (note 8). See also Eckhard Koele, *Personality* (Newton, N. J.: Catholic Protectory Press, 1941).

[41] Scheler (note 9).

[42] This is the approach taken by Bollnow (note 9), and by Joseph Kockelmans, *Contemporary European Ethics* (Garden City: Doubleday, 1972), esp. 349-50. While Kockelmans is clear that Heidegger was not engaged in a normative endeavor, Kockelmans hopes to work out the normative implications of *Being and Time,* which to him implies a fundamental human need to actualize essentially moral modes of *Mitsein* or 'being-with'. This issue is discussed further in our Chapter Three, section 2.

[43] See note 8, as well as Koele (note 40).

[44] As in Moore (note 13), W. D. Ross, *Foundations of Ethics* (Oxford: Oxford University Press, 1939), and H. A. Prichard, *Moral Obligation* (New York: Oxford University Press, 1949).

[45] Ross, *The Right and the Good* (Oxford: Clarenden, 1965), 22.

[46]Ross, *The Right and the Good,* 22.

[47]Jeffrey Reiman, "The Fallacy of Libertarian Capitalism," *Ethics* 92 (1981), 85-95, shows with admirable clarity that it is a fundamental mistake to assume that the notion of 'property rights' should apply in the same way to very large accumulations of capital as it does to small items of petty property.

[48]Maurice Merleau-Ponty, *The Phenomenology of Perception* (New York: Humanities, 1962), esp. Preface and 299ff.

[49]Merleau-Ponty, *The Primacy of Perception* (Evanston: Northwestern, 1964), 75.

[50]Amadeo Giorgi, "Phenomenology and Experimental Psychology," in Giorgi (note 25).

[51]Georg Lukacs, "Existentialism or Marxism," G. Novack, ed., *Existentialism versus Marxism* (New York: Delta, 1966).

[52]Max Scheler, *Man's Place in Nature* (New York: Noonday, 1961). See also Stephan Schneck, *Person and Polis: Max Scheler's Personalism as Political Theory* (Albany: SUNY, 1987); Alfons Deeken, *Max Scheler's Moral Philosophy* (New York: Paulist Press, 1974); and Koele (note 40).

[53]Scheler, *Formalism in Ethics and Non-formal Ethics of Values* (Evanston: Northwestern, 1973).

[54]Scheler, *The Nature of Sympathy (note 9).*

[55]David Hume, *Treatise of Human Nature* (Oxford: Clarendon, 1888), Book III; *Inquiry Concerning the Principles of Morals* (Indianapolis: Bobbs-Merrill, 1957), 109ff.

CHAPTER TWO

COHERENTISM AND IS-OUGHT RELATIONS

As mutiny rages and the crew argues over which compass is to be followed, the term 'coherence' becomes almost a political buzz-word and is bandied about in a variety of different senses. In the last chapter, we saw that the 'coherence' of theories in Rescher's sense can be used as a quasi-positivistic verifiability criterion which would allow some credibility to be attached to theories that fail to conform to the strict positivist criteria of empirical evidence or logical proof.[1] Coherence of this kind seems to be (or tries to be) analogous to the 'parsimony' criterion for scientific theories.

Michael DePaul speaks of a 'coherentism' in moral theory which is not 'foundational' in nature.[2] That is, as we reduce our 'considered moral judgments' to 'reflective equilibrium,' the original moral judgments change in the process. Thus one cannot regard the original judgment as the 'foundation' for the new belief, and it seems clear that the new belief is more nearly correct or 'closer to the truth' than the old one. (Older positivists of the Ayer and early-Hare variety might well insist that this is true only in the sense that the new beliefs, unlike the old ones, are non-self-contradictory.) I purposely choose the phrase 'reduce to reflective equilibrium' to emphasize the similarity between this reduction and the phenomenological reduction discussed in the last chapter. The phenomenological reduction, however, is theoretically more complete than the one DePaul envisions; besides appealing to the virtue of parsimony and stripping a theory of its self-contradictory and 'counterintuitive' implications, the phenomenological reduction is also supposed to strip it of inappropriate and 'inauthentic' presuppositions which might contaminate the moral experience. However, we have seen that this approach, too, has its limitations.

One of the clearest studies of coherentist epistemology in ethical theory has been carried out by Geoffrey Sayre-McCord.[3] In Sayre-McCord's view, coherentists attempt to set up other criteria for the coherence of moral theories besides freedom from self-contradictory and counterintuitive implications. However, in his view, the other criteria fail to withstand critical scrutiny as criteria whose fulfillment would be a desirable thing for moral theories. In Sayre-McCord's analysis, besides the avoidance of self-contradiction, there are two other qualities that authors tend to count as contributing to the 'coherence' of a theory: *completeness* and *interconnectedness*. But the ideal of *interconnectedness*, combined with the demand for consistency, ultimately leads to a demand that the entire theory be derivable from one single fundamental first principle, since, even if two independent principles do not obviously contradict each other, the possibility of their contradiction must still be forestalled by appeal to a higher principle, which then becomes the one true first principle of the theory. And the demand for *completeness* leads to the acceptance of theories which are much more likely to be false than true: Coherence, after all, can lead us only 'closer to the truth'; but a theory which claims to have the *complete* truth when in fact it is only 'close to' the truth obviously will yield false answers to some, many, or perhaps all questions which it is used to answer.

So it seems that the claim of completeness makes a theory less likely to be true rather than more likely. The demand for completeness therefore defeats itself. Sayre-McCord's conclusion, then, is that coherence can be a legitimate standard for judging theories only if it expurgates the interconnectedness and completeness requirements. But then it is left only with the demand for self-consistency, which is not a very exciting basis on which to recommend a moral theory, especially since it is possible to devise a multiplicity of mutually-contradictory but self-consistent theories.

What the various concepts of 'coherence' seem to have in common is that they hope to provide a basis on which to *compare* different theories with each other in the attempt to decide which one is more likely to be true. The epistemological 'foundation' of the theory, strictly speaking, then becomes the sheer fact that the theory comes off better than its rivals in this comparison, if only the criteria for comparison can have been settled beforehand. To avoid any confusion in referring to this kind of 'coherence', perhaps it will be helpful to use the qualifying expression, *'comparative* coherentism.' To provide a basis for comparing the probability of theories, after all, is the ultimate goal of the coherence strategy. What needs to be determined, if we want to know whether such a 'comparative coherentism' is feasible, is whether there are any clear and objective criteria for comparing theories beyond mere self-consistency.

1. Comparative Coherentism and Factual Adequacy

'Comparative coherentism,' as here defined, is the kind of approach to the epistemology of ethics which, in light of the impossibility of proving ethical statements and the untrustworthiness of ethical intuitions, proceeds by comparing the plausibility of all conceivable coherent and/or consistent theories of ethics (or all that have so far been thought of) ---including the thesis that there are no true ethical principles---so as to accept the one that, in view of the best available criticisms and arguments, is most likely to be the correct one. Such a strategy seems to have been used by the most diverse of theorists---Kant, Rawls, Mill, Scheler, and innumerable others, though most of these thinkers have used other epistemological assumptions as well.[5] Comparative coherentism is used, in fact, by any philosopher whose case depends crucially on refuting the reasoning of opposing theories. However, these various philosophers obviously disagree as to the correct epistemological criteria for criticizing theories within such a strategy. This section will attempt to clarify the rationale of comparative coherentism, and to establish some criteria that would be used by a philosopher who is aware that such a coherentism is at least part of his epistemological basis. We shall find that consistency with reliable factual information and avoidance of ad hoc hypotheses are especially important in this regard. The word 'factual' here is used broadly, so as to refer not only to empirical facts, but also to any ontological and logical truths that might be discoverable---any truths, in short, that are not themselves expressions of 'oughts'.

We have seen that Sayre-McCord recognizes only three fundamental criteria for 'coherence' in ethical theories.[6] A coherent theory must be (i) *consistent*, (ii) *epistemically interconnected*, in the sense that all statements in the theory must be justified by the first principle of the theory, and (iii)*complete*, in the sense that it must answer all questions within its domain (which I take to mean all questions for which competing answers could conceivably conflict with the principles of the theory). Of these, Sayre-McCord rejects the second as untenable, and therefore also the third. His conclusion is that coherence should be used as a 'regulative ideal' by moral philosophers, but not as an 'operative constraint.' I shall say more about this point later. But for now, it seems that a fourth criterion is often also used by coherence theorists--- that a theory should not conflict with reliable factual information. And it is this fourth criterion that leads to interesting results.

Most philosophers, whether acknowledged coherentists or not, do in fact use the criterion that a correct ethical principle will not conflict with reliable factual information. For example, those who say 'ought implies can' assume that it is possible (and undesirable) for an ethical statement to conflict with a factual one. This criterion seems to be widely employed to criticize basic ethical principles, not just their application to cases. Thus, many of us would agree with Paul Edwards, J. J. C. Smart and others that, if determinism is true, then ethical theories like Kant's, which emphasize moral blame, would become false or meaningless[7]---as

Kant himself goes to great length to point out.[8] There is an appealingness to MacIntyre's claim that "It would generally be a decisive refutation of a moral philosophy to show that moral agency on its own account of the matter could never be socially embodied."[9]

The interesting point for our present purposes about this widespread belief that an ethical statement can conflict with a factual one is that most of the same philosophers who believe it also believe that a factual statement cannot *imply* an ethical statement. Kant, for example, believes this, as do most contemporary philosophers. Only Searle, Gewirth, and those emotivists who regard 'ought' as by definition an expression of emotion seem to have notably argued otherwise.[10] Yet it is very strange that philosophers should believe that an 'is' can *contradict* an 'ought' but cannot *imply* one, for the following reasons. Suppose A stands for 'it is the case that' and O stands for 'it ought to be the case that.' If $O(x)$ implies $A(y)$ (as in 'ought implies can'), then $-A(y)$ implies $-O(x)$. If we take $-O(x)$ to be an ethical statement, then certainly it is being implied by a factual statement, though perhaps in a trivial sense, given that $-O(x)$ *negates* an ought rather than affirming one. What is less trivial is that it is possible in principle that there is a finite number of logically viable ought statements (including the statement that there is never anything that one ought to do). Let's call this series $O(x_1)$, $O(x_2)$,...$O(x_n)$. (Similar reasoning could be applied even if the series were infinite rather than finite, as we shall see later.) Then it is also possible in principle that all of $O(x_1)$ through $O(x_{n-1})$ contradict factual statements, $A(y_1, y_2,$ etc.). If so, then $O(x_n)$ *must* be true because it is the only one left. (*Ex hypothesi*, one of the n-1 statements that have been eliminated in this process is the statement that there is never anything that one ought to do---an especially difficult but not impossible alternative to eliminate, as we shall see.) And if these inferences are possible in principle, then it follows that it is possible in principle that $A(y_1, y_2,$ etc.) implies $O(x_n)$. Thus a series of factual statements would imply an ought. (The uncertainty of factual information need not detain us. If a series of facts can imply an ought, then a series of probable facts can imply a probable ought.)

Furthermore, it is possible (and still more likely) that some series of factual statements, $A(y_1, y_2,$ etc.) conflicts with *some* of the possible ought statements, say $O(x_1, x_2,...x_{n-3})$, but not with some others, $O(x_{n-2}, x_{n-1}, x_n)$. Then such a series of factual statements would imply 'Either $O(x_{n-2})$ or $O(x_{n-1})$ or $O(x_n)$.' And then if x_{n-2}, x_{n-1}, and x_n *agreed* on a few points, p_1, p_2, and p_3, it would follow that $A(y_1, y_2,$ etc.) would imply $O(p_1, p_2, p_3)$. In this event, a set of factual premises would again imply an ethical conclusion.

Thus there is some series of 'is' statements that definitely does imply at least some *alternation* of 'ought' statements, and it is possible in principle that some series of 'is' statements implies some definite 'ought' statement without reservation. One promising coherentist strategy is to use the conflict between certain factual and ethical statements to narrow the range of possibly correct ethical principles to the point where any statements affirmed by all the remaining alternatives could be accepted as definitely correct, while outstanding disagreements among the remaining alternatives could be resolved by means of some sort of criteria for comparing their plausibility in terms of the logical structure of theories. Later, it will become evident that there are some points of agreement between those sufficiently coherent theories which are not eliminated by virtue of contradicting reliable factual knowledge. Each of these points of agreement therefore becomes an ethical statement whose truth is established by a series of factual statements. And where there is not agreement among the non-eliminated theories, criteria for comparing the probability of the truth of ethical theories can sometimes be applied (but perhaps not always).

A number of problems and objections arise in trying to formulate such a comparative coherentist approach. One problem, which will be discussed in section (a), is to understand how a moral statement can logically conflict with a factual statement, since the subject matter of the two types of statements is apparently different. Section (b) will attempt to establish criteria for comparing the probabilities of competing 'ought' claims not eliminated by conflict with facts, and in so doing to address two interrelated concerns: (1) Even if the eliminative and comparative process should work out as hoped and we were to end up with an ethical theory that is more likely to be true than any other, the resulting theory is still very likely to be wrong in various respects, and we may be doing more harm than good by acting on it. And (2) Sayre-McCord argues for essentially this reason that a coherent theory may not be as good as a loose assemblage of merely consistent (and incomplete) theories.

The key to these questions is that the right thing for a person in an epistemologically imperfect position to do is to act on the basis of the theory (or collection of theories) that is putatively right, i.e., is most likely to be true in light of the best information available at the time, and that the extent to which we are a obligated to obey a principle is proportional (among other considerations) to the extent to which its truth is evident or discoverable on this basis.

Section (c) will establish that there are some points of agreement among all viable theories that remain after the ones that conflict with facts have been eliminated, even though the number of such possible viable theories is technically infinite (e.g., there are an infinite number of possible coherent interpretations of Rawls). It will also be necessary in this context to eliminate the theory that there is nothing that one particularly ought to do, since it would contain no ethical points of agreement with the other remaining theories, which do make positive 'ought' statements. Section (2) will then develop this point in more detail.

(a) Can an 'ought' contradict an 'is'?

The first question that needs to be clarified is how an ethical statement can contradict a factual one. This would seem possible only if the ethical statement in question somehow implicitly posits the existence of some thing or state of affairs that in fact does not exist. But we normally think of the factual existence of such things as affecting only the application of an ought, not its truth or validity. It is possible that adultery could be wrong even if no one had ever committed adultery or ever would.

Let's begin by considering some non-ethical statements that do and do not contradict each other.

(1) The present king of France has a beard

would normally be taken to contradict the fact that there is no present king of France, provided that we interpret the speaker as meaning to suggest that there is one.

(2) All present kings of France have beards

does not logically contradict the fact that there is no present king of France, though it is rendered trivially true or vacuous by that fact.

(3) All kings of France have beards

neither contradicts the fact that there is no present king of France, nor is it rendered trivial by this fact, for the statement could be taken to apply to past, future or possible kings of France. It would, however, become trivial if it were somehow to turn out to be impossible for there to ever be any king of France, past, present or future. And it would become false if the speaker means to suggest that there could possibly be kings of France, whereas (in the hypothetical situation proposed) there could not possibly ever be any.

Now let's consider some ethical statements.

(1a) The present king of France should be obeyed

must be taken to contradict the fact that there is no present king of France, if we interpret the speaker as meaning to suggest that there is one.

(2a) All present kings of France should be obeyed

does not logically contradict the fact that there is no present king of France, though it is rendered trivially true or vacuous by that fact (if we grant that 'should' has some meaning or other).

(3a) All kings of France should be obeyed,

like (3) above, neither contradicts the fact that there is no present king of France, nor is it rendered trivial by this fact, since it could be taken to apply to past, future or possible kings of France. It would, however, become trivial if it were somehow to turn out to be impossible for there to ever be any king of France. It would also become false if it is meant to suggest that there could possibly be some kings of France and if in reality there could not possibly ever be any. In this case, the question of the truth or falsity of the ethical claim would be decided with absolute certainty (assuming that we know with certainty what the speaker meant) simply by knowing that there could never in fact be any king of France. On the other hand, if the speaker only means that *if* there is ever a king of France, *then* he ought to be obeyed, then the truth of the statement cannot be decided on this basis. But it may be decidable on still another kind of factual basis, as a different example more readily suggests.

We often assume that a statement like

(4) The president of France should get what he deserves

would be false if it could be shown that there cannot possibly be any such thing as desert, which in turn might be taken to follow from the factual claim that man has no free will---assuming, that is, that 'ought implies can.' (To save time, let's omit discussion of the soft determinism issue for now and assume for the moment that the concept of desert intended would be negated by determinism in conjunction with 'ought implies can.')

But why do we assume that ought implies can? Logically speaking, an ought statement would not seem *necessarily* to become false or meaningless just because the subject cannot do what he ought, any more than 'All kings of France should be obeyed' becomes false or meaningless just because there is no king of France. In both instances, it seems more accurate to say that the ought statement is vacuous in some strong sense. We saw that statement (3a) does not become false or meaningless in light of the non-existence of kings of France if what is meant is *'If* there are any kings of France, then they ought to be obeyed.' Similarly, the fact that there is no desert would not render (4) false or meaningless if what it means is *'If* there is such a thing as desert, then the president of France ought to get what he deserves.' In both instances, the statement becomes vacuous, but not false or meaningless. Furthermore, it is perfectly legitimate to express the factual element of a moral statement conditionally in this way, so that the question of the truth of the moral principle is not confused with whether there happen to be any instantiations of it---for example, if adultery were wrong but no one ever had or ever would commit adultery. Yet there still seems to be something radically wrong about the vacuousness of (4) that somehow definitively discredits the ought statement---something more radically wrong than in the adultery example in which there happen to be no instantiations.

The reason for this persistent intuition is that there is a type of vacuous statement that is so deeply vacuous that it cannot possibly be true. There is an important sense in which an ethical statement about things or states of affairs that could not possibly exist is vacuous in a deeper sense than those that are about things that might exist, but as it happens do not exist, as in the adultery example. For, if the thing or state of affairs in question can never *possibly* exist, it can be shown that if the statement is true, then so is its contradiction. 'You ought to ride a two-horned unicorn every time you see one' would be false if it were logically impossible for there ever to be any two-horned unicorns, because we would then know with certainty that there will never be any, and therefore that there will never be a situation in which we ought to ride two-horned unicorns. Therefore, it is not the case that we ever ought to ride a two-horned unicorn in any specific situation, so we ought not to ride two-horned unicorns.

The speaker may then protest that what she really means is 'If there *could* be two-horned unicorns, then we ought to ride them.' But, even when construed in this way, the statement still ends up with its own contradiction being true because, as an ethical principle, it is inapplicable. And if we know with certainty that there will never be a situation in which an ethical principle should be applied, then it is never the case that it ought to be applied; thus it ought not to be applied. In this sense, an ethical statement about things or states of affairs that cannot possibly exist is deeply vacuous, i.e., is not only vacuous, but false. In such a case, ought implies can in a strictly logical way.

Someone will object that logicians normally assume that any universal statement which is never applicable to any real situation in the world becomes automatically true because it has no falsifying instantiations. Some logicians, in fact, have questioned this claim[11], but it is generally accepted. Thus the statement that all kings of France have beards, which we have been using as an example, is assumed to be true in case there are no kings of France. So, it might be objected, it is wrong-headed to try to show that an ethical generalization must be false if it is never applicable. Indeed, its lack of applicability should be enough to ensure its universal (though vacuous) truth.

But there is a clear answer to this objection. In the case of factual universals, the universal does not imply a *subjunctive.* I.e., the statement 'All unicorns have two horns' is vacuously true if there *are* no unicorns; but we cannot automatically claim that it *would* be true if there *were* unicorns. In fact, if there *were* any unicorns, then the statement would be false. Ethical statements of the kind we have been discussing, by contrast, do imply their corresponding subjunctives. For example, the statement 'One ought to ride all unicorns,' if it has any kind of meaning whatever, must be interpreted to mean that, in some sense or other, if there *were* unicorns, then one ought to ride them. Now suppose that, at present, there are no unicorns. If we were to say that the statement 'One ought to ride all unicorns' is automatically true because there are no unicorns, we would also have to grant for the same reason that 'One ought to refrain from riding all unicorns' must also be true. But the conjunction of these two statements would imply that, if there *were* any unicorns, then one ought to both ride them and refrain from riding them, which is clearly a self-contradiction.

Besides *logical* impossibility, there is another type of impossibility that may render ethical statements deeply vacuous. Take the statement, 'Everyone ought to be present at her own father's birth.' It is not logically impossible that a person be present at her own father's birth, for to do so would involve no apparent self-contradiction. It is, however, ontologically impossible to do so if it is necessarily and universally true (as implied by some universally correct theory of physics, for example) that backward time travel is impossible. If such a theory of physics happens to be true (whether we know it is true or not is irrelevant), then it will also happen to be true that backward time travel is impossible, though not logically impossible. So any ethical statement that recommends doing that which is impossible, though not logically impossible, becomes deeply vacuous nonetheless, because it cannot possibly be true. Let's call this type of impossibility 'ontological impossibility.'

There is still another type of impossibility that may render ethical statements deeply vacuous and thus false. There are situations in which people say that we ought to do something under the present circumstances, whereas, given the previous history of the universe (which might have been different), it is now either logically or ontologically impossible to do what is recommended in the present circumstances, and the circumstances cannot be changed. For example, if someone tells me that in all circumstances I ought to do what my grandfather recommends, but my grandfather is dead, the action recommended is neither logically nor ontologically impossible per se (some people can do what their grandfathers recommend), yet it is impossible *under the circumstances.* (To save time, let's simply assume, for now, that there can be no telepathic communication with the dead.)

Statements which are impossible under the circumstances are also deeply vacuous, i.e., cannot possibly be true, for the following reason. Ought statements are meant to answer the question 'What should I do?' But if, say, a mechanic tells me that I ought to buy a new car in circumstances where I cannot afford one, then he has not answered my question. The only way his statement can avoid being deeply vacuous in this case is if, other than buying a new car, there is no effective solution to my problem. But if it is the case that I ought to buy a new car unless I cannot afford it, in which case I ought to have ring and piston work done, then the truth under the circumstances is that I ought to have ring and piston work done. By telling me that I ought to do something other than what I ought to do, the mechanic has said something which is false under the circumstances, although it might be true under other circumstances. To the extent that an ought passes itself off as being the best thing to do in a broader class of cases than it really is, it becomes deeply vacuous and false, for the same reason as in the example in the previous paragraph---i.e., its contradiction can be correctly asserted.

There is, of course, *another sense* of 'ought'---the sense used by such utilitarians (and determinists) as Smart and Schlick[12]---which does not imply 'can'. In this sense, 'X ought to be done' simply means 'It would be good if X were done.' In this way, it makes sense to say 'There ought not to be any blind people,' meaning that in a morally perfect universe (which is not the one we live in), there would be no blindness---or, as Newton once said while contemplating the disorderly motions of the heavenly bodies, "Had I been the Deity, I would have made it better." In this kind of sense, we can say that thieves ought not to steal even if predetermined to do so, in the sense that things would be better on the whole if they didn't, or perhaps that they would be more virtuous or that people would like them better (if that is what we happen to mean by 'ought'). So there are some senses in which ought implies can, and others in which it does not. But, to return now to statement (4), it is pretty clear that the person who makes the statement 'The president of France ought to get what he deserves' means it in one of the other senses of ought which, by contrast to Smart's sense, do imply can, so that the statement does imply a contradiction by virtue of its deep vacuousness in relation to the presumed truth of determinism (*if* we presume this truth, that is). By saying that the president should get what he deserves, it says that something should be done about him which is different from what should actually be done about him in circumstances excluding any attribution of desert to him. We ought not to give him what he deserves if no such option exists.

Let's look at another example of an ethical statement that might contradict an empirical reality---an ethical statement that is often made these days.[13]

(5) Criminals should be punished severely enough and only severely enough to deter them and others from future offenses.

What will happen to this statement if, as many criminologists suggest, most criminals are not effectively discouraged by the threat of punishment,[14] and if those who are are deterred not so much in proportion to the *severity* of the punishment, as in proportion to the *certainty* of it?[15] And suppose further, as these criminologists clearly mean to say, that this difference in susceptibility to deterrence among individual prospective offenders is a matter of *degree* rather than a simple either-or. Then we would end up with a moral statement which, in connection with these facts, would become deeply vacuous because, if we were to refrain from punishing those who are more difficult to deter, we would decrease the *certainty* of punishment for those who are easier to deter to the point where some of them would no longer be deterred. (We assume here that prospective offenders perceive the certainty of punishment essentially in terms of the mathematical chances of any similar offender's being punished. Whether this is the case can be debated, but our point is that there are possible combinations of facts that, if the case, would render the ought statement in question deeply vacuous.)

Furthermore, it would be impossible to make punishments severe enough to deter the most irrational offenders, so we could make the punishment infinitely severe without accomplishing our goal. And at the same time, by making punishments this severe, we would violate the second part of the moral statement, 'and *only* severe enough to deter future offenses.' If this second part of the injunction has any meaning at all, then, clearly, infinitely severe punishments would violate it. Nor does it do any good to say that the 'only if' clause would still hold at least for those who *can* be deterred, because the ability to be deterred is a matter of degree, not a simple either-or. So if we make the penalty severe enough to deter even *some* of those who are more difficult to deter, it will then be more severe than necessary to deter those who are easier to deter. For deterrence is not primarily a matter of being discouraged by one's own punishment, but by the punishment of others. And there is no degree of severity that is enough to deter everyone but no more than necessary to deter some particular ones. Therefore, to speak of punishment severe enough and only severe enough to deter offenses is, in light of the empirical realities involved, like speaking of a temperature cold enough to freeze air but not cold enough to freeze water.

It is therefore conceivable (though we have not yet demonstrated that it is the case) that a set of factual statements could imply an ethical statement in the following way. Suppose we were to learn through logic that there are only three possible ethical theories, X, Y, and Z. And suppose we learn in the way just indicated that Y and Z contradict some factual statements that, let us say for the sake of argument, are necessarily and universally true. We have seen that a factual statement can be necessarily and universally true in three ways. (1) Its denial may involve a self-contradiction (e.g., 'There are two-horned unicorns'); or (2) its denial would contradict universally true ontological principles (e.g., 'I am going to return to the time of my father's birth'); or (3) its denial may have become impossible given the previous history of the universe (e.g., 'I am going to seek the advice of my grandfather who is dead.') Then if theories Y and Z contradict factual statements in some such ways, it would follow that X must be the correct theory, if there is any correct theory. Suppose, then, it were logically necessary that there be a correct theory---that a universe devoid of moral value were somehow self-contradictory or impossible. Then we would be completely justified in assuming that X is the correct ethical theory, and for purely factual reasons.

Unfortunately, the situation in ethics is not that simple. What we have is a series of ethical theories, A, B, C, ...N, which may or may not exhaust all the possibilities. And we have some reasons for doubting the truth of some, though they could perhaps be modified to meet some of our objections. Moreover, the fact that we have managed to think of more devastating objections against A than B could be culturally relative. It may be that the personality dispositions of most philosophers in our culture incline toward a peculiar dislike for A, and therefore motivate us to put a good deal of time and energy into criticizing it. Or perhaps there is more grant money to encourage philosophers to think up improved versions of B than A. To further complicate things, it does not seem on the face of it to be self-contradictory or impossible to assert that no ethical statements whatever are true; so, even if we could eliminate all except one, we still would not know whether it is true or not. Worse still, if A and B define their terms in different ways, they may offer us values which in practice sometimes conflict, without there being any higher court of appeal for such a decision. Worst of all, after all the theories that conflict with facts have been eliminated, the remaining theories may be equally credible from the coherence perspective. And, even if some are more coherent than others, there are still reasons against accepting the most coherent credible theory, as Sayre-McCord suggests.[16]

Thus, if comparative coherentism is to yield any knowledge whatever about what we ought to do, it must do several things: It must, first of all, define 'coherence' in such a way that coherence is a desirable feature of theories, all things considered; i.e., in such a way that a coherent theory is more likely to be true than a less coherent one. It must then show either that one course of action must be definitively favored over another according to such criteria, at least in some cases; or, if certain theories are still equally favorable by all such criteria, that these equally favorable theories agree on at least some ought statements. We must now explore these possibilities.

(b) Complications in the coherence criteria

Suppose now that a number of ethical principles and theories have been eliminated because they conflict with facts as in the above examples, and that several viable principles and theories are left from which to choose. Of these, some are coherent in Sayre-McCord's strict sense while others are not.

Should we now eliminate those that are not coherent in this sense? To do so would oversimplify the situation, because the truth is that no theory is absolutely coherent, and few (other than those that have already been eliminated because of logical or factual inconsistency) are absolutely incoherent. Moreover, approximation to coherence as Sayre-McCord has defined it may not be the only criterion by which to evaluate principles and theories. One theory may be slightly less 'coherent' in this sense than another, yet have other advantages over it, as we shall see.

Sayre-McCord is correct in suspecting that the reasons for accepting the best coherent theory are not compelling, if interconnectedness and completeness are taken as essential for coherence in a theory.[17] But suppose the coherence of a theory is a matter of degree rather than something that is either present or not. Suppose a theory's having two rather than one basic assumption does detract somewhat from its coherence, but does not completely eliminate its coherence. Sayre-McCord's reason for positing interconnectedness---and ultimately a monism of first principles---as a requirement for coherence is that, even if two independent first principles do not obviously lead to a contradiction, there is no guarantee that they will not conflict in some particular situation, in which case some third principle is needed to resolve the conflict and then becomes the true first principle of the theory. But, strictly speaking, such a third principle does not necessarily become the first principle in the sense that the other two could be *deduced from it.* It is more often accurate to say that the theory then has three first principles. But this in itself is no reason to regard the theory as completely incoherent. It is still more coherent with respect to first principles than one that must be propped up with, say, fifteen ad hoc hypotheses. It would apparently be more coherent, for example, than Kant's theory, which besides its initial assumption had to be propped up with three ad hoc hypotheses (God, freedom and immortality).[18] And, though it may be less coherent with respect to first principles than one with only one first principle, it may still be more coherent in other respects. For example, the one first principle of the rival theory may demand a daring leap of faith, whereas the theory with three first principles may demand three very conservative leaps.

Someone may argue (as it seems Sayre-McCord would) that if a third first principle is resorted to in order to resolve the contradiction between the initial two, the whole constellation of principles then becomes one large first principle. This would be an importantly misleading way of looking at it, for the following reason. Suppose $O(u)$ stands for 'You ought to maximize utility,' and $O(r)$ stands for 'You ought to respect people's rights.' Then to resolve the conflict, we have a third principle ---'In cases of conflict, apply formula x'---which could be written, 'If $C(u \& r)$ then $O(x)$,' where C stands for 'there is conflict between.' Clearly, these are three logically independent statements, since any one of them could be logically possible without the others. To say that they really constitute one large principle, 'If not $C(u \& r)$ then $O(u)$ and If not $C(u \& r)$ then $O(r)$ and If $C(u \& r)$ then $O(x)$,' is true only in the trivial sense that *any* series of statements can be written as the conjunction of the statements. If this were allowed, no consistent theory would be any more coherent than any other, just as in natural science all theories would have to be considered equally parsimonious and there would be no such thing as an ad hoc hypothesis---which would be absurd. Why it makes so much difference whether one consistent theory has more unjustified assumptions than another will be discussed shortly.

If we grant that coherence is a matter of degree with regard to number of first principles, it follows that the same is true with regard to the completeness of theories. Suppose there are instances in which two first principles of a theory do conflict, yet the theory provides no clear way to know, on the basis of any of its other principles, which of the two conflicting values should get priority in the given circumstances. To show that this happens in a theory would be a legitimate criticism, but again would not make the theory absolutely incoherent. It might be less coherent than a rival theory in this respect but have other advantages that would make it more coherent in other respects. For example, the rival theory might postulate some arbitrary conflict-resolution principle, such as 'On weekdays, give priority to fairness; on weekends, to maximal utility.' But it would be irrational to suppose that such an arbitrary move would make the theory more coherent than one that honestly left the unresolved issues unresolved.

Now to come to the crucial question about all this. Why, in fact, do we feel inclined to regard a more coherent theory as more likely to be true than a less coherent one? I can see no rational reason for this preference other than the reason the same or a similar preference is shared by natural scientists. I.e., a theory is more likely to be true, all else being equal, if it explains diverse information by means of few theoretical postulates than by means of many. Why? Because it is statistically less probable that one *spurious* theoretical assumption could explain all the data in a field than it is that five thousand spurious theoretical assumptions could explain them all. And it is the statistical improbability that such a marvelous feat as to subsume a diversity of data within few postulates might be spurious, as compared with the pedestrian feat of subsuming them within a large and disorderly array of postulates, that makes us conclude---well-advisedly but without absolute certainty--- that, all else being equal, the more parsimonious theory is more likely to be true. However, as discussed elsewhere, all else often is not equal, and in certain instances there are reasons to suspect that the preference for parsimoneity can be a hindrance to arriving at the truth---most notably in psychology, where we are likely to accept a false and parsimonious theory because the facts which might disconfirm it are systematically difficult to objectively observe in that they are susceptible only to subjective introspection.[19]

If parsimony increases the probability of a scientific theory, all else being equal, then some such reasoning should be equally rational in ethical epistemology as well. The reason such attributes as interconnectedness and completeness are admired is that it would seem to be a more improbable feat to be able to subsume a variety of ethical situations within one or a few principles without ever encountering a contradiction, than to subsume them under a large and disorderly array of postulates. Also, as Sayre-McCord suggests, each possible combination of independent postulates must be reconciled by means of an additional decision principle.[20] If we were allowed as large and disorderly an array of postulates as we pleased, then we could believe anything we liked, regardless of what reason might have to say about it. For example, we could believe in a geocentric universe complete with epicircles and any other ad hoc hypotheses needed to make such a view consistent with the facts. This does not mean, however, that we must fall down on our knees and worship a theory just because it is parsimonious, as Sayre-McCord also rightly insists. Number of first principles and ad hoc hypotheses is only one of the criteria by which theories must be judged.

Besides the completeness, logical consistency, factual adequacy and sheer *number* of ungrounded assumptions a theory makes, the *plausibility* (in some sense) of the ungrounded assumptions would seem to be an important criterion that affects the probability of the theory. For it follows from essentially the same probabilistic reasoning used above that a theory whose first assumptions ask us to accept the most on the basis of rash leaps of faith (or 'direct ethical intuitions' or 'considered moral judgments') are least likely to be true, all else being equal. But how do we determine how 'rash' a leap of faith is? Is it a rash leap of faith to grant Rawls' assumption that 'fairness' in the sense of whatever would be preferred in the original position is the same as 'fairness' in the moral sense? Is this less rash than to grant to the Ku Klux Klan that racial integration is immoral? Or to grant to Nozick the assumption that property rights are more important than any other consideration?[21] To say exactly what there is about an initial assumption that makes it 'more a leap of faith' than some other is a difficult and important problem. Some first principles must surely be less plausible than others for reasons *other than* whether parsimonious theories can be made to *follow from* them. We shall see later that there are good reasons to believe that certain value beliefs are very plausible for reasons other than the coherence of any theories that might be based on them.[22] This does not detract from the importance of coherence, because it does not change the fact that a more coherent theory containing a given set of plausible assumptions is more likely to be true, when considered as a total theory, than a less coherent theory containing this same set of plausible assumptions. But it does mean that, the more a theory's justification depends on unfounded 'ethical intuitions,' the less coherent it is, since a person in an epistemologically limited position cannot as well be expected to be confident of the truth of such assumptions. It should be noted, however, that section (c) will show that, because certain principles are shared by all non-eliminated theories, these principles need no support from any ungrounded assumptions, intuitive or otherwise; and that without such areas of agreement, the comparative coherence approach would be considerably less attractive.

Why should we consider ourselves justified in acting according to a merely probable theory---let alone demanding that others do so? Would it not be better not to act at all than to act according to an ethical system that might well be false? In fact, if we act on the basis of a theory just because it is a little more probable than competing theories, then we act on a theory that is more likely to be false than true. For if there are N competing theories which, let us assume for the sake of illustration, are *approximately* equally probable, and if we choose one just because it is a little more probable than the others, then the chances of choosing the right theory are only approximately 1/N, which will surely be less than the (N-1)/N chances of choosing a false theory. Is this in itself not enough to completely discredit the comparative coherence approach?

Three major points need to be developed before this question can be answered. (1) A crucial point which will be developed in section (c) is that there are certain principles shared by all N of the non-eliminated theories, and that these principles are for this reason certain rather than probable. The other two points are as follows.

(2) If a person in an epistemologically limited position does what is putatively right based on the best information available to her, including all arguments and criticisms of all available theories and all the factual information she can assimilate, then she does what is the unequivocally right thing for a person in her position to do, given that a complete description of her situation would include that she lacks access to the absolute truth. The corollary is that the more obviously true a principle is, the more morally binding it is. Consider, for example, the epistemological position of a baseball manager who tells his pitcher to bunt in a situation where the 'percentages' indicate that this is most likely to be the best course to follow; however, the pitcher fails to bunt correctly and the team loses. Did the manager do the right thing? I.e., what 'should' he have done? If ought implies 'can know' (and in the epistemologically limited position, it always does, for reasons discussed in (a) above), then the manager has done the right thing because there is no way to know that the pitcher, contrary to probability, would fail to bunt successfully, nor do the percentages indicate that the pitcher is likely to succeed if he hits rather than bunting. But if the assumption that the pitcher is more likely to bunt successfully than to hit successfully is a correct assumption, then the manager *should* act according to it rather than according to a worse assumption. Thus, by letting the pitcher bunt, the manager did the right thing, though it did not produce the best consequences. In fact, if the manager told the pitcher to hit rather than bunt, whereupon the pitcher miraculously hit the first home run of his career, thus winning the game, we would still say that the manager had made the wrong decision given the information available, and that he *should* not have let the pitcher hit, although luckily no harm was done by the mistake---just as it would be wrong, and contrary to what I should do, to hold a gun with one empty chamber to someone's head and pull the trigger even if, luckily, the empty chamber happens to come up and no harm is done. (Again, there is also that other sense of 'ought' used by Schlick and Smart, in which ought does not imply 'can know' in this sense, but it is not the relevant sense when I am asking myself what I ought to do; if I am unable to find out what I ought to do, then clearly it is not the case that I ought to do it, for to do so would require that I be able to guess that the best available evidence is false---which I ought not to do.)

(3) One further consideration must be weighed before choosing which theory to act by. What should be done in a given situation is determined not only by the probability of the truth of each rival theory, but also by the

amount of value or disvalue each theory claims would be promoted by the action in question. (I use the phrase 'promote value' to include either producing good consequences in a teleological sense, or promoting value by virtue of 'rightness' in any non-teleological sense.) If theory A says that a given action has a positive value of 10, and the theory has a 60% probability of being true, whereas theory B says the same action has a negative value of 100, but only has a 40% probability of being true, then the odds are that I will be more likely to promote more value or less disvalue by following theory B, even though it is less likely to be true than A. In fact, the odds are 40 to 6 in favor of B.

Suppose, for example, and very hypothetically, that I know somehow that it is certain that I should do what benefits myself, and somewhat less certain that I should do what is fair. If the fairness theory says that to murder a person to gain $5 for myself promotes a grotesque amount of disvalue, whereas egoism says that the same act would promote only a tiny amount of positive value, then egoism should be sacrificed to fairness in this case even if egoism is a little more likely to be true. In the simplest case---if egoistic and altruistic oughts were equally uncertain---I could formulate the general principle that I ought never to grotesquely harm others to benefit myself only slightly, and I ought never to grotesquely harm myself to benefit others only slightly. By acting on such principles as these, I would ultimately end up with a definite set of prima facie 'ought' statements which, based on the probabilities involved in the comparative analysis of the various non-eliminated theories, I ought to follow. And at the same time, I would minimize the chances of doing harm if the theory which is most probable according to the best possible such analysis should happen not to be true after all.

This decision principle would also be capable of resolving the conflict between fairness and utility after a certain fashion. Suppose I believe that utilitarianism is more likely to be true than, say, Rawls' theory of fairness, and that I am then faced with the decision whether to slightly increase the total utility by imposing a great injustice on one person---which would produce grotesque disvalue according to the Rawlsian theory. Suppose also that, after completing the comparative coherentist analysis of the two theories, it turns out that Rawls' theory is *almost* as credible as utilitarianism. Then I must decide in favor of Rawls in this case because the odds are that I will promote more value (or less disvalue) by doing so. Only if I were almost absolutely certain that utilitarianism is the correct and absolutely final answer to the questions of ethics, and that Rawls' theory is false, would the odds favor my choosing utilitarianism in this case. By the same token, a Rawlsian who allows that some credibility might attach to utilitarianism would not be able to allow some trivial question of fairness to outweigh huge amounts of utility either (although it is to Rawls' credit that a true Rawlsian, who judges fairness at the 'macro' level, would probably not do so anyway).[23] Moreover, if it is allowed that the right thing for a person in a limited epistemological position to do is to do what is most likely to be right given available information, then by playing the odds in this way we not only do what is putatively right; we do what is unequivocally right in our circumstances.

Unfortunately, there are several major problems with this approach. (A) Suppose, after eliminating counterfactual theories and principles, and after weighing the remaining ones in terms of probability (based on number and plausibility of their first principles and ad hoc hypotheses as well as on their comprehensiveness), and after balancing this consideration against the amount of value or disvalue each theory claims will be promoted by each alternative action, there are *still* a number of theories and principles that are equally viable, with no further grounds for choosing among them. Not only is such an outcome possible; it seems probable. Suppose Rawls' theory of fairness turns out to be the favored theory in some situation. (This is not unlikely even if one believes utilitarianism is more probable, as we have just seen.) But there are an infinite number of equally coherent versions of Rawls' theory, corresponding to the infinite number of amounts of risk that a rational person might be willing to take in the original position.[24] These different amounts of risk partly account for the widely discrepant interpretations of the consequences of Rawls' procedure, ranging from ultra-conservative libertarianism to socialism.[25] Theoretically, if we allow first principles to be completely groundless, *any* amount of risk aversion or lack thereof could be assumed in the original position. In general, in any theory, a groundless first principle can be assumed which would arbitrarily posit the 'amount' of value attributed by the theory to certain actions. The problem, therefore, is that value is not an easily quantifiable phenomenon; its measurement standards in different theories are therefore difficult to make commensurable with each other in a way that is not arbitrary.

(B) There is also the possibility of what we might call 'perverse' moral theories which, although they assume without proof some malicious first principle (e.g., that all Arabs should be executed), nonetheless are as coherent as possible in all other respects. It is conceivable that such a theory might have only one first principle, that it needs no ad hoc hypotheses, is comprehensive ('In *every* situation, do what is most likely to contribute to the eventual execution of all Arabs'), and has a first principle that, barring direct ethical intuition, is about as plausible as, say, Rawls' assumption that fairness in the sense of what would be preferred in the original position has moral value. Then we would have to weigh such perverse theories in the probability assessment, often ending up with perverse actions being chosen.

(C) Another crucial question is whether the theory that there is never anything that we ought to do is just as plausible by the above criteria as any other (or perhaps more so). Granted, it will often make little difference in our calculations if we regard it as equally plausible with, say, two other theories that conflict in a given situation, as in the example of choosing between a slight amount of injustice and a gross amount of disutility. We would still favor the slight amount of injustice even after weighing the equal probability that it makes no difference what we do. But a worse problem is that, if it is possible that it makes no difference what we do, this thesis might be construed as having the same probability as the total probability that it makes any difference what we do according to any theory whatever. In that case, someone might be considered legitimated in not even bothering to weigh the various probabilities in any given situation. Also, we would tend not to make moral decisions except when pressed, and would be prone not to seek out or volunteer to put ourselves in the position to make moral choices. Such reasoning might not be conclusive, but it does somehow underscore that ethical nihilism has a special status in the comparative coherence approach. The whole idea that moral theories can be assigned probabilities becomes highly questionable unless nihilism can be eliminated, because the whole idea of comparing theories with each other presupposes that there is some correct theory.

These objections would perhaps seem sufficient to indicate that the strategy of comparative coherentism, if limited to what we have so far described, simply will not work. Corresponding to every coherent theory that tells us that action X promotes a value of 10, there will be an equally coherent theory (though perhaps groundless, arbitrary and perverse) which is virtually similar to the other one except that it posits a value of 100 or 1,000 for the same action. The units of comparison then become incommensurable. Thus, if all possible coherent theories are allowed into the comparative analysis no matter how groundless and arbitrary are their basic assumptions, the comparative analysis itself becomes arbitrary. On the other hand, if we dispense with the 'amount of value' criterion and use only logical consistency, factual consistency and number of groundless assumptions and ad hoc hypotheses as the criteria, we will always end up with a large and perhaps infinite number of equally coherent rival theories, and thus no basis for choice.

Another way of stating the problem is that, if logical and factual consistency as discussed in (a) are the only criteria with which to *definitively eliminate* possible theories, then there are still *too many* theories left to be included in the probabilistic comparison just outlined. What we need is a way to definitively eliminate still more of the possibilities before proceeding to probabilistic coherence comparisons.

Beyond logical and factual consistency, this can be established only by showing that some ethical statement is definitely true. Perhaps, then, we should explore the part of the comparative coherence strategy which suggests that, once the illogical and counterfactual theories have been eliminated, the remaining ones might necessarily agree on certain points. Perhaps the points of agreement together with their logical implications, though modest, would be enough to rule out what were called 'perverse' theories in objection (B), as well as the ethical nihilism in objection (C). And they might also provide some basis on which to decide between the arbitrary but equally coherent alternatives with which objection (A) was concerned.

The next section will therefore explore to see whether all non-eliminated theories would agree on enough to enable us to eliminate ethical nihilism and perverse theories, and to insist that the remaining theories be less arbitrary in the kinds and amounts of value they posit.

(c) Must there be any value?

For present purposes, let's count as 'moral theories' not only theories based on non-prudential oughts, such as Moore's and Kant's, but also those theories based on prudential oughts, such as egoism and naturalism (notwithstanding, for the moment, Kant's and Moore's insistences to the contrary, which will be considered in due course).[26] By this definition, ethical nihilism would be interpreted to mean that there is never anything that we ought to do either for prudential or non-prudential reasons. According to this usage, ethical egoism (whether particular or universal) would be sharply distinguished from ethical nihilism because it asserts that there are things that we ought to do for prudential reasons, though not for non-prudential reasons. That is, egoism asserts that there are some things or states of affairs that have value in a sense of 'value' defined broadly enough to be common to all moral theories. 'X has value' in this broad sense would mean (prima facie) that 'All else being equal, X ought (either prudentially or non-prudentially) to be realized.' E.g., if I say that something I desire in an egoistic sense has value, I mean that the thing or state of affairs that I desire (prudentially) ought to be realized, all else being equal. If I say that the welfare of future generations has value, I mean that it (non-prudentially, from my perspective) ought to be realized, all else being equal.

Some theorists (e.g., Moore and Kant) say that a prudential ought cannot be a moral ought because the open question can be asked, 'But should I (morally) value that which I (prudentially) value?' or, in other words, because the prudential ought is hypothetical rather than categorical.[27] But suppose for a moment that all non-prudential ought statements are untrue. Then the answer to the open question would *necessarily* become affirmative, for then it would never be the case that I ought to let any other value supersede the realization of what I prudentially value; yet I would not be able to deny that what I prudentially value would *have* value in such a case. Thus it would necessarily be true that I ought to try to realize my own self-interested values in the only sense of 'ought' which would retain meaning once non-prudential ought statements had been rejected. The open question only remains open as long as there is the *possibility* of non-prudential oughts; it therefore cannot serve as an objection against the statement that, if there were no non-prudential oughts, then I ought to do what I prudentially ought. Only if I valued nothing would it be possible to assert that there is nothing which I (either prudentially or non-prudentially) ought to do.

Since every conscious and emotional being (as all human beings are) values something, even if only in an egoistic sense, it follows that to reject both egoistic and non-egoistic oughts simultaneously would be untenable. If I reject non-egoistic oughts, then I must accept egoistic ones. Since nihilism is being taken here to mean the denial of all oughts, both egoistic and non-egoistic, nihilism in this sense becomes untenable and can be eliminated. This may seem a paltry accomplishment. But what it means for the overall project of comparative coherentism is crucial. It means that, if we are willing to consider prudential theories such as egoism in the comparative analysis of all non-eliminated theories, then we can treat the thesis that there is never anything that we ought to do as having been eliminated. So then if some series of factual considerations should allow us to eliminate all positive ought statements except for X, Y and Z, and if X, Y and Z agree on a few points, p_1, p_2, and p_3, then the series of factual statements would imply p_1, p_2, and p_3, which are then prima facie oughts.

Now that nihilism *has* been eliminated, we can ask whether there is anything that all minimally coherent moral theories have in common with each other. First let's define 'minimally coherent.' Here we include both very coherent and less coherent theories, and we include theories that are incomplete in the sense of failing to provide a clear answer to all conceivable moral questions, so long as the theory does not lead to unresolved self-contradictions or counterfactual implications. We should also exclude from the class of 'minimally coherent' theories those whose comparative probability analysis according to the principles of section (b) above would result in the theory's being considered negligibly probable compared with other theories. The purpose of this stipulation is to save us the trouble of considering the effects of highly improbable theories at every turn of our analysis, which would be a waste of time if such theories are ultimately going to be excluded by comparative probability analyses anyway.

Among these highly improbable theories, it would seem inevitable that we must count theories that provide no arguments to support any of their ought claims, yet make a large or infinite number of ought claims. Many intuitionist theories are in this category. Moore, for example, offers a fairly long list of independent prima facie oughts, each epistemically dependent on a direct moral intuition, yet he insists that there are no general formulae from which the priority of these oughts can be derived in specific cases.[28] Rather, a separate intuition is required for each specific priority decision. But each direct moral intuition is still another ungrounded assumption which is logically independent of all the others, for it would be possible to believe one such assumption without believing the others. We would therefore end up with a number of ungrounded assumptions equal to the number of things considered valuable or obligatory plus the number of possible conflict situations, which would be very large and potentially infinite. Since the degree of coherence of a theory with an infinite number of ungrounded assumptions approaches zero, such a theory cannot be considered even minimally coherent.

Someone might argue that an ethical intuitionism such as Moore's really has only *one* ungrounded assumption, namely, that one's ethical intuition is correct in each situation where a decision is to be made. But a person whose intuition is correct in one situation may incorrectly intuit something in another. Since it is possible for one such intuition to be true and the others false, they logically constitute an infinite number of ungrounded assumptions. And this will be true of any theory whose only epistemological basis is an appeal to direct moral intuitions.

On the other hand, this does not mean that we cannot count as minimally coherent those theories that provide an *argument* as to why we should believe our intuitions in certain cases, or even in all cases, for then the belief is ultimately based on the argument, not the intuition. A utilitarian, e.g., might believe that trusting our intuitions will produce the best results on the whole and in the long run. The intuitions in question are then not the epistemic basis of theory, but specific recommendations *derived from* the theory.

In eliminating pure intuitionisms (i.e., those that appeal for each priority decision on a separate intuition) from the class of minimally coherent theories, we must avoid being seduced into the position that any theory is less than minimally coherent if it fails to provide a precise decision rule for every conceivable conflict. There are some conflicts which no theory can resolve. E.g., if a death squad is going to execute one of two innocent men, both unknown to me, and I am forced to choose which one should live, there is no theory that can give me a good decision rule for this case. That is because, in this case, it makes little difference which one I choose. A coherent theory will be unable to decide those cases in which it makes the least difference which decision is made. It will not, however, be unable to decide between, say, a trivial question of fairness for one person and and earth-shaking question of abject misery for millions of people. In general, the more coherent a theory is, the more able it will be to resolve conflicts that make a great deal of difference (according to its own principles), though it may fail to resolve those that make little difference. Moore's intuitionism, however, insists on still another appeal to direct intuition even in those cases of conflict that make a great deal of difference.

There are also minimally coherent theories that do not pretend to be any more than partial or incomplete theories, which map out a certain small domain, in which they claim to know what should be done, and admit that they do not know what should be done outside of this domain. E.g., someone might claim to know what should be done here on earth without considering how these actions affect life in other parts of the universe. This incompleteness detracts little from the theory's coherence, because it is attributable only to the lack of reasonably obtainable information. Theories whose failure to offer decision rules is not attributable to these considerations, however, become incoherent as they multiply fundamental principles and conflicts for which the theory offers no basis for a decision. In sum, a minimally coherent theory is one that does not lead to irresolvable self-contradictions or to counterfactual implications, and does not require a very large or potentially infinite number of ungrounded assumptions in order to resolve important conflicts arising from information that is reasonably available.

Now let's find out whether all minimally coherent theories as so defined have some things in common with each other. Here I shall concentrate on one particular value claim that they will end up having in common. It is interesting and suggestive to note that all minimally coherent theories can be categorized in terms of how the things they regard as intrinsically valuable relate to consciousness; and for this reason, we shall see that each of them presupposes that the existence of conscious beings must have value. Minimally coherent theories can be divided into four types:

(A) Theories that assert that consciousness or conscious beings themselves have intrinsic value (often called personalist theories);

(B) Theories that assert that *some type or features* of consciousness are intrinsically valuable---e.g., happiness or pleasure (egoism and hedonistic utilitarianism) or authenticity (certain types of existentialism);[29]

(C) Theories that assert that there is something whose intrinsic value is independent of the value of consciousness or of any type or feature of consciousness, but which could not exist without there being some conscious beings---e.g., fairness in the distribution of happiness (Rawls), or the performance of certain obligations (deontologies that emphasize rights and duties);

(D) Theories that assert that 'value' has a relational rather than a simple ontological status---e.g., because 'valuable' means 'desired by someone' (ethical relativism, emotivism and emotivistic utilitarianisms).

Some of these types of theories can be combined, of course. There are emotivist deontologies, deontic theories which also seek to maximize happiness, personalisms which also value happiness and fairness, etc. Nonetheless, the intrinsic values posited by all these theories must be defined somehow in relation to conscious beings. For only a purely intuitionistic theory of the less-than-minimally-coherent type can posit intrinsic values that would have no relation to conscious beings (e.g., that aesthetic value would have moral value even if no conscious beings existed to contemplate the aesthetic value).

The existence of (at least some) conscious beings is necessary in order for any of the above intrinsic values either to be actualized or to even *be* values (whether actualized or not). For, if consciousness did not exist, then the ought statements that express these values would all become deeply vacuous.

On the other hand, while the existence of consciousness is sufficient to ensure the value of some of these values, it is not sufficient for all of them. The existence of consciousness is enough to ensure the truth of the statement posited by theories of type (A), that consciousness has intrinsic value, because it is an empirical fact that at least many conscious beings desire to be conscious beings; thus, from our above refutation of ethical nihilism, it is evident that either the continued existence which these conscious beings desire is intrinsically valuable, or some more important intrinsic value supersedes it. In either case, the existence of the conscious being is prima facie intrinsically valuable.

This step in our reasoning is crucial and should not be passed over too quickly. Some may object that it is misleading to say that the existence of consciousness is sufficient to ensure the value of consciousness, because conscious beings are equally necessary for the existence of both positive and negative values, whatever they are. Given an instance in which the existence of a conscious being led only to negative value (i.e., moral evil), one would not be constrained to say that the existence of the conscious being had net positive value.

To clarify this problem, we must distinguish between (1) the existence of value as that which *ought* to be actualized all else being equal (as contrasted against a state of affairs such that there is never anything that we ought to do); and (2) the existence of *things and states of affairs that have* value, i.e., the *actualization* of values in sense (1). The existence of consciousness is sufficient to guarantee that there will be value in sense (1), but not necessarily that there will be things or states of affairs that are valuable, i.e., the actualization of values.

It can be argued that it is better that there be value in sense (1) than that there not be value in this sense. For, if there is value in sense (1), then it is possible that there may be valuable things and states of affairs in sense (2), whereas if there is no value in sense (1), then these sense (2) values will be impossible. It is also true that the existence of sense (1) values makes possible *negatively* valuable things in sense (2) (i.e., evils). However, if the sense (2) negative value so far outweighs the sense (2) positive value that it would be better for there to be no sense (1) value to begin with, consciousness always has the option to simply cease existing, thus erasing all sense (1) values according to all minimally coherent theories, and thus bringing the sense (2) net value back to zero. Given this ability on the part of consciousness, it is better in net terms for there to be value in sense (1), because without it there can be no valuable things and states of affairs in sense (2). Therefore, consciousness or at least some conscious beings have prima facie value in all minimally coherent theories.

Does this mean that *all* instances of consciousness have value? That may depend partly on which theory one adopts, and on how much sense (2) value the instance of consciousness in question promotes. What is clear is that consciousness either has prima facie intrinsic value (be-

COHERENTISM AND IS-OUGHT RELATIONS 57

cause, as discussed above, conscious beings desire to be conscious), or some other value supersedes the intrinsic value of the consciousness. But other values which might supersede the value of the consciousness in question according to any minimally coherent theory are in turn dependent for their existence on conscious beings (either the one in question, or some other conscious beings, or both). In any case, conscious beings have prima facie value, i.e., value which exists unless some other value supersedes it.

This principle may seem almost as inconsequential as the elimination of nihilism. But consider its implications in the context of the comparative coherentist strategy. It immediately eliminates many of the most perverse theories since they would be inconsistent with it. Other perverse theories become less coherent and thus less probable as a result of it because they have to proliferate ungrounded decision principles and additional basic assumptions in order to avoid conflicting with it, and they must posit some explanation of how the value of whatever it is they propose (e.g., the execution of Arabs) supersedes the value of the conscious beings involved. Each such explanation makes the theory vulnerable to some corresponding objection. E.g., if the theory explains that the execution of Arabs has value in that the action would make conscious beings in general happier, then the theory opens itself to objections; perhaps the happiness in question could be achieved in some other way which would not require the annihilation of something that has prima facie value. Besides becoming vulnerable to a plethora of such objections by accommodating itself to the prima facie value of consciousness, the perverse theory also in the same process becomes less perverse. For now the theory that all Arabs should be executed has been forced to modify itself into something essentially resembling a utilitarianism which, in addition to the usual assumptions of utilitarianism (that happiness has intrinsic value and that we should value the happiness of others as well as ourselves), it also posits that the happiness of an arbitrarily specified group has less value or does not have value; it thus becomes less coherent than ordinary utilitarianism because of these ad hoc hypotheses. So the import of the (now much more mildly) perverse theory in the probability calculations as described in section (b) above would become inconsequential because of the improbability and mild perversity of the perverse theory. In trying to accommodate themselves to the prima facie value of consciousness, all perverse theories will encounter a similar fate. For the various possible value systems that accommodate themselves readily to the value of consciousness yield the four general types of more traditional (and less perverse) moral theories mentioned above.

Someone may suppose that a perverse theory such as the one just mentioned could be construed as at least minimally coherent because it does affirm the value of at least some conscious beings (i.e., non-Arabs), and all that was established in the above argument was that at least *some* conscious beings have prima facie value. But the problem here would be that, if one were to consider the abstract possibility of a world devoid of non-Arabs, the conscious beings in such a world (or at least many of them) would value their own consciousness, and therefore this consciousness would still have prima facie value. In order to deny the value of these conscious beings, then, the perverse theory must posit other prima facie values which presumably would take priority over the lives of these conscious beings. And this is where the perverse theory becomes enmeshed in the complications just discussed, multiplying ad hoc hypotheses and ungrounded assumptions in order to yield its desired conclusion. Indeed, the prima facie value which these other presumed values must outweigh in such a theory would have to be presumed so extremely important that the theory must become extremely incoherent in the attempt to argue that they are more important than the conscious beings in question, in the face of the fact that any other value presupposes the value of conscious beings.

It is not necessary at this point to comparatively evaluate the four types of minimally coherent theories. The important point is that there is something which all minimally coherent theories do agree on, even at a point in the analysis when the only counterfactual theory that has been eliminated is ethical nihilism. Essentially, nihilism is eliminated by the fact that all conscious and emotional beings posit value. The remaining minimally coherent theories then agree that there could be no value without such beings. Value statements derivable from this point are thus ultimately derivable from a factual statement.

We can then set about to (1) eliminate all theories not consistent with all such implications (e.g., perverse theories); (2) eliminate those theories which are not consistent with factual and ontological truths that may be discovered, according to the general strategy discussed in section (a) above (Chapters Three and Four will make a beginning in this direction); and (3) with regard to those aspects of the non-eliminated theories that still conflict with each other, instigate comparative analyses in terms of the coherence (qua probability) of theories as suggested in section (b). Even after such a complex and far-flung project has been carried out (we can by no means complete it in this one book; it is really a scheme for uniting the findings of the entire community of scholars), there is no guarantee that we will be able to answer all conceivable ethical questions. Completeness is not a necessary feature, and perhaps not a desirable feature of coherent theories. Moreover, some of the answers we do arrive at will probably change as future generations discover further factual and ontological truths. But we will be doing what is putatively right based on the best information currently available to us---which, from the standpoint of the person in an epistemologically limited situation, is the right thing to do.

A number of serious objections might still be raised against the refutation of nihilism outlined here---the same objections that would be raised against any attempt to derive 'ought' from 'is', notably Gewirth's attempts. There are in fact similarities as well as differences between this argument and Gewirth's. The next section will establish that none of the objections against Gewirth are applicable here.

2. The Elimination of Nihilism as an 'Is-Ought' Relation

Gewirth's *Reason and Morality* has been criticized by a number of prominent philosophers.[30] The upshot of most of these criticisms is predominantly negative, though many do damn Gewirth with praise before in effect announcing that his well-intended and adeptly-attempted project is a failure. I shall argue, however, that there is a core of truth in Gewirth's approach nonetheless. The refutation of nihilism just outlined attempts to accomplish *part* of what Gewirth's argument attempts, without opening itself to the same objections. It avoids these objections because what it asserts is much more modest. There is no attempt either to prove the existence of *rights* or to overcome *egoism*.

Gewirth argues, essentially, that if a rational agent recognizes that certain goods are necessary for her agenthood, then she cannot without self-contradiction deny that those goods have value (to her). Thus she cannot avoid affirming that it would be a valuable thing (to her), all else being equal, if others would refrain from interfering with her having those goods---which is to say that she must claim that others have a duty to avoid interfering with her having them, and thus that the agent in question has a right to such goods. But if the agent cannot avoid affirming that she has a right to these necessary goods, and if this right follows from what it means to be an agent, then she must admit that the same rights follow from any instance of agenthood. Thus she must admit that all agents have these same rights, and therefore cannot without self-contradiction deny that she herself is constrained to respect them.[31]

This argument is one of the latest attempts to, as J. J. C. Smart so colorfully puts it, 'pull a normative rabbit out of an analytic hat.'[32] Though it has been widely criticized, many of the criticisms have been answered with remarkable persuasiveness by Gewirth.[33] Granted, these answers are not completely adequate, as we shall see, but they show so well the resilience and persistence of Gewirth's fundamental intuition, that one wonders if there is not an insight there after all, though perhaps Gewirth has not developed it in exactly the right way. In what follows, I shall first touch briefly on some important respects in which Gewirth's response is adequate, and some in which it is not. I shall then try to explore how his original argument might be reframed in such a way as to avoid the main criticisms, becoming thereby not a refutation of egoism, but of nihilism.

(a) A brief review of criticisms of Gewirth

The most forceful and prominent type of criticism of Gewirth's core argument focuses on his inference from the agent's valuing the goods necessary for her agenthood to the conclusion that the agent has a right to those goods. As W. D. Hudson puts it, 'But how can the mere fact that anyone insists upon having something give him a right to it?'[34] Gewirth's response is that critics who make this charge have misunderstood the meaning of this inference. What he means to conclude here, he says, is not that the agent *has* such rights, but rather that the agent must, on pain of self-contradiction, *claim or affirm* that she has such rights. And if only this much is granted, then it follows that the agent must also grant the same rights to others, since she has committed herself to the notion that such rights belong to her *by virtue of being an agent,* and thus that the same rights must also belong to any other agent by virtue of that agent's being an agent.[35]

Technically, this response is not completely adequate. In the first place, if all Gewirth means to assert, when he moves from the agent's valuing the necessary goods to her claiming a right to them, is that the agent is logically committed to *claiming* that she has such rights (whereas in fact she may not *actually* have them), then it does not follow that she must grant that other agents have the same rights. All she has to grant in this case is that other agents are committed to *claiming* that they have such rights. Since, by Gewirth's own admission, they may not *actually* have such rights, then there is no reason for the agent in question to *believe* that they actually have them.

Secondly, and of more ultimate importance in my view, it seems that the word 'right' must have an *exceedingly weak meaning* if the agent's claim that she has a 'right' to certain goods is to follow from her recognition that these goods are necessarily *valuable or good.* And the correlative 'duty' of other agents must use a correspondingly weak sense of 'duty' if the notion that people have such a duty to respect the agent's rights follows from the mere notion that it would be *a good or valuable thing* if they were to respect them. In effect, all it would mean in this case to say that someone has a prima facie 'right' to certain goods---given such a weak sense of 'rights'---would be that, all else being equal, *it would be good* if other people were to help her obtain those goods. But this does not entail that other people are *obligated* to help her; that would be a much stronger claim.[36] Thus it does not entail that one is obligated to respect others' 'rights'---only that it would be good, all else being equal, if one were to do so. But, of course, when others' 'rights' conflict with one's own, all else is not equal. So there is really no sense at all in which this reasoning, given such a weak sense of 'rights,' ever commits one to the belief that one even *ought* to respect others' 'rights' in cases of conflict with one's own---let alone that one is *obligated* to do so.

Against the first of these two objections, Gewirth superficially seems to be arguing that the agent in question must at least grant that other agents are just as legitimately entitled to claim the rights as she is, since it is only *by virtue of being an agent* that she claims them. But, strictly speaking, the original agent does not have to grant this. She might have to grant it if what she believed were that having the rights in question follows logically from being an agent. But in Gewirth's argument, the agent is not committed to the idea that having certain rights follows logically from being an agent. She is only committed to the idea that *claiming* to have certain rights (even if one does not actually have them) follows logically from being an agent. So each agent needs only to grant that other agents *claim to have* certain rights (which they may not actually have).

To be sure, it would be strange, and perhaps inconsistent, for the agent in question to believe that *she* is logically committed to claiming a right which *she* actually does not have (and knows that she does not have), for then she might have to both believe that she has the right and believe that she does not have it. But there is no inconsistency in believing that *another* agent is committed to claiming a right which she actually does not have. The problem with Gewirth's reasoning at this juncture is that he proceeds as if the initial agent in question were committed to the idea that one has certain rights by virtue of being an agent. But all the agent is really committed to is that being an agent causes it to be *in one's self-interest to claim* rights, or to believe that one has them, whether one actually has them or not. Therefore, the fact that other agents are just as committed as I am, by virtue of their self-interest, to claiming to have the same rights that I claim to have, does not entail either that they actually do have the same rights that I have, or that I must believe that they actually do have the same rights that I have. It is especially important to notice that an agent is not committed to believing that others' 'right'-claims are objectively legitimate and therefore ought to govern the original agent's actions in the same way as do her own 'rights'-claims.

Gewirth *might* have chosen to get around this objection by claiming somehow that I must admit that other agents really do have as much of a right to the necessary goods as I have, perhaps because they are just as legitimately entitled to claim the right. But, even if such a move could be successfully defended, it would only serve to underscore the truly modest amount of *meaning* in Gewirth's sense of the term 'right'. When I paraphrased Gewirth's argument at the outset, I purposely used the very weak expression, 'It would be a valuable thing [to the agent], all else being equal, if others would refrain from interfering with her having those goods---which is to say that she must claim that others have a duty to avoid interfering with her having them and thus that the agent in question has a right to such goods.' I chose this weak phrasing because, the weaker the definition of 'rights' and 'duties' one chooses, the better Gewirth's argument seems to go through. That these are very weak definitions of these terms indeed is evident from the fact that, according to Gewirth, an agent can infer from its being *'a good thing,'* all else being equal, for people to do something, to the conclusion that they have a *'duty'* to do it and that the agent has a *'right'* for them to do it. If this is a valid inference, then 'A has a right for B to do X,' which is equivalent with 'B has a duty to A to do X,' in turn means nothing more than that 'It would be good (for A) if B would do X'---or rather, in fairness to Gewirth, 'It would be an *essential* good (for A) if B would do X.' So, even if I must grant that others have the 'right' for me to do X, all I am really saying is that it would be (an essential) *good* (for them) if I were to do X. And when I say that others have just as much of a 'right' for me to do X as I have for them to do X, all I am really saying is that it would be just as much an essential good (for them) if I were to do X, as it would be an essential good (for me) if they were to do X. But if this is all Gewirth's argument has established, then two types of questions still seem to be left open: (1) Granted that it would be (essentially) good for A if I were to do X, am I *obligated* to do what is (essentially) good for A? And (2) granted that it would be (essentially) good for A if I were to do X, *ought* I to do what is (essentially) good for A? We can also formulate quantitative versions of these two questions: (1a)*To what extent* am I obligated to do what is (essentially) good for A? And (2a)*How much* of my time and energy ought I to devote to doing what is (essentially) good for A?

Not only does Gewirth define 'rights' and 'duties' in such weak senses as to leave these types of questions open; he also seems to run them together. For he seems to think that the fact that it would be good (for me) if others would do X implies not only that they *ought* to do X, but also that they are *obligated* to do X. It seems plausible enough to infer from 'It would be good if I were to do X' to 'I ought to do X' ---provided, that is, that we define 'ought' in a weak enough way. For example, it would be good if I were to get in my car (it is now 1:00 a.m.), drive downtown, find a homeless person, find her a place to spend the night, and give her the money she needs to pay for it. (I.e., it would be good *for that person* if I were to do so.) So, given a sufficiently weak sense of 'ought', we could say that, all else being equal (i.e., if I have nothing 'better' to do), I 'ought' to do it. But in order to say this, we would have to define 'ought' in such a weak sense that it would be very far from entailing that I am *obligated* to do it, and thus have a *duty* to do it. Obviously, there are many things that it would be good for me to do, and therefore which I 'ought' to do in this weak sense, but it is not so obvious that I would be shirking some 'duty' if I fail to do all of these things. Quite the contrary, it seems absurd to assert that I have a duty to do everything that it would be good for me to do. Even a moral saint could hardly measure up to such an extreme notion of duty or obligation. Gewirth's argument, as it stands, therefore does not quite seem to work.

(b) The sense in which the value of consciousness is undeniable

In light of the above considerations, the first thing that needs to be done, in order to preserve Gewirth's basic intuitive insight, and at the same time to save it from these objections, is to simply eliminate the notion of 'rights' from the argument altogether. For the distinction just drawn between obligatory and non-obligatory oughts may raise some hope that Gewirth's 'is' could ground an 'ought' if the 'ought' were defined weakly enough. But then the 'ought' is too weak to entail a 'duty'. And where there is no duty, there are no rights.

Instead of using the notion of 'rights', Gewirth could fall back on the assumption (in a moment I shall show how easily the assumption could be grounded) that, all else being equal, it is good to do what is essentially good for some agent. From this assumption, he could then simply argue that, since it would be essentially good for A if I were to do X, then, all else being equal, it would be good if I were to do X. Thus I 'ought' to do X, in the weak sense, all else being equal.

The first problem facing this argument, of course, would be to get around Moore's open question argument. The fact that X is 'good for A' in the sense that A actually values X does not entail that X is morally good or right or that it ought to be done. A may value heroin, but she ought not to get it. But our modified version of Gewirth's argument gets around such examples. First of all, that A merely happens to value X would not make X good or something that ought to be done. Rather, that A must necessarily value X in order to be an agent makes X good and something that ought to be done. Take an extreme example: Suppose X stands for avoiding nuclear war (which is essential to the existence of all agents). Then if X is not done, there can be no more agents. Thus X ought to be done, not because (A) it would be self-contradictory for any agent to say that (all else being equal) X ought not to be done, but because (B) the existence of agents has intrinsic value. Here we would have to assume the intrinsic value of the existence of agents, but, as we shall see, this is not such a difficult assumption to ground.

The reason we must steer clear of (A) here is that it appears inevitable that it would ensnare us in essentially the same difficulties for which Gewirth has already been criticized. If X stands for avoiding nuclear war, then obviously it would be self-contradictory for a true agent in Gewirth's sense to eschew it. But suppose X stands for sending enough food to Africa to save its starving masses without grossly inconveniencing ourselves. In this case, in order to argue that it would be self-contradictory for me to oppose the policy (all else being equal), we would have to revive the inference to rights and duties which we are now trying to avoid.

On the other hand, suppose we opt in favor of (B)---that anything that is essentially good for agents is (all else being equal) good *simpliciter* and something that ought to be done, just because the existence of agents has intrinsic value. I suggested above how such an assumption could be grounded.[37] Essentially, what it amounts to is that, regardless of what system of values one chooses (provided that it is even minimally coherent), there can be no value without conscious beings' existing---no pleasure, no happiness, no fairness in the distribution of anything, no self-actualization, no 'having a life,' etc. So any value that there is presupposes the existence of conscious beings. Since conscious beings are needed in order for there to be any value, then conscious beings have value if anything does, in any sense of the word 'value' that has any meaning.

64 COHERENCE AND VERIFICATION

Now the open question argument insists that my valuing X does not entil that X is valuable in an objective sense, because the question remains open as to whether I ought to value X. I.e., X may be objectively bad even though I subjectively value it. But suppose X is my own consciousness. Then either (i) *there is an objective system of values* in terms of which people ought to act, or (ii) *there is no objective system of values* (any correct one, that is), in which case the only value is subjective. If (ii) obtains, then the open question can be closed. For, in this case, anything that anyone values becomes valuable (all else being equal). Thus anything that anyone values is (all else being equal) good in the only sense of 'good' that has any meaning in this case. And, by the weak definition of 'ought', one ought to promote what is good. Since consciousness is the most basic of all goods, on which all other value would depend under condition (ii), then a world devoid of conscious beings would be a world in which no value would be possible. Thus, since a world containing value (and hence containing conscious beings) is better than one devoid of value, it follows that the existence of conscious beings ought to be promoted before anything else, simply because of its own prima facie value. And this in turn entails that we should promote all conditions which are necessary to beings' achieving and maintaining an optimal level of consciousness. Just how much consciousness would constitute an 'optimal level' remains to be worked out. But the notion of an optimal level of consciousness can be extended to include all conditions necessary to its achievement, which plausibly includes optimal amounts of pleasure, happiness, opportunities for self-development, and empathic relationships with other people.[38]

On the other hand, if (i) obtains, then there are objective values which may override people's subjective values. But there can be no objective value without conscious beings any more than there can be subjective value. And, if a world containing value is better than one devoid of value, then it is better for the necessary conditions of this value to exist than not to exist. So whether (i) or (ii) obtains, in either case conscious beings have prima facie value, and in fact constitute the most basic value on which all other values depend. Thus the existence of conscious beings ought to be promoted before anything else because of their own intrinsic value.

I add 'intrinsic' because it is a phenomenological datum that consciousness experiences its own existence as having at least subjective value even if nothing further results from it; thus such existence has value, at least prima facie, even if nothing further results from it, i.e., intrinsically. (Later we must decide whether this implies that, all else being equal, the more conscious beings there are, and the more fully conscious these beings are, the better. Of course, when the number increases too much, then all else is not equal. For miserable material conditions, which are aggravated by overpopulation, tend both to thwart the self-actualization of consciousness in those who do exist, and to create negative value in the form of pain. These issues will be discussed in Chapter Six.)

Many will object that, since the existence of consciousness is equally presupposed as a condition for positive *and negative* value, one therefore cannot say that it has prima facie positive value. However, it can easily be seen that it is better for conscious beings to first exist and then to make the choice as to whether to continue existing, than never to exist at all. For, given that they first exist, they have the power to cease existing at any time if the negative too hopelessly outweighs the positive; whereas, if they initially do not exist, they do not have the power to come into being. Therefore, it is prima facie better (i.e., conducive to more value) if conscious beings exist until and unless they choose to cease existing. When I say that conscious beings have prima facie value, I count as one of the conditions that would override the prima facie value any situation in which a conscious being's existence brings about such overwhelming negative value that it is well justified in choosing at that point to cease existing.

Several important problems remain unresolved if we take this general direction. Perhaps the worst of them stems from our weak sense of 'ought'. (But in fact, we saw that Gewirth also must use such a weak sense if he is to have any hope of making his argument go through.) Given such a weak sense of 'ought', we can say that we ought to promote value, and we can say that all conscious beings, to the extent that they are conscious, have value. And to the extent that they are potentially more conscious than they are, it would be a valuable thing and something that we ought to do (all else being equal) if we were to help them become still more conscious. Nonetheless, such a system would not initially appear to answer any of the *quantitative* and *distributive* questions about ethics. When there is a conflict between one person's having the goods necessary to maintaining and enhancing her consciousness, and another person's having them, on what basis can we decide who gets the goods? I.e., on what principle are goods to be distributed? Secondly, to what extent ought we to promote valuable states of affairs according to this weak sense of 'ought'? It seems that all oughts in such a system would have to be supererogatory rather than obligatory, since the weak sense of 'ought' cannot ground any absolute duties. We could say something like 'You ought to contribute some of your income to the poor,' but not 'You have an absolute duty and the poor have a corresponding right for you to contribute at least X% of your income to the poor.'

In answer to the question 'How much?' it seems that, on the basis of the reasoning presented so far, we can only answer, 'The more the better.' Or, if someone has strangled eight people in their bathtubs, we can say that he ought not to have done it, but only in the sense that it would be better if he had strangled only seven, and better still if he had strangled none at all. We have not yet established any principle on the basis of which we could say that there is a definite number of people that he has an absolute duty or obligation (in some sense) not to strangle. Or, again, Sartre and his friends in the Resistance murdered many French civilians during the German occupation,[39] but since it was done in such a good cause, on balance, these murders could not, on the basis of any reasoning we have seen so far, be considered violations of any duty on their part. We can say that it would have been better if they could have found a way to accomplish their objectives without murdering people, but we can neither say how much better, nor claim that these people had a right not to be murdered. All values would thus seem to blend in some great utilitarian melting pot in which there is no definite amount of good that one ought to do, and no single act that one must definitely do or not do. Certainly, an adequate system of ethics should be able to establish a stricter code of conduct than this.

Should we succeed in answering these questions, we would be accomplishing something that Gewirth's original argument ultimately failed to accomplish. To refresh our memories quickly on this point (the ground has for the most part been covered elsewhere),[40] consider as an extreme example an ante bellum American slave with a cruel master who works him too hard, feeds him too little, prohibits him from learning to read, and horsewhips him as punishment. Is this slave not, nonetheless, an agent? Of course he is, for he makes many moral decisions in relation to his fellow slaves, his own relation to the power structure, and any non-slaves with whom he comes into contact. But if the slave is an agent, then he must already have the amount of freedom and well-being necessary to his being an agent. Therefore, according to Gewirth's reasoning, he would have no right to demand more, and we would have no correlative duty to help him attain more. In short, the institution of slavery would be morally legitimate. The only actions definitely prohibited by Gewirth's argument would be killing the slave or injuring him so severely that he is no longer capable of making decisions and acting on them.

Gewirth might respond that we have the duty to allow the slave enough *freedom to act* on whatever decisions he makes. But this would require more freedom than any of us have. For there are certain decisions that we would all make, if only we had the freedom to act on them. So Gewirth's original argument, which makes use of the concepts of correlative duties and rights, really does not answer the quantitative and distributive questions that it might at first seem to answer.

On the other hand, if we pursue the modified line of argument I have suggested, we might be able to make some progress with these kinds of questions. One way in which the modified argument avoids problems crucial in Gewirth's original argument is that the modified argument concludes, not that each conscious being (and conscious beings include agents) must *claim* that the goods necessary to her being a conscious being (or agent) have value, but rather that the goods necessary to the consciousness (or agency) of each conscious being *actually do* have value. For we saw that, whether the value system we choose is an objective one or a subjective one, it will still end up endorsing the claim that conscious beings have value, since without them there could be no other value. So, neglecting for now the question as to how I personally fit into the picture, I must admit that other conscious beings also have value. For if I were to die tomorrow, the existence of those other conscious beings would still be presupposed by any value that would remain in the universe at that point, in the only sense of the word 'value' that would have meaning in that context.

Someone may object that I am equivocating 'value' in the same way that Gewirth equivocates 'good'. I.e., just as Gewirth says 'good' meaning 'good for me' or 'good for some other agent (though perhaps not good for me),' I am saying that the existence of other agents is 'valuable' *simpliciter* when really it is only valuable *for them*. But the difference is that the revision of Gewirth's argument is able to close the open question where needed. If there are objective values, then conscious beings other than myself have value. If there are no objective values, then subjective value is the only value there is. So if I were to die tomorrow, there would still be value in the only sense of 'value' that would have meaning absent objective value. Thus I must recognize that, in either case, the existence of other people's consciousness has the same kind of value that my own has, and thus that it would be a valuable thing (all else being equal) if I were to facilitate their conscious existence. Whether this entails any *duty* on my part is a different question. But I 'ought' to do it in the weak sense of 'ought'.

It follows from this reasoning that all conscious beings, to the extent that they are conscious or have the potential to be conscious, have the same *kind* of value, and that (with the possible exception of myself), they all have *amounts* of value proportional to their consciousness or potential to become conscious. The fact that we now have a way to compare the *amount* of value that different conscious beings have provides the grounding that we need for a *distributive* system (neglecting for the moment the problem of how I personally should fit into the distribution system). We can define fairness as the principle which requires that the conditions necessary for a continuing, optimal level of consciousness (not just agency) ought to be provided to all conscious beings (again, with the possible exception of oneself) *to the same extent*. That is, the oughtness of the 'ought' in question applies to an equal extent to all of them.

There is an intuition, of course, that warns of a distasteful elitism here. What if one person has the potential to be 'more fully conscious' than another? (This problem would seem to arise with regard to virtually any coherent self-actualization or perfectionist system of ethics.) I think the strength of this intuition arises from two points the prereflective understanding of which always accompanies the intuition. The first is that no one should set herself up as judge of the extent to which individuals are conscious or have the potential to become so. Elitism arises largely from the natural but erroneous tendency to identify 'consciousness' with 'intelligence' in the sense of problem-solving ability. But intelligence in this sense has nothing to do with the individual's degree of consciousness. A good computer can solve most problems better than any of us, but is not therefore more fully conscious (contrary to the view of some extreme functionalists). Wagner seems to have been less adept than Mozart at such intellectual abilities as memory and calculation, since the latter often amused his friends by memorizing an entire score at one reading, and could instantly solve the most complex problems of counterpoint while improvising. But none of this makes Wagner's music expressive of any less depth of emotion than Mozart's. Similarly, it would be a gross error to judge the amount of feeling existing in an idiot by observing her intellectual ability. Nor should one assume that someone like Epictetus, because of his outward appearance of calm, did not have deep feelings.

The second important point that seems to ground the natural intuition that elitism is distasteful is that we tend to assume that a more fully conscious being *needs* less assistance in the fulfillment of her conscious potential than does a less fully conscious being. This is at least true to the extent that competence in dealing with one's total emotional life tends to correlate with one's degree of consciousness. So it seems (rightly, I think) incorrect to say that we should help those most who need the help least. We must therefore modify the distributive principle so that we ought to facilitate the continued, fully-conscious existence of all conscious beings proportionally to the extent to which they are conscious or capable of becoming so, but also proportionally to the extent that they need our help. (The need for this modification will be shown in Chapter Five, where this point will be developed more fully.)

Some classes of conscious beings obviously have less potential for consciousness than others. Notably, most types of animals are capable of achieving only a very small amount of consciousness compared with people. Therefore, their existence, while it does have some intrinsic value, has less intrinsic value than that of people.

If this principle of fairness is essentially capable of being developed into a solution of the *distributive* problem (obviously, what has been said so far does not develop it), then what about the *quantitative* problem? Given that it would be good (or valuable) if I were to help people (or 'rescue' them, to use Gewirth's term), how does this imply, and to what *extent* does it imply, that I have a *'duty'* or am *'obligated'* to go around helping and rescuing people?

At this point, one viable strategy might be to borrow a page from the Rawlsian book. If we know how goods ought to be distributed, then we know in principle how the best possible society ought to be structured. Once the structure of this society has been delineated, such a delineation would define what political rights and obligations this ideal society would force and/or encourage people to have toward each other. We could then say that we ought to try to make our present society match the ideal society in this respect to the greatest possible extent. Thus we ought to have a society that enforces those rights and obligations which can be calculated as likely to produce the fairest possible distribution of goods. Only in this way (and certainly not *prior to* answering the distributive question) can we hope to answer the quantitative question with respect to rights and obligations. Once we know what rights and obligations the ideal society would impose, we are in a position to say that a person is 'definitely obligated' to refrain from strangling *any* people in their bathtubs, and not merely that one 'ought' to refrain from strangling too many, all else being equal.

We should also note that any interrelationship between conscious beings who affect each other's freedom and welfare constitutes a 'society' in this sense, and therefore ought to be brought into conformity, insofar as possible, with the fairest possible distribution system for necessary goods (i.e., goods that facilitate conscious existence), and thus with the system of rights and obligations most likely to accomplish the fairest possible distribution of such goods.

The only 'rights' and 'duties' that can be established in terms of the revised form of the argument, then, are those which we can say ought to be enforced by the ideal society, i.e., the one in which the distributive principle is most fairly embodied. In the realm of personal morality, which one normally expects to go beyond the demands of social justice, there are indeed additional oughts. For example, one ought to contribute to worthwhile charities. But to speak of these oughts as 'duties' (as is sometimes done in ordinary language) is to use a much weaker sense of 'duty' than it has in the context of socio-political rights and duties---so much weaker, in fact, that 'It is one's duty to contribute to worthwhile charities' means no more than that 'One ought to contribute to worthwhile charities.' In the socio-political context, by contrast, 'It is one's duty to support the needy' can be framed in such a way that, because of the distributive principle arising from the equal value of everyone's consciousness (with the possible exception of my own), it ought to be translated into legislation stipulating that one will be forced to do what is necessary to support the needy and punished for evading the duty.

There is one glaring problem whose solution has not yet been hinted at here. Ironically, it is the problem Gewirth originally set out to solve: the problem of egoism. We have seen that the revised argument establishes beyond reasonable doubt that not only my own consciousness, but also that of other people, has value not only prudentially (to the person in question) but also *simpliciter*. But the large problem we bracketed at that point was that we could not establish that the consciousness of others has the same *amount* of value as my own. Why should I sacrifice the fulfillment of my own consciousness in order to help others fulfill theirs? Indeed, why should I even inconvenience myself for this purpose? The fact that I acknowledge that others' having the necessary goods to fulfill their consciousness 'has value' does not necessarily obligate me to *do* any particular thing about it. And, given that I am not obligated to do anything about it, why should I trade off that which is both subjectively valuable to me *and* valuable simpliciter, in order to realize that which is valuable simpliciter, to be sure, but not valuable *to me*?

Moreover, although in an abstract sense I must acknowledge that the existence of all conscious beings (with the possible exception of myself) have essentially the same kind and amount of value, in practice there seems no reason to suppose that I either could or would support sociopolitical policies that would be formulated as if I personally did not exist. Before I can support any such policies, it seems necessary that there be some reason for me to count myself as merely one citizen among many, having only the same value as the others. Otherwise, will I not end up making all decisions, including social and political ones, in terms of my own self-interest? In short, why be moral?

In truth, neither Gewirth's argument, nor my revised argument overcomes egoism. Gewirth's argument does not overcome it because, as we saw, the 'duties' that it grounds are not 'duties' in the obligatory sense, but at best only in the weak sense that it would be good or valuable if I were to do certain things. Nor does it answer the quantitative and distributive questions. The revised argument does provide a basis for answering the quantitative and distributive questions, but only when I leave myself out of the picture; it does not prove that I should distribute goods equally (or in any other particular proportion) *between myself and others*.

The problem of egoism is therefore a separate issue, and one that in principle cannot be solved by any is-ought argument. Moreover, the question of egoism really has more to do with why I should be moral in the sense of what is to *motivate* me to be moral, than it does with how it is that I understand what *is* moral to begin with. But, granting at least temporary failure on the part of the revised approach to Gewirth's argument to resolve the problem of egoism (which is a problem for any moral philosophy), consider what the revised argument does accomplish.

In effect, the revised argument seems to achieve essentially what Gewirth set out to do (except for the problem of egoism): It derives prima facie oughts (granted, modest ones) from the realm of 'is' statements. The logical structure can be outlined as follows:

1. Either there is a correct system of objective values, oughts and duties, or all values derive their value by being subjectively valued by someone.

2. In either case, the existence of conscious beings is prima facie presupposed by any value that there is, and therefore is itself valuable. I.e., it is better that there be conscious beings than not, because without them there can be no value whatever. (Several objections against this inference were answered.)

3. By definition, one ought to promote that which is valuable.

4. Thus, one ought to promote the optimal amount and degree of conscious existence, and, extrinsically, all conditions necessary to conscious existence.

5. Since all conscious humans (with the possible exception of oneself) have the same kind and amount of value, one ought to promote their necessary conditions equally and in proportion to the extent that they need one's help. (The status of oneself in this schema has still to be worked out and will be addressed in Chapter Three below.)

Granted, the argument proposed here is quite a radical revision of Gewirth's reasoning. Perhaps Gewirth does not need to revise his views to this extent. After all, the logical problems in Gewirth's original argument are not universally recognized as such (especially not by Gewirth himself) and may yet be successfully defended. But the key problem in any such defense is how to close the 'open question.' The revised argument presented here does seem capable of closing it, by contrast to Gewirth's version. It also seems capable, in principle, of grounding answers to the distributive and quantitative questions with which Gewirth's original theory seems to have more trouble than it originally seemed to have.

3. *Cumulative Summary and Transition*

We have now seen that, aside from arbitrary emotional whims, which are not genuinely normative judgments, no ethical statement can be demonstrated either logically or through objective-empirical observation, nor is intuitionism an adequate basis for such beliefs. The idea of comparative coherentism seemed a promising strategy for deciding on the relative probabilities of theories, except that there were too many approximately equally coherent theories, and there was no commensurable basis on which to compare the probability of these coherent theories with that of ethical nihilism. Now that nihilism has been eliminated, not only does it remove the latter obstacle, but it also may give us some basis on which to compare the remaining theories.

Ultimately, the epistemological basis for the elimination of nihilism, i.e., for the thesis that conscious existence definitely has (either prudential or non-prudential) prima facie value, is essentially a phenomenological datum: the sheer fact that conscious beings do value things (especially their own existence). This fact is not something that is known through *objective* observation in a strict empiricist sense, nor can it be proven logically. It is known through a very easily accessible phenomenological analysis of the nature of one's own subjectivity. This point will be explored further in the next chapter.

Two other major obstacles remain, however. The first is that egoism has not yet been eliminated. This problem has two main subdivisions. (a) No particular proportion can be established between the extent to which I ought to promote what is good for myself and the extent to which I ought to promote what is good for others. And (b) if psychological egoism is the case, then it might not be possible for a person to be motivated to act according to any non-egoistic value system.

The second major unresolved obstacle is that, even if egoism can be overcome, there will still remain a number of approximately equally coherent theories whose probability cannot be compared in any meaningful way. It is therefore necessary to discover some *factual or ontological* truths with which some of the remaining theories conflict, so that the field can be narrowed still further.

These two major remaining problems are the Charybdis and Scylla referred to earlier: the 'Why be moral' question, i.e., the question of the motivational ability to act according to non-egoistic motives; and the determinism/compatibilism problem as it relates to the 'ought implies can' issue. Note that both these monsters are brute-factual ones, involving not normative questions per se, but moral-psychological ones.

The first chapter of Part II, then, will concern itself first with an investigation of some necessary or 'ontological' features of the motivational dimension of consciousness, and then with the implications of these features for ethics, whose effect will be to overcome egoism and give people a motivation (which they prudentially ought to cultivate) to find out what is objectively morally right and act accordingly (while at the same time this subjective motivation does not *dictate* what in the end is going to turn out to be considered morally right by the person in question). The remaining chapter of Part II will consider the other moral-psychological problem---determinism/compatibilism---and the ethical implications of this factual or ontological issue. We will then be in the possession of enough factual information to chart a fairly narrow course between Charybdis and Scylla. These facts will narrow the number of normative options to the point where the remaining ones will be susceptible to a meaningful comparative-coherence analysis, which we shall then attempt in Part III.

I also hope to make evident at each juncture of these analyses that if (contrary to my usual habit) I should commit some error, other philosophers may simply correct my mistake in such a way that the *correct* conclusion at each juncture will still fulfill the same ultimate purpose, i.e., eliminating those normative theories which are not compatible with the facts so as to guide the ship on the *true* narrow course between Charybdis and Scylla.

NOTES

[1] N. Rescher, *The Coherence Theory of Truth*.

[2] Keekok Lee, *A New Basis for Moral Philosophy* (London: Routledge & Kegan Paul, 1985) attempts to erect a coherentist epistemology for ethics based on the similarities between ethical and scientific reasoning. Such schemes have been critiqued by Gilbert Harman, "Moral

COHERENTISM AND IS-OUGHT RELATIONS 73

Explanations of Natural Facts---Can Moral Claims Be Tested Against Moral Reality?" (See Chapter One, note 4); by Nicholas Sturgeon, "Moral Explanations," D. Copp and D. Zimmerman, eds., *Morality, Reason, and Truth: New Essays on the Foundations of Ethics* (Totowa, N.J.: Rowman and Allanheld, 1985); and by David Wong, *Moral Relativity* (Univeresity of California Press, 1984), among others.

[3]DePaul, "Reflective Equilibrium and Foundationalism."

[4]Sayre-McCord, "Coherence and Models for Moral Theorizing."

[5]If we grant that the principle of non-egoistic ethical hedonism does not follow logically from the assumption of an egoistic psychological hedonism, then the reasons for preferring utilitarianism rest heavily on Mill's critique of Kantian and intuitionist theories in the opening pages of his *Utilitarianism* (New York: Dutton, 1931), 3-4. At the same time, Kant's case rests crucially on the refutation of prudential ethics (see note 26); Scheler's on the refutation of both Kantian and utilitarian ethics in his *Formalism in Ethics and Non-formal Ethics of Values* (Evanston: Northwestern University Press, 1973), 12ff; and Rawls' on the refutation of utilitarianism, Kant, and intuitionism (which theoretically would include even the more sophisticated intuitionisms such as Scheler's phenomenological one)---as evident in the discussion by Sterba (see note 21), 5-10.

[6]Sayre-McCord, "Coherence and Models for Moral Theorizing." See also *Essays on Moral Realism* (ed.) (Ithaca: Cornell University Press, 1989).

[7]Paul Edwards, "Hard and Soft Determinism," in Sidney Hook, ed., *Determinism and Freedom in the Age of Modern Science* (New York: Macmillan, 1961), 161-62; J. J. C. Smart, *Ethics, Persuasion and Truth* (London: Routledge & Kegan Paul, 1984), 116.

[8]Kant, *Foundations of the Metaphysics of Morals* (New York: Bobbs-Merrill, 1959), 59-83.

[9]Alasdair MacIntyre, *After Virtue* (Notre Dame: University of Notre Dame Press, 1984), 23.

[10]J. R. Searle, "How to Derive 'Ought' from 'Is'," *Philosophical Review* 73 (1964), 43-58; Alan Gewirth, *Reason and Morality* (Chicago: University of Chicago Press, 1978); C. L. Stevenson, *Facts and Values* (New Haven: Yale University Press, 1963).

[11]E.g., Fred Sommers, *The Logic of Natural Language* (Oxford: Clarendon, 1982).

[12]Smart; Moritz Schlick, *Problems of Ethics* (Englewood Cliffs: Prentice Hall, 1939), Chapter 7. We should note that Schlick

might not agree that his sense of 'ought' does not imply 'can', but this is only because he construes the meaning of 'can' in an unusual way, leading to the soft determinist and inevitably utilitarian consequence that people ought to do things that external factors beyond their control have forced them to be incapable of willing to do.

[13] E.g., James Sterba in *The Demands of Justice* (Notre Dame: University of Notre Dame Press, 1980), 81, says "Punishment is to be generally restricted to the least amount of harm sufficient (1) to maintain general deterrence among those who would be tempted to commit similar crimes and (2) to prevent recidvism among criminals." John Hodson in *The Ethics of Legal Coercion* (Dordrecht: D. Reidel, 1983) and many others have proposed similar deterrence principles in criminal justice theory.

[14] E.g., Lee McPheters, "Criminal Behavior and the Gains from Crime," *Criminology* 14 (1976), 137-52; Charles McCaghy, *Crime in American Society* (New York: Macmillan, 1980), 97-99; William Chambliss, *Crime and the Legal Process* (New York: McGraw-Hill, 1969).

[15] Charles Tittle and Alan Rowe, "Certainty of Arrest and Crime Rates: A Further Test of the Deterrence Hypothesis,"*Social Forces* 52 (1974), 455-62; Charles Logan, "On Punishment and Crime (Chiricos and Waldo, 1970): Some Methodological Commentary,?" *Social Problems* 19 (1971), 280-84; "General Deterrent Effects of Imprisonment,"*Social Foces* 51 (1972), 64-73.

[16] Sayre-McCord, "Coherence and Models for Moral Theorizing," 181-185.

[17] Sayre-McCord, 172.

[18] Kant, *Critique of Practical Reason,* 126-138.

[19] R. D. Ellis, "Phenomenological Psychology and the Empirical Observation of Consciousness."

[20] Sayre-McCord, "Coherence and Models for Moral Theorizing," 172.

[21] As bluntly stated by James Sterba, "Recent Work on Alternative Conceptions of Justice,"*American Philosophical Quarterly* 23 (1986), 1.

[22] See section 2 of this chapter and Chapter Three, section 2.

[23] Robert Wolff, *Understanding Rawls* (Princeton: Princeton University Press, 1977), 77ff.

[24] D. Kay, "Playing Games with Justice,"*Social Theory and Practice* 6 (1980), 33-52.

COHERENTISM AND IS-OUGHT RELATIONS

[25] See Chapter One, note 7.

[26] Kant, Foundations, 59-83; G.E. Moore, Principia Ethica (Cambridge: Cambridge University Press, 1956), 67.

[27] See note 26.

[28] Moore (note 26), 162ff.

[29] See Chapter Three, section 2.

[30] Alan Gewirth, *Reason and Morality* (Chicago: University of Chicago Press, 1978); Edward Regis, Jr., "Gewirth on Rights," *Journal of Philosophy* 78 (1981), 786-94; E.M. Adams, "Gewirth on Reason and Morality," *Review of Metaphysics* 33 (1980), 579ff; Sid B. Thomas, Jr., "The Status of the Generalization Principle," *American Philosophical Quarterly* 5 (1968), 181; Jan Narveson, "Gewirth's Reason and Morality---A Study in the Hazards of Universalizability in Ethics," *Diologue* 19 (1980), 652-74; W. D. Hudson, *Modern Moral Philosophy* (Garden City: Anchor, 1970); Jesse Kalin, "Two Kinds of Moral Reasoning: Ethical Egoism as a Moral Theory," *Canadian Journal of Philosophy* (1975), 345ff; see also the critical essays by various authors and the response by Gewirth in Edward Regis, Jr., *Gewirth's Ethical Rationalism* (Chicago: University of Chicago Press, 1984).

[31] The essentials of this argument are contained in *Reason and Morality*, 1-128, and in Gewirth's "The 'Is-Ought' Problem Resolved," in *Human Rights: Essays on Justification and Applications* (Chicago: University of Chicago, 1982).

[32] Smart, *Ethics, Persuasion and Truth* (see note 7), 8.

[33] Gewirth, "Replies to My Critics," in *Gewirth's Ethical Rationalism*, 192-255.

[34] W. D. Hudson, "The 'Is-Ought' Problem Resolved?" *Gewirth's Ethical Rationalism*, 127.

[35] Gewirth, "Replies to My Critics."

[36] A similar point is made by Jan Narveson, "Negative and Positive Rights in Gewirth's *Reason and Morality*," *Gewirth's Ethical Rationalism*, 96-107.

[37] See Chapter Two, section 1(c).

[38] R. D. Ellis, *An Ontgology of Consciousness* (Dordrecht: Nijhoff, 1986), esp. Chapters 4 and 5. See also Chapter Three, section 2 of this book.

[39] Simone deBeauvoir, *The Ethics of Ambiguity* (New York: Philosophical Library, 1967), verifies that many such murders were carried out by the Resistance, and justifies them essentially on the basis of a quasi-utilitarian calculus.

[40] See especially D. D. Raphael, "Rights and Conflicts, "*Gewirth's Ethical Rationalism,* 84-95.

PART II

METAETHICAL IMPLICATIONS OF PSYCHOLOGICAL FACTS

CHAPTER THREE

FIRST FACT: THE MOTIVATION TO BE MORAL

One side of the Strait of Messina is guarded by Scylla, who, representing herself alternately as a beautiful nymph and as a terrible monster, will let no ship pass unless it can first answer the question 'Why be moral?' The reefs are strewn with wrecked pieces of ethical vessels that failed this test. Some, lured by the charm of the nymph herself, have answered the question by positing that she should be moral because, at heart, she is really motivated to do things which are moral although she may not realize it. In each of these cases, Scylla's reply has been to show her true colors by devouring the crew and smashing the ship, since that is what she is motivated to do. These, in fact, are the ships of which she is most contemptuous, because they sail under false pretenses, claiming to be normative vessels whereas in reality they are only amateur psychological ones, and claiming to know better than the professionals ---and, more to the point, better than Scylla herself---what she really wants, though they contradict what she *thinks* she wants. Concerning whether she ought to do *everything* she 'really' wants to do (even if not nice) they have little to say, having already committed themselves to the thesis that she wants to do what she ought, and therefore ought to do what she wants.

Then there are those other ships which, when confronted with Scylla in her monster form, cry out that she ought to be moral whether she is motivated to be moral or not. But, of course, they have forgotten to erase the slogan 'OUGHT IMPLIES CAN' which is still emblazoned conspicuously on their hulls, so that Scylla, inflamed by these words, cannot imagine how she is to be moral if her total motivational condition impels her to be immoral.

Let's begin our own journey by carefully circumscribing our reasons for needing to consider the question 'Why be moral?', and thus the problem of egoistic motivation, in the context of moral epistemology, so as to guard against pursuing beyond the bounds of our necessary purposes what is an interesting issue in its own right. The crucial reason to discuss the problem of egoistic motivation in relation to moral epistemology can be stated succinctly as follows:

(1) If psychological egoism is true, and if ought implies can, then it appears, at least on the face of it, that no one ever ought to do anything other than what is in her own self-interest. Therefore, no *non-egoistic* moral system is possible. But, if psychological egoism is granted, then it also follows that an *egoistic* moral system is pointless and a waste of time, since it would only tell people to do what they are going to do anyway. Thus *all* moral systems, egoistic or non-egoistic, are either impossible or pointless.

(2) Even in the senses of 'ought' which technically do not imply 'can', (as in 'there ought not to be any incurable diseases'), it would still be pointless and a waste of time to tell people what they ought to do if they cannot do it and therefore are not going to do it no matter what we say.

If psychological egoism is true, then, whether or not ought implies can, all ethical discourse appears on the face of it to be either (a) false or (b) pointless and a waste of time. And it is only for this reason that we must consider the question of egoism, stoically resisting the temptation to become involved in the many issues pertaining to egoism that would be irrelevant to this ultimate purpose.

At the same time, we must also continually remind ourselves that it is not enough to show that there is some minuscule *logical possibility* that egoism might not be conclusively true. If the truth of any ethical theory we posit presupposes the *falsity* of egoism in one sense or another, and if egoism in this sense is just as likely to be true as false, then the theory in question is just as likely to be false as true. Not only are people not likely to be motivated to obey a theory that is just as likely to be false as true; it is quite arguable that they *ought not* to obey a theory that is just as likely to be false as true; i.e., it is not the case that such a theory ought to be obeyed. But, since the central claim of every ethical theory is that it ought to be obeyed, such a theory becomes completely false in its central claim. Thus it is not enough to show that egoism *might conceivably* be false in the relevant sense; we must show positive reasons to believe that there is enough of an altruistic motivation in human beings to counteract the unfortunate implications of egoism just mentioned. For this purpose, we must investigate certain aspects of the nature of consciousness which are crucial to grounding in a *positive* way the motivation to be moral.

1. The Problem of Egoism

According to the reasoning just outlined, if human nature were constituted in such a way that each person could in each case act only in accord with her own self-interest, then no coherent and non-trivial system of moral philosophy would be possible. We could, of course, advocate rearranging the society so that there would be less conflict among the egoistic interests of individuals. But we could not *coherently* (and in truth) advocate that anyone should support such a program unless it were in her egoistic interest to do so. And if it were in her egoistic interest to do so, then we would only be telling her to do what we knew she was going to do anyway, which would indeed be to advocate an ethical system, but a completely *trivial* one. In general, if human nature were completely dominated by a true egoism, in the sense of a motivation to pursue only one's own interests, then there would be no purpose in prescribing what anyone ought to do, because it would be possible only to endorse all and only those actions which we know people are going to commit anyway. Thus any such system would be trivial. Of course, we might be able to get people to act contrary to their self-interest by convincing them that a false assessment of their self-interest is the correct one; but to do so would be to put forward an *incoherent* (because obviously false) view. Or we might be able to prudentially clarify people's assessment of their self-interest so as to change their minds about what they were going to do; but this would change only their analysis of the *facts* of the case at hand, and would therefore constitute a purely factual assertion, not a normative one.

It will be helpful throughout this discussion if we notice at the outset that egoism would still have these same devastating implications for ethical theory even if it is defined in such a broad way that it is compatible with altruistic feelings and behavior. Suppose, for example, that egoism is defined this way: 'To act egoistically is to act in such a way as to satisfy, to the best of one's ability, one's strongest motive in each situation.' By this definition, a man who sacrifices his life to save the life of a friend is acting 'egoistically', although his action must also be viewed as *altruistic* in that he is not acting to *benefit* himself (i.e., make himself 'happy' or 'pleasant' in some sense). There is no contradiction between egoistic and altruistic motivation if egoism is defined in this broader way (though such an egoism does not entail hedonism). For this reason, many philosophers regard such an egoism as trivial and of no important consequence. It may even be viewed as a tautology that all *motivation* is egoistic if egoism is defined to mean acting according to one's strongest *motive*.[1]

While I agree that it may be stretching ordinary usage to call such a broadened position 'egoism', I do not think that it is trivial by any means. In fact, the real motive for calling it 'egoism' is that it has the same unfortunate implications for ethics that other egoisms have. If there is a law of human nature which states that everyone must always act according to her strongest motive, then it would at least *appear* that we have a problem: If I tell someone she ought to do X, but X is not what she is most strongly motivated to do under the circumstances, then I am telling her that she ought to do what she *cannot* do. On the other hand, if I tell her to do X in circumstances where X *is* what she is most strongly motivated to do, then I am merely telling her to do what she was going to do anyway. In either case, ethics is pointless and a waste of time. As we saw at the outset, this is the essential problem that egoism poses for ethical theory. If 'egoism' by the broad definition just mentioned poses this same problem, perhaps it is just as well that we allow it to be called egoism. For, whatever it is called (I shall refer to it as 'egoism in the broader sense'), we still have to deal with it. It would be fruitless to try to sidestep a problem simply by depriving it of a name.

If we understand egoism in the *narrower* sense to mean that everyone always does whatever she thinks (or, in some sense, feels) will best promote her own 'self-interest,' this egoism is difficult to distinguish from egoistic *hedonism*. If any distinction can be drawn between the two views, the distinction would obviously hinge on the difference between 'self-interest' in the narrow definition and 'happiness' (or 'pleasure', if indeed there is any difference between happiness and pleasure). We might say, for example, that a president who is motivated purely by a desire to be well spoken of in history books is motivated by a desire to attain his own self-interest, but not by a desire to attain 'happiness'---if, that is, we define 'happiness', as is normally done, to denote some *experience* or complex of experiences. The president would then be acting egoistically in the narrower sense, but would not be acting hedonistically. Both these types of motives would be distinguishable from an egoistic motive in the *broader* sense. If the president is guided in all his actions by an overriding concern for the well-being of future generations, this motive is neither hedonistic (by any meaningful definition of 'happiness'), nor is it egoistic in the narrower sense, since the well-being of future generations cannot be equated with the president's own self-interest. It is, however, egoistic in the broader sense, for the president is acting in accordance with his strongest motive, which is to promote the well-being of future generations. (Again, if this is his motive, it will be a waste of time to tell him that it ought to be; and if it is not his motive, it will also be a waste of time to tell him that it ought to be. So even egoism in the broader sense remains a problem.)

The similarity between egoistic hedonism and egoism in the narrower sense arises from the fact that to seek happiness (or 'pleasure') is to seek something that is in one's own self-interest. But the converse is not true. To seek what is in one's self-interest is not necessarily to seek happiness, if one is not the kind of person who places ultimate priority on the desire for happiness in one's emotional makeup. A masochist, for example, may pursue his own self-interest without pursuing his own happiness. Many existential psychologists, such as Rollo May, have given this distinction between happiness and self-interest a crucial place in their motivational theories, emphasizing that to seek happiness as one's only goal is not in one's self-interest; that it would be better to sacrifice some happiness if that is what is necessary to keep one's life from becoming a state of contented---but zombie-like---semi-consciousness.[2]

Egoism in the narrow sense is therefore a sub-category within egoism in the broader sense. Egoistic hedonism, in turn, is a sub-category within egoism in the narrower sense. The truth of any one of these doctrines would seem to have the above-outlined implications for ethical theory, unless we can devise some way around them.

It is also important to avoid confusion between 'egoism in the broader sense' and determinism (which will be discussed in the next chapter). The thesis that actions are predetermined does not necessarily imply that they are predetermined *in the way* specified by egoism in the broader sense. It is also conceivable that someone might argue that a person can become an egoist in the broader sense without having been predetermined to do so.

(a) Inadequacy of received solutions

It is all too easy to refute attempts to demonstrate the truth of egoistic *hedonism*, whether it is psychological or ethical egoistic hedonism that is at issue. With regard to egoism in the broader sense, however, these traditional refutations become less than adequate.

The great grandfather from whom all egoistic hedonists have evolved was Aristippus the Cyrenaic.[3] Aristippus began with an epistemological perspective which said that all knowledge and experience come to us through *sensations*. Even knowledge of rational and mathematical principles is obtained by means of a kind of inner sensation or quality of felt experiencing; thus it makes sense to say, 'I *sense* the validity of your argument.' More obviously still, the empirical knowledge of things in the world comes to us by means of sensations. Therefore, all we know in the strict sense are our own sensations. We then *infer* that the sensation stands for something in the real world which causes the sensation, but all we can know of the truth of this assumption, again, is through still other sensations.

Our knowledge of the worth or value of things, then, must also come through sensations, says Aristippus. But since a sensation consists of a 'movement of the soul,' it follows that sensations can be distinguished into three types of movements: (1) violent, turbulent sensations, i.e., painful ones; (2) moderate sensations, i.e., pleasant ones; (3) faint or barely perceptible sensations, i.e., indifferent ones. Aristippus then argues that no one would voluntarily choose the first or third type of sensation over the second. Anything that is experienced as worthwhile must therefore be the type of thing which causes us to experience this second type of sensation, namely pleasure. Since only the second type of sensation can be desired, and since only sensations can be known, it follows that only sensations of the pleasant type can be known to be desirable or worthwhile, and therefore only pleasure can be desired. But, by a mode of reasoning familiar to all students of Mill, Aristippus concludes that if only pleasure *can* possibly be desired, then only pleasure *ought* to be desired.

Aristippus is unclear by modern standards as to whether his assertion that hedonism is an iron-clad and inviolable psychological law is an assertion based on empirical observation, or a deductive-logical proof, or perhaps both. It will be instructive to consider both kinds of arguments, since both kinds have been used by various hedonistic philosophers at various times.

Considering the hedonist thesis as an *analytic* claim, i.e., a claim which purports to be deductively provable, the argument would seem to rely on one of two syllogisms. Either (i) no one can at any time desire displeasure, therefore everyone must desire pleasure at all times; or (ii) any action which a person commits by his own choice is committed because he *chooses* to commit it, therefore he *wants* to commit it; thus, once the action has been committed, the person has gotten what he wanted, and therefore has done what *pleased* him, i.e., what gave him *pleasure*. No one can choose to do anything other than what he *wants to do*.

Several objections can be brought against each of these arguments. Regarding argument (i), John Watson has pointed out that (A) a tacit presupposition is involved, and one which we have no reason to assume is true. Watson points out that, while it may be true that people always seek their own pleasure *all else being equal*, Aristippus has not shown that in fact all else *is* always equal. For example, it may be that a person will never choose displeasure *unless* some overriding moral consideration prompts him to do so.[4]

(B) Another objection is that, logically speaking, the argument takes the form: 'Man never desires any non-X, therefore he can desire nothing other than X.' The same reasoning would imply that, since man never desires bad whiskey, he can desire nothing other than good whiskey. The fallacy involved is a false limitation of alternatives: Aristippus tricks us into assuming that we can never desire anything other than either pleasure or displeasure, just as the analogous argument just cited tries to trick us into thinking that man must desire either good whiskey or bad whiskey. Of course, Aristippus does offer some argument that we must desire either pleasure or pain by assuming that we cannot desire anything that produces an indifferent sensation or no sensation at all. But, as J. C. Gosling points out, this claim is probably false, since my desiring the well-being of future generations is an obvious counterexample; the well-being of future generations will produce in me no sensation whatever, yet I desire it.[5]

(C) A related and perhaps more fundamental criticism of this type of hedonist argument is that, while it may be true that no one would willfully choose to be in excruciating, agonizing pain, it does not follow that no one can tolerate a *moderate* amount of pain or discomfort if some other consideration (such as a moral consideration) prompts us to do so. Correlatively, a tacit presupposition of argument (i) which may not be true (and probably is not) is the assumption that there is no specific *amount* of pleasure which is *enough*. That is, there may be a certain quantity of pleasure that people want to achieve in their lives, but they may be indifferent to any further pleasure beyond this optimal amount. In the case of any *specific* pleasure, such as eating or sexual activity, a certain amount satisfies us and we seek no more beyond this point. Why might this not be true of pleasure in general? Once we have achieved the amount of pleasure we want, at any given time, why not channel the remaining energy into achieving other purposes, such as justice or the truth? The hedonist will respond that if I reach the point where I have eaten enough food to satisfy my hunger, for the moment, and decide to turn my energies toward some less pleasant activity, such as studying, this simply means that, at this point in time, studying gives me more pleasure than eating any more food---or at least that I expect to get more pleasure in the long run by studying now. But whether or not this additional hedonist assumption is true depends either on analytic argument (ii) above---the argument that insists that if I do what I *want* to do, then I am doing what brings me the most *pleasure* by definition; or it depends on some empirical evidence or other which we have as yet to cosider. First, let's briefly review (for most philosophers are well aware of it) what is wrong with analytic argument (ii), and then we can consider the relevant empirical evidence.

Analytic argument (ii) is generally regarded as invalid because it commits the fallacy of equivocation, changing the meaning of the word 'pleasure' and/or the meaning of the word 'want' in the middle of the argument, so as to appear to be supporting a claim which it does not really support. The argument says that if I do something through my own choice, then I am doing what I 'want' to do; therefore, since 'pleasure' means by definition what I 'want', then I do whatever I choose to do for the sake of pleasure. The fallacy is that in the first statement (that if I choose to do something then I must 'want' to do it), 'want to do X' means nothing more than 'choose to do X.' But in the second statement, 'want to do X' means 'get pleasure out of doing X.' For example, if I choose to sacrifice my life for a cause, suffering, let us say, an excruciatingly agonizing death in the process, then by the *first* definition of 'want', I do 'want' to sacrifice my life and therefore I do 'want' to suffer the agonizing death. But in the *second* sense of 'want' (i.e., 'that which gives me pleasure'), it is clear that I do not 'want' to suffer the agonizing death (i.c., I do not enjoy it; it does not give me pleasure), but rather I do it in spite of the fact that I do not 'want' to do it in this important sense. 'Want' clearly refers to two different meanings in the two roles it is assigned in the argument, but in order for the argument to be valid, the meaning would have to remain the same throughout. The argument that whatever I want to do must bring me pleasure by definition plays on the ambiguity of 'want' in order to give the deceptive appearance of proving that we always want pleasure, whereas in fact all it proves is that we always choose to do whatever we choose to do---which in reality says nothing.

Any *analytic* argument which begins by defining 'pleasure' (or 'happiness') in the usual way---i.e., as a positive quality of feeling or as a complex of positive feelings which can be concretely, subjectively experienced---and then attempts to prove egoistic hedonism in this sense, must inevitably be guilty of the same equivocation. It simply is not self-contradictory to claim that someone seeks something other than 'pleasure' (or 'happiness') in the usual senses of these words. One may, of course, redefine 'pleasure' (or 'happiness') to mean 'satisfying one's strongest motive,' but then one is not arguing in favor of egoistic hedonism as we have defined the terms; one is in that case arguing in favor of 'egoism in the broader sense,' which will be considered later.

But now let's consider the reasoning of those who believe in egoistic hedonism not for a priori logical reasons, but for empirical reasons. (In this category we also may as well include those who would be egoists for phenomenological reasons, since the kind of phenomenological evidence offered would be a kind of observation or experience.) In this case, the claim is that it is an *observable fact* that man seeks his own happiness (or pleasure). The first question usually asked here is: Is it an observable fact that man always seeks his own pleasure or happiness, or is it merely an observable fact that man *sometimes* or *frequently* does so? Any counterexample should suffice to discredit a universal claim. And there do seem to be many cases in which people do things that do not bring them pleasure, and which the people in question believe they are doing for reasons quite removed from any consideration of anticipated pleasure resulting from the action. The hedonist might be able to show that perhaps in some of these instances the person is only *apparently* doing something contrary to her own pleasure or happiness, but that in reality she expects to get something out of it in the long run. Against this, however, we can think of examples in which the person obviously knows that she is not going to get pleasure in the long run out of the action---for example, when someone sacrifices her life for a cause. The hedonist may insist that many people who sacrifice their lives expect to get rewards in Heaven for doing so. Even so, it is very dubious that anyone would believe that sacrificing one's life for a cause is the only way to get to Heaven, or even the most pleasant or least unpleasant way to get there. Besides, there are atheists who have sacrificed their lives for causes---for example, the Russian revolutionaries described by Camus in his play *The Just Assassins.*[6] The hedonist may then claim that those who make sacrifices really 'enjoy' making the sacrifices because the fact that anyone chooses to do something implies that she wants to do it, which implies that it makes her happy or brings her pleasure. But this is exactly the same as analytic argument (ii) which was already refuted. Or the hedonist might claim that somehow the person has miscalculated, thinking that the sacrifice was really going to bring her more pleasure or happiness; but there are so many instances in which it is manifestly obvious to even the most unintelligent observer that the actions in question are *not* going to produce pleasure or happiness, that this claim would become empirically implausible in grotesque proportions.

Most philosophers are aware of the arguments just presented, in some form or other, and frequently take great 'pleasure' in tripping up their egoistic-hedonist sophomore students with them. But we must be careful not to delude ourselves into making egoism per se into a friendly straw man. There are more formidable versions of egoism than this facile hedonistic variety. In particular, a much more sophisticated variation of the egoistic way of thinking is shared by many contemporary psychologists. Their thesis is that, while it is true that people sometimes do other things besides seek pleasure, all human actions are still ultimately *caused* by a lifelong process of *conditioning* in which the resulting pattern of behavior and motivation can be traced to an *original* desire for pleasure and for the avoidance of pain (or, to be more precise, a tendency to seek positive reinforcement and avoid negative reinforcements and punishments).[7] For example, such a psychologist might argue that, although I might sacrifice my life for a cause, which clearly does not give me pleasure, the reason I choose to sacrifice my life for the cause is that I have been rewarded repeatedly throughout my life for performing actions which are considered noble or self-sacrificing, and which conform to the moral principles accepted by my society or subculture. Self-sacrificing behavior is therefore ultimately *motivated* by the selfish desire for reward, although the individual is not aware that this is the motive. Unlike the more straightforward type of egoistic hedonism, this kind of theory can be and is frequently submitted to rigorous experimental verification methods.

The most obvious criticism of such theories *as forms of hedonism* is that they must define 'positive reinforcement' operationally---which is to say, 'positive reinforcement' means *by definition* any environmental condition which tends to increase the frequency of a behavior.[8] It is thus true *by definition* that any organism will behave in such a way as to maximize its positive reinforcements, whatever they might be. It is now fairly well known that a vast number of experimental findings exist in which a 'positive reinforcement' cannot by any stretch of the imagination be identified with 'pleasure' in the experiential or phenomenologically-felt sense.[9] One reason experimental psychologists for many years were able to ignore these kinds of paradoxical findings (e.g., chickens would rather peck than eat)[10] is that their strict behaviorism did not allow them to even talk about 'pleasure' in the experiential sense, for this is a subjective condition which according to traditional logical positivism cannot be operationalized or objectively observed and measured. But the upshot of this kind of consideration is that 'positive reinforcement' cannot be identified with 'pleasure', and therefore reinforcement theory in psychology is not a form of hedonism.

It *is*, however, a form of *egoism* whose implications would be just as important for ethical theory as any other form of egoism. For it certainly does assert, either that all actions can *ultimately* be traced to the motivation to promote one's own 'self-interest' (i.e., to obtain the 'positive reinforcement' and engage in the corresponding 'consummatory responses'[11]); or it asserts that all actions result from the organism's tendency to 'satisfy its strongest motive' in each situation. In other words, it is either a non-hedonistic egoism in the narrow sense, or an egoism in the broader sense.

We saw earlier that any distinction between egoistic hedonism and non-hedonistic egoism in the narrow sense must hinge on a distinction between 'pleasure' (or 'happiness') and 'self-interest'. But it should be clear by now that, if 'self-interest' is not interpreted to mean pleasure or happiness (as defined experientially), then it must be defined simply as *whatever* the organism seeks. If 'self-interest' is defined as pleasure or happiness, then egoism in the narrow sense collapses into hedonistic egoism, and therefore falls victim to the same objections discussed above. On the other hand, if 'self-interest' is defined to mean *whatever* the organism seeks, then egoism in the narrow sense collapses into egoism in the broader sense. For in this case all it is saying is that the organism behaves in such a way as to 'satisfy its strongest motive.' And it is not necessary to become involved in a discussion of experimental psychological data in order to see that this thesis, as mentioned earlier, is a tautology, though not a trivial one. After all, the 'strongest motive' (i.e., 'positive reinforcement') is operationally defined as that which the organism seeks, to the extent that the organism seeks anything at all.

Many philosophers would let it go at that, since the analytic tendency of twentieth century philosophy has so strongly conditioned us to assume that any tautology must be a trivial one. But we saw earlier why this one is not trivial. If the organism is constituted in such a way that it always tries to satisfy its strongest motive (to the extent that it tries to do anything at all), then the dilemma for moral theory remains as real as in the case of any other egoism: To tell the organism to do what its constitution impels it to do is pointless and a waste of time; to tell it to act contrary to what its constitution impels it to do is not only a waste of time and pointless, but also incoherent.

Many attempts to refute or circumvent this implication of egoism in the broader sense have focused on the notion that, even if what we do is determined by our strongest motive in the given situation, there are many instances in which we derive satisfaction from achieving a certain goal only because we have previously freely *chosen* to set this particular goal for ourselves rather than some other goal. One of the classic versions of this argument was originally formulated by Joseph Butler.[12] Butler does not disagree with the inference that psychological egoism would imply ethical egoism, but he denies that psychological egoism is true in a sense that would be relevant to this implication. It is an empirical fact, he reminds us, that people often do want to do things which benefit others. The confusion of the egoist, he says, stems from the assumption that just because I get personal satisfaction out of doing something, this personal satisfaction must therefore be the sole motivation for doing it. In Butler's view, just the reverse is true; if I get pleasure out of benefiting others, it is *because* I want them to be benefited in the first place; I do not want them to be benefited in order that I will get pleasure out of benefiting them.

The problem, however, is that Butler's response does not accomplish what he wishes it to accomplish. Butler thinks that, having now refuted egoism, he can go on to construct an ethical theory which prescribes that people sometimes should do certain things which are contrary to their own self-interest. But that depends on what is meant by 'self-interest', as we have seen. If self-interest is the same thing as pleasure or, for that matter, happiness, then obviously people do sometimes act contrary to their 'self-interest'. (This definition, however, would equate *egoism* with *hedonism*.) But if 'self-interest' means the achievement of an end defined by one's strongest motive under the given circumstances---for example, a masochist's desire that a ton of bricks be dropped on his head ---then people *cannot* act contrary to their self-interest, now defined in terms of the strongest motive. For the egoist in the broader sense need not deny that altruistic actions are possible. One can act altruistically if that happens to be one's strongest motive under the circumstances. If a mother sacrifices herself for a child, she is satisfying her strongest motive under the circumstances; and it is only natural that someone with the drives and instincts of a mother should be motivated to feel altruistic toward her children. The point is that, if someone's strongest motive is *not* to do X, then, according to the egoist in the broader sense, there is no point in telling her that her strongest motive *ought* to be to do X, unless by fabrication we can convince her that she 'really' wants to do X when she does not---in which case we would be making a (false) factual claim rather than a (true) normative one.

Another standard response to egoism in the broader sense is to insist that, although we may technically act according to our 'strongest motive,' *what* motive *is* the strongest motive, and indeed what motives we have to begin with, are the result not of some causal mechanism but of free will; and that this free will freely chooses to be guided by the moral law.[13] Indeed, if the metaphysical assumption that motives are chosen through free will is granted, then this move would fairly obviously get us out of the egoist dilemma. No doubt, that is why the assumption of free will is and has been so popular among Western philosophers. (Of course, the Arabs, by and large, got along well enough without it for many centuries, but that is a different story.)

But think what such a metaphysical assumption might cost! Besides the tortuous and controversial logic and additional assumptions needed to work free will into a coherent concept of the mind-body relation, there is also the problem that, as far as any supporting arguments are concerned, determinism seems at least as likely to be true as free will.[14] So, even if free will is *logically possible* (and this is as much as most of its supporters are prepared to even attempt to show, when they are speaking clearly), what this means is that we have decided to let *all ethics*---in fact, even the very *possibility* of any meaningful normative judgment---rest on a flimsy metaphysical assumption that comes off in debates sounding little or no more likely to be true than its denial. And this in turn leads us, as ethical theorists, to prescribe that people obey some resulting theory which rationally can be considered no more likely to be true than are its basic assumptions, and therefore to prescribe that people act according to a theory that is no more likely to be true than false. But, as mentioned earlier, it can well be argued that it is *not the case* that people ought to act according to any theory that is just as likely to be false as true.

If it is possible to save ethics from the implications of egoism in the broader sense *without* forcing all ethics to depend on a dubious metaphysical assumption (in the next chapter, I shall discuss just *how* dubious it is), then it would certainly seem advisable to explore such a possibility. To develop this alternative solution is the purpose of the next sub-section. But first, there is one other popular solution that ought to be touched on.

Many philosophers hold that, even if our actions were determined by psychological conditioning which is ultimately reducible to some interaction between 'drives' and/or 'instincts' on the one hand and a pattern of positive and negative reinforcements on the other, it would still be possible to *condition ourselves* to be the kind of persons we think we should be, to have the desires we think we should have, and to take pleasure in the kinds of things we think we should take pleasure in. This argument also would counteract the anti-moral implications of egoistic hedonism, if valid. This line of thinking was originated by Aristotle, who said,

> As regards the pleasures, pains, appetites and diversions,...it is possible to be the kind of person who is overcome even by those which most people master; but it is also possible to master those by which most people are overcome.[15]

Which type of person one is, according to Aristotle, depends on conditioning or habit---a hypothesis strikingly congruent with most modern psychological theories of learning, particularly those of Hull and Spence.[16] But whether or not someone has cultivated this habit or that habit depends in turn on what kinds of moral training one has had, and on what kind of training and conditioning one has imposed on *oneself*. If one wishes to be the kind of person who enjoys reading, for example, then one will begin by reading frequently, knowing that eventually one will reach the point where one enjoys reading. In this way, we choose our needs and desires, by cultivating them in ourselves through conditioning. But if it is possible to cultivate our own needs and desires, it is also possible to train ourselves to be the kind of people whose needs and desires do not conflict with moral responsibility.

This type of argument, however, while it may save ethics from the devastating implications of egoism in the narrow sense, does not save us from egoism in the broad sense. What the argument is really trying to show is that, even if psychological egoism is true, it would still be possible to coherently advocate a non-egoistic ethical system because this 'Aristotelian principle' (what psychologists call 'contingency management' ---the ability do condition oneself) would allow us to choose to train ourselves, within certain limits, to take pleasure in those things that we initially think we ought to do, and to find displeasure in those things that we think we ought not to do. To the extent that the self-imposed conditioning regimen succeeded, then, to act out of our self-interested desire for pleasure would be to act according to a system of ethics which at some remote time in the past (prior to the self-imposed conditioning regimen) we had chosen to adopt. In the same way, a serious basketball player is trained in such a way that he enjoys playing the fourth quarter of a grueling game, which for the ordinary, untrained person would be agonizing because of the physical exhaustion involved.

But there is an obvious problem with this use of the Aristotelian principle as a reconciliation of psychological egoism with non-egoistic ethical principles (not to deny that the Aristotelian principle has other important applications in moral psychology). The problem in this context is that, if all human actions were really completely egoistically motivated (in the broader sense), then the initial decision to train oneself in this way or that would never be made unless the person perceived that to do so is ultimately in her own self-interest in the sense of offering to satisfy the strongest motive at that particular point in time. So if we tell the person that she ought to train herself in one way or another, we are either telling her to decide to do something she *cannot* decide to do, and thus making a trivial statement; or we are telling her to do what her own initial egoism would have motivated her to do anyway, which is also trivial; or we are advising her that her self-interest really lies elsewhere than where she thought it lay, which is indeed to make a coherent and non-trivial statement, but one that is factual rather than normative; or we are misleading her into thinking that what is in her self-interest really is not, which is to make a false factual statement, intermixed with a normative statement that would be trivially true if our misleading factual claim were true, but which under the stated circumstances is false and incoherent.

Someone might argue in a more complex way that a moral philosopher might know that some coherent normative statement, that people ought to do X, is true, and then falsely advise people in such a way that they believe the noble lie that it is in their self-interest to do X, or that they believe it is in their self-interest to train and condition themselves to enjoy doing X, so that thenceforth it *will be* in their self-interest to continue doing X. Thus the statement that people ought to do X could be a coherent and non-trivial ethical statement in spite of psychological egoism. The problem with this argument is that, if people can really only do what they perceive to be in their self-interest, then the philosopher can believe that she ought to propagate the noble lie only if she believes it is in her self-interest to do so. So if it is in the philosopher's self-interest to get people to do X, then the statement that X ought to be done is trivial because the philosopher was going to get them to do it anyway. And if it is not in the philosopher's self-interest to get people to do X, then the statement that people ought to do X is trivial because there is no way they can do it, given these circumstances.

While this last argument as it stands is inadequate as a refutation of the implications of egoism in the broader sense, I believe it points us in the general direction of a correct solution. In fact, the reader may have already guessed the direction this solution is going to take.

(b) Toward a workable solution

Suppose I have bet my friend Bill $100 that I will do what is morally right. And suppose that, after reading some philosophical treatises, he and I come to the conclusion that what is morally right is to go to Mecca. Since I am motivated to win the bet (for egoistic reasons), I resolve to go to Mecca because that is what we have decided is right. But, just as I am about to get on the train (the fare is $99), Bill rushes onto the platform with still another philosophical book which refutes the arguments that had originally convinced us that I ought to go to Mecca. This book now conclusively demonstrates that people ought not to go to Mecca. The arguments convince me, so I do not go to Mecca.

Bear in mind our original purpose for studying the egoism issue in the present context. What we wanted to know was whether, if psychological egoism is true, it would be pointless or a waste of time to tell people what they ought to do. Here we find a case where, even if psychological egoism in *any* of the senses discussed above is true, it is still not pointless or a waste of time for someone to tell me what I ought to do. Since I had an incentive (admittedly an egoistic one) to do whatever turned out to be (objectively) morally right, it was not a waste of time for the author of the first book I read to tell me I ought to go to Mecca. If his arguments were strong enough to convince me that going to Mecca is the *objectively correct* thing to do, then I would do so, even if it would have been more to my egoistic advantage if it had turned out that I should not go (since then I would save the $99 train fare). For I wanted to do what was really morally right in order to win the bet. Nor, at the same time, was it a waste of time for the author of the second book to tell me that I ought not to go. If I found these arguments more cogent (again, in an objective sense), then I would act accordingly. For I would still want to do what is really morally right in order to win the bet. In the end, whether I go to Mecca or stay home depends utterly on which action is judged to be morally right in an objective sense. And that is all that we needed to establish in order to answer the riddle originally put to us by the Scylla of 'Why be moral?' Even *if* all my actions are egoistic in the broad sense (we have already seen that they are not all egoistic in the narrow sense), it is still possible for me to be motivated to do what is morally right whether or not it would otherwise be more in my self-interest than some other action---*provided*, that is, that the action in question costs me less than $100.

Now, someone might object, it *would* be a waste of time for anyone to tell me I ought to go to Mecca if the fare is over $100. But this is not necessarily true. Suppose, before discovering the argument that I ought to go to Mecca, my friend Bill first discovers a book which provides convincing arguments to the effect that I ought to attend an Aristotelian training school (which charges a fee of $99) which will help me to train and condition myself to get more pleasure out of doing what is right than I ever could get out of any amount of money. After completing this conditioning regimen (which is based on the most enlightened and scientific principles of 'contingency management'), Bill then shows me the argument to the effect that I should go to Mecca, though the fare is $1,000. But now it no longer makes much difference to me how much it costs, for I now desire to do what is right more strongly than I desire money. In fact, I now no longer care whether I win the original $100 bet. I have become a person who is (technically, egoistic-in-the-broader-sense) motivated to do *whatever* is right, and damn the cost. So it certainly cannot be pointless or a waste of time for anyone to tell me what I (objectively) ought to do---and why---even though all my motives might be (technically) egoistic in the broader sense.

The objection at this point, however, will be: What if the fee for attending the Aristotelian training school is over $100? Well, that is the crucial question. How strong, in fact, is the initial motive to be moral, and is this motive strong enough to get us through the Aristotelian training in spite of the initial unpleasantness (i.e., the 'cost') of this training?

The initial motivation to be moral is not, of course, a bet we have made with someone. But I shall argue, in the next section, that it is at least as important, psychologically, as any bet could be in motivating action. The motivation is the (technically, egoistic-in-the-broader-sense) altruistic feeling of empathy with all other conscious beings, which prompts us to want to find out what is right and then do what is right in relation to all conscious beings. Even *possible* conscious beings who do not yet exist are not excluded from this empathic feeling. The argument is not, however, that I ought to do X because I am motivated to do X (the argument that has sunk so many ships). It is rather that I ought to do X because a rational examination of the relevant objective issues tells me that the statement that I ought to do X is likely to be true. The empathic feeling which motivates me to find out and do what is right in relation to all conscious beings will equally well motivate me to do X, Y or Z, depending on which appears likely to be objectively correct.

2. *The Motivation for Altruism*

In order to establish that consciousness is motivated strongly enough by altruistic feelings to overcome its motivation to seek happiness and pleasure (i.e., 'self-interest' in the narrow sense), we must establish that there is something that consciousness wants more strongly than it wants happiness, at least to the extent that it *is* conscious; and that it wants to *be* conscious to an optimal extent. If consciousness wants to be conscious to an optimal extent, and if lesser degrees of consciousness are not enough to satisfy this need, then it is prudentially in the self-interest of consciousness (in the broader sense of 'self-interest') to do whatever is necessary in order for it to be conscious to this optimal extent. It can then be shown that, in order for it to be conscious to this optimal extent, it is necessary for consciousness to feel a universal empathy with conscious beings in general, to the extent that they are conscious beings. It is not enough to have empathic feelings toward certain selected individuals or groups.

Several theses, then, must be demonstrated. (a) Consciousness exists in the manner of an unfolding process or pattern of change rather than as a stasis. Consciousness also wants to exist, in the sense of continuing to be conscious to an optimal extent; but wanting to continue to exist means that it must unfold and change in a certain kind of pattern, for it cannot exist as mere stasis. (b) Conscious processes need to be *symbolized,* i.e., physically embodied in appropriately-structured physical activities, in order to be experienced to an optimal extent. The most appropriate symbolic activities for this purpose require the achievement of empathy with conscious beings other than oneself. (c) In order to achieve the degree of empathy needed with other conscious beings *qua* conscious beings (and not qua beings whose consciousness is inauthentic) consciousness must attain and maintain an empathic feeling with the abstract idea 'authentic conscious being'; this universalized empathy entails an empathy with all conscious beings to the extent that they are conscious.

(a) Consciousness must avoid stasis

The notion that consciousness exists in the manner of a process rather than a stasis, to the extent that it exists qua consciousness at all, is one that I have discussed at much greater length elsewhere[17] but into which we should avoid any unnecessary digression at this point. Any discussion of the ontological status of consciousness (or, for those who dislike the word 'ontology', of the 'manner in which consciousness exists') will interrelate with issues in the philosophy of mind, the 'theory of cognition' and action theory, which are notoriously controversial areas. But we need to stay with relatively uncontroversial assumptions, lest we end up grounding ethical theory in such a way that the resulting normative claims are almost as likely to be false as true, and are thus morally non-binding, since in that case no agent would be much constrained to believe that the resulting normative claims are true. Fortunately, the claim that consciousness, to the extent that it exists, exists in the manner of a process or pattern of change is hardly controversial at all. Only those who are very strict Cartesian dualists could coherently deny this claim, and strict Cartesian dualism is easily shown to be untenable. As for such diverse philosophers of mind as James, Searle and Dennett, Feuerbach and Hegel, Aquinas and Ibn Rusd, there is essential agreement on the proposition we need: Consciousness is a pattern of change which takes the body (and the things which form physical systems with the body) as the substrate for the change. It is not really necessary for us to become involved in the controversies that divide these various thinkers. It is their common element that interests us. For James, consciousness is a 'function' of the body, as it is for Dennett.[18] Dennett compares the relationship to that between a person's voice and the person's vocal cords: One could say neither that the voice is identical with the vocal cords, nor that the voice could exist independently of the movement of vocal cords (or of something *like* vocal cords in the relevant respects).[19] Similarly, Dennett's nemesis, Searle, agrees at least that consciousness is "caused by processes going on in the brain."[20] Feuerbach expresses essentially the same relationship when he says, "The real relation of thought to being is as follows: Being is subject, though is predicate."[21] Similarly, Feuerbach's nemesis, Hegel, admits in his *Logic* that spirit and nature relate as predicate and subject, insisting, however, that this does not imply that nature (i.e., the physiology of the body) *causes* the spiritual phenomena.[22] It may be that spirit 'appropriates' whatever physical elements it finds existing in the brain and uses their functioning to suit its purposes. Still another way of expressing the relationship is put by Aquinas. Following Ibn Rusd's interpretation of Aristotle, the soul is both 'an activity' for Aquinas and 'the form of the body.'[23] As an example of how non-controversial this position is, notice that it is equally compatible with Aquinas' libertarianism and Ibn Rusd's determinism.

Some of the philosophers just quoted believe that the pattern constituting consciousness is *caused by* the physiological functioning of the brain. For others, the causal relation is just the reverse. Some hold that the direction of causation can move both ways alternately or in sequences. Still others hold that the relation is not a causal one at all, but rather one of identity. But what all these views have in common is the idea that consciousness is a pattern of activity whose substrate is the body. This relationship can be understood as analogous in many ways to the relationship between a sound wave and a wooden wall through which the wave is propagated. The sound wave is in some important respects not 'identical' with the wood as it passes through it; many other media *could* have propagated the same wave just as well. Thus one would not speak of a theory of 'sound-wood identity,' except in the odd sense in which the sound wave can be viewed as a 'pattern of wood activity' as it passes through the wood (just as U. T. Place calls consciousness a 'pattern of brain activity').[24] Nor need one necessarily regard the wood as the primary *cause* of the pattern of the wave, although the medium does have some effect on it (passing through a wooden wall tends to weaken high frequencies more than low frequencies, etc.), and in *some* instances the medium of the wave may be viewed as its cause, as when a speaker vibrates. At the same time, the sound could not exist *without* the wood (or some medium) either, so there can be no *dualism* of sound and wood. However, the medium can be replaced with some other medium, just as the body can replace some or all of its cells while maintaining essentially the same stream of consciousness and a very similar (if not exactly the same) personal identity. And there are many things that can be said about the sound that cannot be said about the wood---for example, it travels a great distance, while each wood molecule vibrates only a tiny distance, and in a perpendicular direction. Analogously, there are things that can be said about states of consciousness that cannot meaningfully be said about the bodies of which they are predicated, as Dennett, Malcolm and others point out.[25] So, whether they are identity theorists, interactionists, epiphenomenalists, libertarians, determinists, or process theorists, philosophers of mind tend to agree on the central core of their concepts of what mind *is*---a complex pattern of change which in one way or another is able to use the physiological functioning of the body as substrate for the change.

That this generally shared view of the ontological status of consciousness is an essentially correct view can be seen from a quick and approximate consideration of some necessary conditions for any adequate solution to the 'mind-body' problem. If we take seriously the correlation of mental processes with law-abiding physical processes (especially in the brain), several possible explanations for the relationships between these phenomena present themselves. *Theories of psychophysical identity* hold that a mental event and its corresponding physiological event are really the same thing as each other, thus eliminating the problem of their interrelations. But then it is necessary to say, with Davidson, that the mental and physical events *appear* in two different ways because of the difference between the subjective and objective perspectives. The problem here is that, if there really *were* no difference between the subjective and objective aspects of the event, then they would not *appear* different from the different perspectives---just as one might say that, if there were no real difference between the front and back of a house, then the house would not appear different from these different perspectives. It is true, of course, that the *same* side may appear different from different perspectives, but only if there is a real difference between the perspectives. But in the case of the objective and subjective dimensions of the mind/body phenomenon, the same thing would not appear different from the subjective and objective perspectives if there were not some difference, however slight, between the subjective and objective to begin with. Even if this difference should consist in the subjective and objec-

THE MOTIVATION TO BE MORAL

tive dimensions' being only different aspects of the same thing, this would still contradict the thrust of the identity theory as far as resolving the above conflict is concerned. Even if they are different aspects of the *same* thing, they are still *different* aspects of the same thing. This, at any rate, is the objection of the opponents of this theory.

Epiphenomenalism would solve the problem by saying that no mental event is ever necessary or sufficient to bring about any subsequent mental event, but that these mental events are both causal side-effects of their corresponding physiological events (in the brain, for example), thus explaining the lawfulness in the patterns of consciousness on a purely physical basis. The problem here is that a mental event is still either *physical* or *non-physical*. If it is *non-physical*, it would have no physical mass, in which case it should not be susceptible to physical forces (the same argument that would apply against any dualism). (Also, a mental event could be neither necessary nor sufficient for its corresponding physical event, since the prior physical event would have to be necessary and sufficient for the subsequent one; therefore the subsequent one could be neither necessary nor sufficient for its corresponding mental event and therefore could not cause it.) On the other hand, if a mental event is viewed as *physical*, then we have just another way of stating an identity theory, which is subject to the criticisms mentioned just above.

Interactionism, in the strict sense of the term, would explain the dilemma by suggesting that a mental event can cause a physical one, which then causes a second mental event, which then causes a third mental event, which causes a third physical event, etc. The problem here, of course, is that the second physical event in this chain would then not cause the third physical event, and we do not seem to find such numerous breaks in the causal chains of brain events as this would require.

Alvin Goldman's *'nomic equivalence'* theory solves the problem by denying that if one mental event is sufficient for a second one then nothing else can be necessary for the second mental event and vice versa. I.e., he denies the normal assumption of an 'exclusivity principle' for causal relations which would state that if one event is necessary for a second, then nothing else can be sufficient for the second event, and vice versa. Instead, Goldman holds that this exclusivity principle can be denied when the two events in question are 'nomically equivalent', i.e., when they are inseparable aspects of the same phenomenon, like the temperature and pressure of a gas.[26] Goldman argues that the relationship between mental and physiological events works in the same way. While this is a consistent and coherent possibility, the drawback is that there are instances where even this denial of the exclusivity principle does not resolve the dilemma. There are often instances where X causes both Y and Z, thus Y and Z are indeed inseparable from each other (since X cannot cause one without the other under the circumstances), yet Y and Z cannot be treated as 'equivalent' even in a nomic sense.

Still another approach to this problem, which would incorporate certain elements of several of the above ones, is the approach strongly implicit in the work of Merleau-Ponty and Henri Ey,[27] and is the one I have called the 'process-substratum' approach.[28] What it really does is to take the coherent aspects of each of the above approaches, culling them of their objectionable commitments. It holds simply that the mental and the physical relate as a process to its substratum. Thus a mental event and its corresponding physiological event might have neither an identity relation nor a one-way causal relation. The process-substratum relation would not be dualistic, nor would it entail the physical acausalities of interactionism. The pattern of the process might remain essentially intact even while replacing or reorganizing many of the components of its substratum, yet the process would be affected in complex ways by physically-caused changes in the substratum. It affirms, with Davidson, that either a mentalistic or a physical explanation may be possible in principle, though one or the other may be more convenient under given circumstances. But it would deny that process and substratum are the same thing viewed from different perspectives; rather, they are inseparable but distinct aspects of a total phenomenon, like the front and back sides of a house. Their inseparability consists in one's being the pattern in the change of the other. And, because they are inseparable, whatever is necessary and sufficient for one is also necessary and sufficient for the other. Consciousness is no more 'the same thing as' the brain than the pattern of a bird's flight is the same thing as the bird, or than the graph of the two factors of an exponential equation is the same as the graph of the equation itself. It is for this reason that to experience a state of consciousness is different from observing the behavior of someone's brain, or even of one's own brain. Does this mean that consciousness could not in principle be explained physically? Not necessarily, if by 'explain' we mean predict and control. But, even if enough information could be collected to do this, to control something is not necessarily the same as to understand *what it is*. For our present purposes, as will become obvious, the important thing is precisely to understand what consciousness is.

When we say that consciousness is a 'process' which takes physiological events as its 'substrate' or 'substratum', we do not thereby deny that the physical events themselves may be processes which take still lower-order processes (e.g., the exchange of electrons between atoms) as *their* substrate. What we mean, rather, is that consciousness is a *higher-order* process than the physical events that constitute its substrate. A person's foot, to be sure, is not the simple, solid substance that it appears to be, but rather is an incredibly complex process in which subatomic particles (which themselves may be complex processes rather than substances) zoom around at high velocities. Nonetheless, the activity of 'walking down the street' is a still *more* complex process which takes the foot as *one* of its substrates.

The reason for emphasizing this relatively non-controversial point is that, if we interpret consciousness as merely one physical process among others, and do not remember that it is a higher-order pattern of change *in* such lower-order processes, then we tend to be misled into thinking of the motivation of consciousness as exhibiting the same tendencies as the 'motivation' of these lower-order physical processes. And if we carry the same reductive schema all the way through the biological level to the chemical and physical levels, we will end up trying to assume that consciousness, like chemical and physical processes, seeks to 'reduce' itself to a lower energy level. This is the general tendency of motivational theories based on the concept of 'drive reduction,' which of course has been a very dominant type of theory among physiological psychologists, although a few, like Hebb, have refused to let drive reduction be the single 'driving'-force (as it were) of motivation.[29] In drive-reductive theories, the ultimate aim of consciousness is to reduce its 'drives', defined as 'physiological deficits external to the nervous system.'[30] Freud, who did as much as anyone to popularize this way of thinking, repudiated it later in life in *Beyond the Pleasure Principle*,[31] but was not taken seriously. What Freud finally realized, however, is that, if the real motivation of consciousness is to *reduce* drives, and if a state in which all drives are completely reduced requires no further conscious activities, then the goal of life is the annihilation and *death* of consciousness. If this were all there is to motivation, it would be easy enough to bring all the 'physiological deficits' to their completely reduced status (i.e., ultimately, to bring all the electrons of all the atoms in the organism to their lowest possible energy levels). Suicide, for example, would do the job nicely and quickly, and would quickly enough become painless.

The problem, of course, is that consciousness wants to reduce its drives, but also *to remain conscious while doing so*. Moreover, given the choice between reducing its drives and continuing to be conscious, consciousness normally chooses the latter, unless the pain involved is absolutely excruciating. Thus consciousness prefers some degree of *pain* over complete absence of consciousness. And since consciousness is a high-energy, relatively complex process rather than a low-energy, relatively simple process, and less still a zero-energy, completely simple *stasis*, it is a fundamental error to construe motivation as seeking stasis---as 'homeostatic drive' theory, in its original and root meaning, is meant to do. Consciousness, in fact, seeks to *avoid* stasis at all cost. This need to avoid stasis is perhaps seen most clearly in the phenomenon of boredom. It is a regularly observable fact that people will readily trade pleasure and happiness in exchange for novelty, adventure, increased complexity of experience, and in general what might be called 'experientially meaningful change,' even if the change is not likely to produce as much pleasure and happiness, in the sense of 'reduction of physiological deficits,' as does the status quo which is being fled from. One can, of course, cling to the idea that this is because boredom is 'unpleasant' and 'unhappy' in expanded, non-physiologically-reductive senses of these words. But to do so is to expand 'pleasure' and 'happiness' to the point where the reductionist project is abandoned, and where clearly non-drive-reductive, anti-stasis, and possibly painful experiences are defined as constitutive of 'happiness'.

What is clear is that the tendency to seek new directions (probably within certain limits), to optimize the amount of consciousness which one experiences, and thus to avoid stagnation into stasis, is at least sometimes a *stronger* motive than is the desire for pleasure in any sense of 'pleasure' that can be linked to the reduction of physical drives. Moreover, there is naturally a certain amount of conflict between these two tendencies. For, as Freud saw, the reduction of drives tends by its very nature to be eventually accompanied by a reduction in the amount of consciousness which occurs, unless there is some contravening tendency.

It is also important to note that we cannot experience pleasure or anything else unless we first *exist*. For this reason also, then, consciousness *must* give priority to its need to *be*, i.e., to exist *qua* consciousness, as over against its desire for pleasure, happiness, or any other particular experience.

If we want to describe what it is that consciousness most strongly wants at any given moment, then, the answer must be framed in terms of the desire to unfold in accordance with a certain pattern of change such that the ensuing state of consciousness will be suitably intense from the subjective point of view. If consciousness stagnates into stasis, this flow is blocked and inhibited. But it is easy to observe phenomenologically that to unfold in this appropriate way is not always easy. It requires a certain amount of self-understanding on the part of the initial state of consciousness to know what to do in order to facilitate this unfolding in the right way.[32] For example, if I mistake my desire for intellectual activity as a desire for a chocolate milk shake, the ensuing consciousness is not likely to fulfill the pattern of change that is sought.

Now let's define 'authenticity' to mean being honest with oneself, experiencing what is really in one's consciousness rather than denying it, repressing it, pretending that it is not there, or somehow distracting oneself from it. It follows that inauthenticity is counterproductive to consciousness' project to unfold in the pattern of change called for by its desire to exist as process and avoid stasis. For inauthenticity will obviously work against the self-understanding of the initial state of consciousness that we just said is necessary in order for consciousness to have much hope of unfolding in such a way as to avoid stasis. Consciousness must therefore desire to exist authentically, and this desire too must be counted as normally more important than the desire for pleasure or happiness, although, again, *excruciating* pain or misery will outweigh it.

Having established this much, we are now prepared to develop, in the next two sections, a line of argument which finally will lead to the grounding for very powerful altruistic emotions. These emotions then entail a strong desire to be moral (without dictating what *is* moral). The phenomenological elaboration of the analysis of the structure of human consciousness posits that authenticity is a more primal value than happiness or self-interest (in the narrow sense). The basis for this assertion is that the desire to exist (which is presupposed by all other desires which are egoistic-in-the-broader-sense) entails a desire to be authentic, since the ontological status of human consciousness is process as opposed to stasis and since authenticity is necessary if consciousness is to guard against the continual temptation of stagnation into stasis. Authenticity implies being in touch with one's own consciousness. For this purpose, as the next sub-section will show, authentic ways to symbolize, concretize, and *explicate* this consciousness must be used. This, finally, requires ethical involvement in the world, honest relationships with other people, and concern for other conscious beings in general. At this point in the argument, however, we face a severe difficulty: Granted that the needed authenticity of consciousness ultimately requires empathic and concernful relationships to certain selected individuals or groups, how does this entail that I must follow any universally binding principles in my relations to *all* people?

Sub-section (b) will trace the reasoning leading from the logical and phenomenological analysis of consciousness to ethical involvement. Sub-section (c) will then confront the difficult problem of grounding the *universal scope* of the motivation to be moral, which is grounded in the feeling of empathy.

(b) Consciousness requires symbolization.

The conception of consciousness as a process or pattern of change implies that man continually seeks to create novelty and is not bound to a drive-reduction schema which would force on us a 'human nature' which necessarily posits one choice, such as happiness or pleasure, as the only possible value. Among those who have been misled by this hedonistic tendency in motivational theory, even Kant was tricked into embracing a psychological drive-reductionism with regard to human motivation, and therefore had to posit God, freedom, and immortality in order to compensate for the supposed 'natural law' that man must always seek his own 'self-interest.'[33] But the question of whether human behavior can be explained in terms of drive reduction is entirely distinguishable from the question as to whether all human behavior is *caused*. Kant erred in assuming that if all human behavior were caused, then it must follow that it is all motivated by the need for physiological drive-reduction, which would lead to egoistic hedonism. Here, then, is an instance where an *ontological* or *factual* question has a profound effect on which ethical system we must choose: *Is* man characterized by such-and-such 'human nature' consisting of 'drives' and of prescribed desires ultimately derivative through learning from the drives? The drive-reductionist faces the bleak choice between hedonism and some form of duty ethics reinforced by the ad hoc postulation of God, freedom and immortality. The non-reductionist, who denies that man by his very nature must always seek an experience called happiness or pleasure, has access to a motivation to be moral which makes possible a non-hedonistic system including such values as fairness, self-actualization, personhood, and even community, if these values turn out to be features of a correct ethical system from a purely moral point of view.

It is also important to notice another crucial difference between this motivational analysis and the emotional theories underlying the emotivisms discussed in the first chapter. Besides the fact that in our present analysis we are not *basing* ethics on emotion per se, but only making ethics possible, there is another distinction. According to the process conception of consciousness outlined above, not all emotions are equally *good* or *valuable* from the prudential point of view. Pushpin is not as good as poetry. Emotions are prudentially good to the extent that they contribute to the *authentic* functioning of consciousness as a whole. Consciousness, as we saw, exists to a greater extent when it functions authentically. Authenticity entails self-honesty, which in turn demands that the person explicate, concretize, and symbolize (via concrete media such as words, gestures, or pictures) her consciousness in the context of authentic relationships with other people, since the immanence of consciousness tends to correlate with the ways in which it is transcendently symbolized. Such a tendency toward correlation between subjective consciousness and the objective manifestations through which it is symbolized is an ontologically necessary feature of consciousness because consciousness cannot take place, and certainly cannot unfold in authentic directions, if not adequately symbolized in concrete ways. This point has been demonstrated more fully elsewhere;[34] the rationale behind it is briefly as follows.

Consciousness needs symbols in order to unfold. If I want to formulate my ideas or feelings on any subject, symbolizing activities---such as using (materially embodied) words---must be engaged in. For example, if I try to remember something that I have forgotten, using words helps me do so. In explaining to someone how to operate a complex machine, actually going through the physical motions helps me remember what these motions are and is sometimes indispensable to remembering. Similarly, a chess player uses the pieces on the board as physical symbols to help him formulate his mental strategy. If I want to remember how I felt in the Fall of 1969, actually listening to Tchaikovsky's Fifth Symphony virtually brings it all back to me. Likewise, a child is encouraged to pray to a deity and subsequently learns to believe in the deity. Symbolizing the conscious state of belief makes it more likely that she will eventually have that conscious state. In each case, a physical activity, the motion of matter (whether the mouth, the hands, the brain, or a system of perceptual organ and perceptual object) serves to symbolize a state of consciousness in order to help that state of consciousness to occur (i.e., to exist as consciousness).

If no consciousness can take place without some concrete symbolizing activity to explicate it, then everything I do also has its effect on the kinds of consciousness which that action symbolizes or fails to symbolize and therefore indirectly renders possible or impossible. Regarding the effect on any concrete action on the *authenticity* of my consciousness, the crucial question becomes: What kind of symbolizing function is a given activity capable of assuming? How broad is the range of possible consciousness (and therefore of possible persons) capable of being symbolized and explicated by this activity, and are any of these possible persons really my own authentic choice?

As a general rule, the array of available symbols (activities in the world that I can use to define myself) tends to limit the range of possible thoughts and feelings that can maintain themselves within the physical embodiment that these symbols facilitate: (1) An initial state of consciousness must be concretely symbolized in the world in order to be fully experienced and to unfold in a way that will optimize the subsequent consciousness into which it unfolds. (2) If the initial consciousness is not concretized in this way, it will either die out or change into a less fully aware form, thus reducing the extent to which I exist *qua* consciousness. (3) If at any given time the activity in which I am engaged on the one hand and on the other hand the values which my consciousness authentically entertains are not capable of assuming the relation of symbol to symbolized, then I must either cease doing the activity, or cease having the value or consciousness which fails to get symbolized, and thus concretized and facilitated, as a result of the activity. (4) If for some reason I am not allowed to cease doing the activity, and therefore must cease having the state of consciousness in question, then either I must decrease the extent to which I am conscious, or I must attempt to deceive myself into having thoughts or feelings which are capable of being symbolized by the activity which I must perform. It is therefore difficult to play a role on a continuing basis without *becoming* the role. Becoming the role can be avoided only if symbolization opportunities can be found which do not fit the role, or to be more precise, which are not constrained by the role.

A conscious being therefore needs to find adequate opportunities, through really-embodied, concrete activity in the world, to symbolize and explicate its consciousness so that it can continue to exist and to change in the directions authentically called for by that consciousness itself; the conscious being also wants to find as many effective opportunities for symbolization as it can. Moreover, this need for symbolization/explication is the *most urgent* need and desire of a conscious being, since our very survival qua conscious beings depends upon its fulfillment. No other gratification or value-fulfillment can be experienced (or at least *fully* experienced) unless consciousness first truly *exists* in order to (fully) experience whatever it experiences. Whether the value structure ultimately discovered or created by consciousness is going to turn out to be egoistic, altruistic or both, consciousness at least knows from the beginning that only to the extent that it is authentic will it find itself able to discover or create value. Authenticity is thus motivated by the structure of conscious existence itself. The value which consciousness places on its own authenticity is presupposed by any other value it might be able to establish. Consciousness therefore wants to symbolize and explicate itself.

Eugene Gendlin suggests that dialogue with other persons is the most effective overall way to symbolize our consciousness and therefore to concretize, explicate and carry it forward.[35] (This concept of Gendlin's profoundly influenced Carl Rogers and the non-directive therapy movement in psychology.) By establishing genuine give-and-take communication and understanding, Smith helps Jones to remember, for example, how he got where he is in his stream of consciousness, where he has come from, why he chose this direction, how it relates backward in the pattern, what the overall meaning is, etc.; meanwhile Jones is helping Smith in the same way---all of which is possible because a common term that unites them is the meaning of the intersubjective relationship itself.

In order for this degree of understanding to take place, a corresponding degree of mutual empathic consciousness must be established. By 'empathic consciousness' I mean simply that Smith must attempt to achieve insight into the meaning of Jones' expressions by putting himself in Jones' place and imagining what subjective states of consciousness might be symbolized by these expressions; in short, he must be able to empathize with Jones' consciousness, as Husserl and Merleau-Ponty both maintain is a prerequisite for linguistic communication.[36] That such empathy is to some extent *possible* is a datum, since each of us has experienced it. It is presupposed by the fact that we have learned to talk. Precisely what experienceable meaning is designated by 'empathic consciousness' becomes quickly evident if we imagine an instance where we fail to establish it or purposely suspend it, as when a doctor makes an incision or when a soldier kills in war. Such an empathic consciousness is a condition for the possibility of authentic interaction. Without it, distraction through Heidegger's 'idle talk' would block the flow of both people's consciousness within the interaction, and the full existence of the consciousness Smith and Jones are trying to explicate could not reach its potential fruitions. (This is not to deny that idle talk has any place in an authentic progression; it may be chosen as one moment of the flow at some time.) The best example of such mutual explication might well be the Platonic dialogue. If this kind of communication is to be possible, each person must achieve some degree of empathic identification with the other, at least during the time when they are interacting with each other. Here we use the word 'identification' in its somewhat loose contemporary sense, as for example in 'identification with the oppressor,' not in the sense of a really-existing *unity* between two minds such as Scheler's *Einsfuhlung*. In fact, the meaning which the other person is trying to communicate is only comprehended (rightly or wrongly) if we projectively imagine what subjective meanings her discourse is supposed to concretely embody for her. (By adding 'rightly or wrongly,' we disengage the present inquiry from any metaphysical speculation as to an already-existing unity among diverse conscious beings such as the one Scheler proposes.)

If this reasoning is valid, then the initial assumption that consciousness is a process rather than a stasis not only implies that not all values are drive-reductionistic (since some seek to increase rather than to reduce the *activity* which consciousness is); it also implies that consciousness must find ways to symbolize and explicate itself in order to continue this activity and must do so authentically; that authentic and concrete interaction with other people is necessary to such a symbolization process; finally, that empathic identification with these other people is a necessary prerequisite for this kind of interaction. But at this point, the most difficult question of all arises: Even granting that empathic identification with other people is necessary for the authentic functioning of consciousness and that this empathic identification leads to ethical comportment toward these other people---to a sort of personal loyalty toward them---, how does it follow that we must *always* comport ourselves ethically toward *all* other people? That I want to establish empathic relations with other people would no more seem to imply that I *must* establish these relations with *all* others, than my wanting an apple implies that I *must* eat *all* apples. What is to prevent me from forming a small circle of friends toward whom I am loyal, and whom I use as my cultural context for symbolization purposes, and proceeding to ignore or even transgress against the rest of society altogether, as do many organized criminals in their criminal sub-cultures? This is the question we must consider in the next sub-section.

(c) Universalized altruism as the motivation to seek moral truth

Loyalty to an in-group or to an individual by preference over outsiders is one possible dimension of consciousness (one possible symbolizing relationship that can help consciousness to unfold in those patterns which it is capable of symbolizing). The attempt to establish some form of interface with the whole of humanity, with humanity in the abstract (a universal empathic identification) is another. To close off either dimension---personal loyalty, or interrelation with all of humanity---is to reduce one's possibilities for growth, complexity, variety and change. If I am to empathize with conscious beings precisely insofar as they exemplify the idea of 'conscious being,' then I must empathize with the idea as a universal in order to learn which aspects of particular conscious beings do indeed embody the idea. Immanuel Levinas' 'infinite curvature of intersubjective space'[37] becomes finite if we cut off communication possibilities and limit them to a narrow, explicitly defined in-crowd.

The universal empathic identification is not a mere quantitative increase in the sheer number of explication opportunities available to the individual, but rather a qualitatively different *kind* of explication possibility. For example, in writing this book, I may at some point reread it from the perspective that would result from imagining how my friend X would react to it; by viewing the book through X's eyes in this way, I may achieve a fuller understanding of the problems, contradictions, unclear meanings and unsupported presuppositions (and, of course, self-deceptions) involved in my thinking and presentation. By again rereading the book from the standpoint that I can imagine another friend Y would take toward it, I see it from a still different perspective and therefore am able to evaluate it still more fully. Each person whose perspective I imaginatively assume (through empathic identification) sparks whole new trains of thought, originally unthought of, thus allowing my consciousness to unfold and progress through the dialogical function. (This progression is consciousness's aim and desire, since, *qua* process as opposed to stasis, it must desire to keep unfolding; it cannot exist as stasis.) All of this, however, presupposes the ability to perform the empathic identification.

But what all these particular empathic identifications are ultimately aimed toward is a general or *abstract* empathic identification in the same way that the correlation of different perspectives on the same object, as Merleau-Ponty says, aims toward the ideal of seeing that the object exists in a world where all perspectives coexist and coalesce in the full being of the object in space.[38] Similarly, my dialogical relations with other individuals, *besides* being ways of using the other person for my own symbolizing/explicating purposes, must simultaneously also aim to treat my empathic identification with that individual as one perspectival element in my empathic identification with the abstract phenomenon, 'all humanity' or 'humanity in general' or 'the complete array of possible ways of being authentically human.' The universal empathic identification therefore relates to that in an individual which authentically expresses the abstract concept, 'conscious being.' It values her not because she is who she is, but because (to a greater or lesser extent) she is one more instance of the abstraction, 'authentically unfolding stream of consciousness.' It empathizes with a form which her being exemplifies rather than merely with the actual individual present at hand. The empathic identification which is relevant to universally binding ethical principles which I choose to impose on myself (on pain of inauthenticity and the resulting atrophy) is the kind that values the person because she is a person, not because she is the particular person she is.

Thus there are at least two kinds of empathic identification: (1) Personal loyalty, which seeks to serve the object of the identification (because it cannot avoid vicariously feeling her pleasure and pain) and does so even if her 'form' (i.e., the structure of her personality) changes beyond recognition; (2) empathy with all humanity as such (agape) ---with the abstract idea of humanity. (Socrates, in the *Symposium*, does not seem to recognize the kind of personal loyalty which continues to identify with a person even after she has completely ceased to manifest the formal features which one originally admired, as for example when one's parent has become a vegetable in a lung machine. While the present analysis does not argue that personal loyalty can serve as the basis of a demonstrable and binding set of universal ethical principles, there is no need to deny that affection for a particular, concrete being might in fact exist either.) Here, then, we have two kinds of relationships which can be used to explicate, concretize, symbolize and carry forward my subjective consciousness in its authentic unfolding. To neglect either possibility would be to close myself off from my own possibilities as a consciousness; it would render certain ones of the motivated directions of my consciousness-progression impossible by depriving them of the opportunity for symbolization and embodiment, and therefore of the opportunity for concrete existence. Whatever might be someone's motivation for closing off this source of symbolization for a whole realm of conscious progressions, that motivation cannot be authentic, since it would be self-defeating from the standpoint of the existential analysis of consciousness as a process as opposed to a stasis. (There is no reason to suppose that these two explication tendencies ever need conflict with each other; if they did, however, a denial of universal empathy in favor of personal empathy would result in a corresponding lessening of the authenticity of the personal empathy itself, implying that the universal would then have to be the better choice as opposed to the personal. The only readily conceivable case of such a conflict would be an instance where a friend or relative demands that we commit come outrageous crime against humanity.)

This completes our meta-ethical grounding of an existential theory of the motivation to respect the moral law, since all we still needed to demonstrate was that in order for a person's consciousness to unfold authentically (as it necessarily wants to do), she must symbolize and explicate this consciousness through dialogical relationships, not merely with *certain specific* significant others in her life, but with the whole of mankind, viewed as an abstraction. We demonstrated that this in fact must happen because phenomenological analysis of any particular empathic identification shows that it opens toward the horizon of a universal empathic identification.

The motivation to respect the moral law, whatever it may turn out to be, does not dictate *what* the moral law is going to turn out to be. For there is an emotion which flows naturally from the universal empathic identification which motivates us to attempt to impose as nearly as possible a universal *justice* among all people, since the universal empathic identification does not discriminate among individuals and is not felt more toward one than another. Yet the problem of what *constitutes* a just distribution of value-promotion among people, and of what my proper role in this distribution system ought to be, has not yet been touched upon in the least.

This chapter has shown only that, luckily, human nature is constituted in such a way that it is possible to have *some* objectively valid system of morality which is not reducible to arbitrary emotional whims and ultimately to egoist motives. In the next chapter, we shall begin the process of narrowing the field of possible theories by confronting the Charybdis of determinism, which has laid waste many a theory. The remaining chapters will continue this process of elimination within the broad umbrella of the coherence epistemology outlined in Chapter Two, and will begin the project of comparing different kinds of theories in terms of their overall coherence as defined there.

NOTES

[1] Alisdair MacIntyre, "Pleasure as a Reason for Action," *Against the Self-Images of the Age* (New York: Schocken, 1971), 174-83. Also Donald Crosby, *The Spectre of the Absurd* (Albany: SUNY Press, 1987).

[2] Rollo May, *Power and Innocence* (New York: W. W. Norton, 1972); *Love and Will* (New York: W. W. Norton, 1968); "The Origins and Significance of the Existential Movement in Psychology," in May, ed., *Existence* (New York: Simon and Schuster, 1958), 3-36.

[3] For detailed discussion of Aristippus, see John Watson, *Hedonistic Theories* (Glasgow: Macmillan, 1895).

[4] Watson.

[5] J. C. Gosling, *Pleasure and Desire* (Oxford: Clarendon, 1969), esp. 83-85.

[6] Albert Camus, "The Just Assassins," *Caligula and Other Plays* (New York: Random House, 1958).

[7] It is true, of course, that the status of these 'causal' relationships is still debated in philosophical action theory. But whether such conditioning results in the corresponding behaviors is not, according to learning theorists, a philosophical question, but an empirical one to be resolved by means of statistical reasoning and scientific method.

[8] Robert White, "Motivation Reconsidered," *Psychological Review* 65, 297-333.

[9] Ellis, *An Ontology of Consciousness*, Chapter 4, enumerates many such studies.

[10] J. B. Wolfe and M. D. Kaplon, "Effect of Amount of Reward and Consummative Activity on Learning in Chickens," *Journal of Comparative Psychology* 31, 353-61, shows that, quite literally, chickens would rather peck than eat.

[11] See White, 297, for the problematic nature of this 'consummatory response' notion in behavioristic psychology.

[12] Joseph Butler, *Five Sermons* (New York: Liberal Arts Press, 1950).

[13] E.g., Crosby, *The Spectre of the Absurd* (note 1).

[14]Indeed, more likely. See Chapter Four, section 1.

[15]Aristotle, *Nicomachean Ethics,* Martin Ostwald, trans. (New York: Bobbs-Merrill, 1962), 194.

[16]Hull's theory is distinguished primarily by the thesis that not only the 'reinforcing' quality of a behavior, but also the sheer fact that the organism has repeated the behavior a number of times (for whatever reason)---i.e., the 'habit strength' of the behavior---increases the frequency of the behavior. For a good explanation, see H.J. Eysenck, *The Dynamics of Anxiety and Hysteria* (New York: Praeger, 1957).

[17]Ellis, *An Ontology of Consciousness.*

[18]William James, "Does 'Consciousness' Exist?" John McDermott, ed., *The Writings of William James* (New York: Random House, 1968), 169-70.

[19]D. C. Dennett, *Content and Consciousness* (London: Routledge & Kegan Paul, 1969), 8-18.

[20]John Searle, *Minds, Brains and Science* (Cambridge: Harvard, 1984), 18.

[21]Ludwig Feuerbach, *Principles of the Philosophy of the Future* (Indianapolis: Bobbs-Merrill, 1966), 47.

[22]G. W. F. Hegel, *Logic* (New York; Humanities, 1967), 151ff.

[23]Thomas Aquinas,*Treatise on Man,* Question 75.

[24]U.T. Place, "Is Consciousness a Brain Process?" *British Journal of Psychology* 47, 44-50.

[25]Dennett (note 19); Normal Malcolm, "Scientific Materialism and the Identity Theory," *Dialogue* 3, 115-25.

[26]Alvin Goldman, "The Compatibility of Mechanism and Purpose," *Philosophical Review* 78, 468-82.

[27]Maurice Merleau-Ponty, *The Structure of Behavior* (Boston: Beacon, 1967); Henri Ey, *Consciousness: A Phenomenological Study* (Indiana University Press, 1978).

[28]Ellis, *An Ontology of Consciousness.*

[29]D. O. Hebb, *A Textbook of Psychology* (Philadelphia: Saunders, 1966).

[30]White (note 8).

[31]Sigmund Freud, *Beyond the Pleasure Principle* (New York: Bantum, 1959).

[32]As elaborated, e.g., by Gendlin, *Experiencing and the Creation of Meaning* (see Ch. One, note 27); also Gendlin, *Focusing* (Toronto: Bantam, 1979).

[33]Kant, *Critique of Practical Reason*, 74ff, shows that Kant's understanding of psychology was essentially drive-reductionistic in nature.

[34]Ellis, *An Ontology of Consciousness*.

[35]Gendlin, "Experiential Phenomenology," in *Phenomenology and the Social Sciences*, ed. M. Natanson (Evanston: Northwestern, 1973).

[36]Edmund Husserl, *Cartesian Meditations* (The Hague: Nijhoff, 1966), 114-20; M. Merleau-Ponty, *Signs* (Evanston: Northwstern, 1964), 97.

[37]Emmanuel Levinas, *Totality and Infinity* (Pittsburgh: Duquesne, 1969).

[38]Merleau-Ponty, *Phenomenology of Perception*, 327-34.

CHAPTER FOUR

SECOND FACT: THE ETIOLOGY OF PERSONALITY

It will become increasingly obvious that the single most important determinant of a person's ethical beliefs is whether, to what extent, and in what sense she believes in determinism. Many philosophers have pretended that this is not the case, and that ethical systems can somehow be neutral with respect to determinism. At a superficial level, for example, it appears that Rawls' rational reflector in the original position can carry out his cost-benefit analyses without knowledge of whether determinism is true. Yet philosophers who really believe strongly in free will find too much emphasis in Rawls on entitlement and not enough on desert,[1] and are uncomfortable with the assumption that fairness in the distribution of happiness or benefits is the all-important value,[2] that "No one deserves his place in the distribution of natural assets,"[3] and that "Undeserved inequalities call for redress.... Since inequalities of birth and natural endowment are undeserved, these inequalities are somehow to be compensated for."[4] If complete determinism is true, of course, then a morally evil personality would be just another 'inequality of birth and natural endowment' for which the society is obligated to compensate the person, according to Rawls' reasoning.[5]

We shall soon see that the increasing occlusion of the determinism issue in recent philosophy results neither from the issue's having been resolved, nor from its lack of importance, but rather from the frustration and sheer fatigue that opponents feel in not being able to convince each other. This incommensurability of opposing arguments in turn reflects the fact that the notion of determinism has been ill-defined for the purposes of establishing dialogue and assessing the implications of the view for ethical theory. The purpose of this chapter is first to redefine determinism in a relevant and productive way, to examine the evidence for this redefined determinism, and to see how it is relevant to the choice of a system of value priorities.

Recent philosophers and physicists have adduced evidence that nature does not operate according to strict causal principles in terms of which every physical event would be completely, necessarily and sufficiently determined (under the given circumstances) by some prior physical event.[6] Rather, they insist that, to paraphrase Clerk Maxwell's colorful expression, electrons are pushed around in their orbits by demons.[7] From the physical point of view, there seems to be some evidence for a genuine randomness in the behavior of subatomic particles.[8] From the philosophical perspective, the argument is expressed concisely by Pierce: There must be uncaused events, either at the beginning of the history of the universe, or throughout its history; either way, the possibility of uncaused events must be admitted.[9]

However, most philosophers are well aware that this controversy concerning the randomness of the ultimate physical events is really quite tangential to the question of determinism as it relates to human actions and conscious processes. For these actions and processes exist at the level of large aggregates of sub-atomic particles and events. As Searle sums up this point,

> The statistical indeterminacy at the level of particles does not show any indeterminacy at the level of the objects that matter to us---human bodies, for example....It doesn't follow from the fact that particles are only statistically determined that the human mind can force the statistically-determined particles to swerve from their paths. Indeterminism is no evidence that there is or could be some mental energy of human freedom that can move molecules in directions that they were not otherwise going to move.[10]

But it is interesting to notice that, after having rejected the mere denial of Laplacean determinism as a relevant consideration, Searle then accepts another argument which, if valid, would endorse free will *only because the argument refutes Laplacean determinism.* It is the old argument from the 'feeling of freedom'---that there is always the feeling that, no matter how rigorously our actions have been predetermined, we still feel that we *could have* acted different from the way we did. It was this same consideration that so horribly de-railed Von Wright's otherwise elegant theory of causation in the 1970s, and led to the absurd debate over 'backwards causation.'[11]

For both Searle and Von Wright, the 'feeling of freedom' supposedly becomes an *argument* when we see that it leads to an element of 'unpredictability' in human choices. To quote Searle again, "If somebody predicts that I am going to do something, I might just damn well do something else. Now, that sort of option is simply not open to glaciers moving down mountainsides or balls rolling down inclined planes."[12] Based purely on this one argument, Searle then concludes that "there must be some freedom of the will because we all experience it all the time."[13]

Of course, if this argument were valid, then it would also be possible to construct a completely mechanical gadget which would have free will. Imagine a machine equipped with a computer keyboard into which one types one's prediction as to what the machine is going to do. Suppose the machine is capable of doing only two things---flashing a light or ringing a bell. One may type either 'You are going to ring the bell' or 'You are going to flash the light.' Clearly marked on the keyboard is a simple switch, the 'acquiescence-rebellion' or 'A-R' switch. When the switch is in the 'A' position, the computer does exactly what the user predicts it is going to do, if and only if the prediction follows from a correct knowledge of electricity and the machine's internal circuits, which are clearly visible on the exposed circuit board in back. We can even remove the components and test them if we like. However, if the switch is in the 'R' position, the machine automatically does the opposite of what we predict. If we type 'You are going to ring the bell,' it flashes the light instead, and vice versa. So, when the switch is the the 'R' position, it is impossible to predict what the machine is going to do---assuming, of course, that we make the prediction known to the machine by typing it into the keyboard. Since the 'unpredictability' argument applies to this machine in exactly the same way as it does to human beings, it follows that if the unpredictability argument is valid, then the machine just described has free will.

It is true that, if we see that the switch is in the 'R' position, and then type 'You are going to ring the bell,' we *secretly* know that it is going to flash the light. But according to the unpredictability argument as applied to humans, to make such a secret prediction would be cheating, since the whole effect of the unpredictability argument as applied to humans presupposes that the prediction must be made known to the entity about whom the prediction is made. If we were allowed to keep our predictions secret from the entity about whom the prediction is made, the   unpredictability argument would not establish free will for human beings any better than it would for the free will machine just described. As long as the prediction is kept secret, then we who are making the prediction, if we really had *all* the needed information about the predictee, would understand the person's character well enough to know whether she is the kind of person who would be devious enough, and clever enough, to decide to trick us by doing the opposite of what she thinks we have predicted.

The problem is that, in the final analysis, all that the 'feeling of freedom' and the resulting unpredictability argument prove is that it is always possible that I could have chosen differently if I had *wanted* to. It does not show that how I would end up *wanting* to choose had not already been predetermined. It shows that I may be free from *presently external* forces, but not from *internal* forces which in turn may have been predetermined in the *past*.

What all these considerations amount to is simply a further confirmation of Searle's original observation: Laplacean determinism is not the relevant kind of determinism to be contrasted against freedom of the human will. But what other kind of determinism is there? The next section will attempt to develop a more relevant definition of determinism, so that we can say once and for all: If this kind of determinism is true, then free will is not; and if free will is true, then *it* is not.

Some readers may be tempted to assume that this discussion of determinism is merely an eccentric digression from our overall topic of ethical epistemology. It must be emphasized, however, that the resolution of the determinism issue is crucially determinative within the broader project of eliminating counterfactual theories and interpretations of certain extremely fundamental moral concepts, as will become manifestly evident in due course.

1. *Psychological Determinism*

The recent boost in the popularity of free will owes in large part to two kinds of arguments. (1) Some philosophers have begun to insist that some human actions (speech acts, for example) may unfold in sequences that are independent of physical causation in the following sense: As Michael Simon puts it,

> Understanding a conversation or a succession of intelligent utterances requires that we apprehend a set of meaning relations, and hence relations that are internal rather than external. The connections between these events have the character of connections of ideas, not matters of fact....Since speaking is itself a kind of action, we can take it that we have found that something other than causality is appropriate for an understanding of at least some actions.[14]

While there may be some truth to this point of view, it does not follow (nor does Simon suggest that it follows) from the assumption that strict, physical causation may not be completely sufficient for an 'understanding' of such phenomena as speech, that determinism is false or that all human actions and action sequences are not completely predetermined by factors other than the person doing the acting. But that is precisely the question we must pursue if we want to know whether determinism is true in any sense which would affect our choice of a value theory. For that purpose, there is a second and more relevant kind of libertarian argument.

(2) Thomas Talbott does argue that determinism cannot be reasonably maintained in the face of mental events as 'acausally' understood. His argument, when buttressed by such acausal analyses as Simon presents, becomes a serious, but instructively uncompelling, challenge to the deterministic way of thinking.[15] Talbott points out, justifiably enough, that the traditional determinist argument to the effect that any action which is not caused must be attributable to 'pure chance' (and therefore no more 'free' than a rigorously caused action) is merely a trivial tautology. Those who advance this argument, he says, ignore the fact that,

if an action is committed for a reason, and therefore 'caused' in a trivial sense, the person may nonetheless remain free from causal necessity to *choose* to 'cause' his own action in this trivial sense. Thus the *person* intervenes between the random, uncaused event (his choosing as he does), and the resulting action (which his choice 'causes' in the trivial sense). This shows that the argument from 'pure chance' does not refute human freedom or responsibility.

Talbott's point is well-taken, in that the argument from pure chance is a tautology. However, Talbott systematically ignores the fact that a person's decisions may be determined by what or who that person *is*, while what the person is may be ultimately attributable to causal and/or chance factors 'beyond his control.' The problem with the usual argument from pure chance is that, rather than showing that a person's uncaused actions are attributable to chance factors *beyond his control*, it merely shows that the actions are attributable to chance. The problem is essentially that the determinist thesis based on this kind of argument is empty of empirical content. The following analysis will attempt to give determinism empirical content by defining it in such a way that, if true, it must show that the 'causal' and 'chance' factors to which a person's decisions are attributable are indeed *beyond his control.*

Determinism can be argued either on empirical or on a priori grounds. Those who opt for a priori grounds realize that if determinism is to mean a genuinely philosophical position, rather than a mere empirical-scientific hypothesis (whose universal truth ultimately could never be proven), then one should be able to support the thesis with reason alone, in a way that remains valid regardless of the truth or falsity of any empirical facts.[16] At the same time, however, such a conceptualization of determinism should not be devoid of all empirical *content*, as is the argument that uncaused events are instances of 'pure chance.' Nor should it become enmeshed in the hopeless attempt to prove the thesis of 'logical fatalism'---that it is somehow logically or quasi-logically 'necessary' that every event occurs just as it does. Richard Taylor has notably commented on this kind of position,[17] which in the 1960s and 70s set off a running and perhaps irresolvable controversy.[18] Even if such a 'logical fatalism' were true, it would be unlikely to disturb any libertarian's sense that her actions are nonetheless free; for, in order to be provable, it would have to broaden the meaning of 'necessity' so far as no longer to exclude freedom. As Keith Lehrer argues, this kind of thesis *could* be stated in such a way as to give it a tangible empirical meaning so as to exclude freedom, but only by forfeiting any hope of being logically provable.[19] Similarly, Fritz Perls has criticized Freud's position on determinism because, by claiming to be a logical necessity, it becomes a 'tautological platitude' so extreme as to be devoid of any real content, meaning or serious philosophical consequences.[20]

The task of our inquiry is thus twofold: first, to formulate an alternative concept, a psychological determinism which has empirical content, yet can be defended with a purely logical argument; second, to see whether such a determinism can have serious philosophical consequences. To accomplish this goal, we must find a middle ground between empty logical determinisms on the one hand, and on the other hand the empirical-scientific thesis that every event must have a sufficient cause---which has empirical content but would be impossible to support with reason alone. The next sub-section will attempt to define the alternative formulation of determinism which can meet these specifications, and the subsequent subsection will then provide the argument to show that 'determinism' in this revised sense is indeed the case. This argument will attempt to demonstrate as a logical necessity that past external factors (roughly characterizable as 'environment') and past internal factors (roughly traceable to the interaction of environment and 'heredity') have at any given time already completely predetermined what a given person is, even if neither logical fatalism nor strict causality is true. The key to the empirical content of the thesis is whether these environmental and hereditary factors are indeed 'beyond the person's control.'

(a) Toward a relevant definition

The empirical-scientific way of conceptualizing determinism is to think of it as an application to human beings of the thesis of sufficient causation; this application takes 'determinism' in the same sense as with natural phenomena but applies it to human beings.[21] I shall suggest (in partial agreement with the purely logical determinists just discussed) that to conceptualize psychological determinism as dependent on sufficient causation in the natural-scientific sense is neither necessary nor fruitful. For whether an event is caused to occur or whether it occurs by a random stroke of luck is inconsequential in the ultimate outcome of the dispute between free will and determinism.

The free will advocate would in some cases want to deny the explanatory adequacy of both causality *and* pure chance, whereas the determinist need not claim supreme importance for either causality or pure chance. The following concept of determinism is designed to retain the essential empirical import of the determinist position, but without the unnecessary additional claim of strict causality, and without becoming a mere tautology:

> *Every decision a person makes is completely attributable to causal and/or chance factors over which the person has (and has had) no control.*[22]

Like logical determinisms such as fatalism and the 'pure chance' argument, this thesis strongly asserts a deterministic view of human agency without necessarily aligning itself with the thesis of universal mechanistic causation. But unlike logical determinisms of those kinds, the thesis as stated above has empirical content. That the factors responsible for a person's decision are 'beyond his control' is by no means tautologous or self-evident.

THE ETIOLOGY OF PERSONALITY   115

Here are definitions for the main terms of the thesis, to be used in the subsequent argument:

Definition of 'attributable to': If we consider the relationship between 'caused by' and 'attributable to,' we find that if A causes B, then B is necessarily attributable to A, whereas if B is attributable to A, it *may or may not* be caused by A. For example, if something is attributable to chance, we would not usually say that it is 'caused by' chance, and some authors maintain that to speak of an agent as 'causing' his own thoughts, deliberations, or actions is to obfuscate the meaning of the word 'cause.'[23]

However, almost anyone would agree that an agent's thoughts are at least *attributable* to the agent in some sense, even though they may not be referred to as 'caused by' her. And hardly anyone will seriously deny the principle that if A is attributable to B, and if B is attributable to C, then A is attributable to C. By our definition of determinism, then, the psychological determinist's contention is that if a choice, A, is attributable to the whole agent, B, and if the total state of the whole agent B at the instant when she makes the choice is completely attributable to a series of other factors, C, D, and E (some of which may be previous states of the same agent), and if these in turn are completely attributable to F, G and H, then A is just as completely attributable to F, G and H as if it had been directly 'caused by' them. The determinist therefore hopes to demonstrate that F, G and H are beyond the agent's control.

'Attributability' in this kind of determinism can be *complete* without being *direct,* and it need not be limited to attributability to a *causal* factor, so long as the factor is beyond the agent's control. 'Attributable to' really means little more than 'truly said of.' For example, if we attribute the winning of football games to a team's defense, we assert that the team's defense wins football games or is a primary element of an entity (e.g., the team as a whole) which wins games. We do not necessarily imply that the defense 'causes' the team to win games, or that it 'causes itself' to win games.

If we define the word 'attributable' in this way, then for all practical purposes the first part of the determinism we have stated---that every decision is completely attributable to causal and/or chance factors---now reduces pretty much to a tautology. It is not false, but it contains little information, since determinists would always consider any event 'attributable to mere chance' if no other event tended to cause, influence, or exert some kind of control over the outcome of the event.[24] (By this criterion, neither an act which is freely chosen nor one which is rigorously caused would be considered attributable to chance.) The substantial content of the thesis therefore hinges on the second part: that these causal and/or chance factors *are beyond the agent's control.* Thus it is essential that we specify the meaning of this phrase, for it is here that the real meaning of our thesis is to be found.

Definition of 'factors beyond the agent's control': When the determinism thesis says 'factors beyond the agent's control,' it refers to two kinds of factors: (a) those which are not caused to be the way they are, in part or in whole, by any choice of the agent, nor influenced in any way by any choice of hers; and (b) those which are indeed influenced by or attributable to some choice of the agent, but to one which it is causally necessary for the agent to make *given other* factors which are beyond her control under condition (a). Even the free will advocate should agree that a factor is beyond the agent's control if it is completely causally necessitated (and, of course, if the agent herself is not one of the causal factors in question).

Falsifiability of the thesis: The thesis stated in these terms is falsifiable in case there should turn out to be some actions which are due to causal and/or chance factors *not* beyond the agent's control. If I have an automobile accident because someone tampers with my braking mechanism, the event is obviously due to a causal factor beyond my control. But if I crash into another vehicle because of slow reflexes, stupidity or carelessness on my part, the libertarian can argue that although my slow reflexes, stupidity and carelessness may 'cause' the accident, these causal factors are not beyond my control, for it is *within my power* to exercise good judgment and to be prepared to react quickly, rather than being content to remain slow, stupid and careless. In fact, if I find myself endowed with the latter traits, I can purposely set forth to eradicate them in myself; or if the task proves hopeless, I can learn to avoid situations beyond my mental capacities. Against this point of view, the psychological determinist has a strong argument. I shall try to present this argument in enough detail to see whether it is really logically compelling.

(b) The argument

From the principle of noncontradiction and the supposition that there is time, it follows that, given any person---say, Joe Freeman---,either (I) Freeman began to exist (as a decision-making entity) at some time, T, or (II) he has always existed. Such a sharp division of the possibilities may seem to leave out a third alternative---that without having always existed, Freeman may nonetheless come into being gradually, rather than suddenly springing full-blown from the head of Zeus, as (I) tends to connote. But whether Freeman begins to exist gradually or suddenly, the result will be the same, for in either case there remains a time T, before which Freeman could have made no decisions. Whether one wishes to set this time at the instant of birth, at the beginning of the development of the embryo, or at the age of reason is inconsequential to the argument.[25] (The question whether T must be presumed as some sort of absolute point in a Cartesian or Euclidean coordinate system can be avoided by defining the points in time as arranged ordinally but not necessarily cardinally in relation to each other, for our present purposes.) Let's consider, then, the two overall possibilities, each in turn: (I) that Freeman began to exist at some time, and (II) that he has always existed:

I. FOR THE CASE THAT FREEMAN BEGAN TO EXIST AT SOME TIME:

From the principle of noncontradiction in conjunction with the assumption that the word 'cause' has some meaning or other, it follows that, given any feature of Freeman or of his acts (where 'feature' is taken to mean anything whatever that could truly be predicated of Freeman at some time---that he is six feet tall, that he drove his car into a tree yesterday, or that he believes in Mohammed), this feature is either caused or not.[26] This idea of 'features' might seem to pack in a gratuitous presupposition until we consider that, given the above definition of it (as anything that could possibly be predicated or correctly said of Freeman), any denial that Freeman has features would be a denial that anything can be predicated or correctly said of Freeman. Obviously, whatever is true of Freeman could conceivably be said about him, and any such truth---whether it be one small truth about the person, or the sum of all truths about the person---is what we mean by a 'feature'. For example, that Freeman drove his car into a tree yesterday is a feature of Freeman, and this feature is either caused (by Freeman, or by some other factors, or both) or it is not caused.[27]

But by this definition of 'feature', our statement that every feature must be either caused or not would seem an unwarranted use of the excluded middle unless it leaves room for features that may be 'partly caused.' This is only an apparent problem, however, for if a feature is partly caused, then it is analyzable at least in principle into the respects in which it is caused and the respects in which it is not caused; these respects then become features (predicates) in their own right which are either caused or not. We could say, therefore, 'Given any feature of Freeman or of his acts, this feature is either caused, or not caused, or analyzable into features that are either caused or not.' But this extra cumbersomeness is unnecessary, so I shall let the third alternative be tacitly understood. For practical purposes, the feature is either (A) not caused or (B) caused. And if it is caused, then the causal antecedent is either (1) something other than Freeman, or (2) the whole agent, Freeman himself, or some feature (or complex of features) of Freeman which was already operating at the time when the decision was made. Let's consider each case:

A. FOR THE CASE THAT THE FEATURE IS NOT CAUSED:

If the feature is not caused, then it is not caused by the agent or by any other causal factor either. To say that it is not caused by the agent is to say that it does not originate with his will. (We are taking the liberty, for the sake of economy, of using 'caused by the agent' in the broadest possible sense, i.e., as synonymous with 'attributable to the agent.') If it is not caused by any other factor either, it is attributable only to chance. All features which are attributable to chance factors are beyond the agent's control, since they are not caused to be the way they are in part or in whole by any choice of his, nor influenced in any way by any choice of his. (This argument is not vulnerable to Talbott's criticism because, rather than asking whether an uncaused *action* is attributable to pure chance, it asks whether an *agent's character* is attributable to pure chance if uncaused; in this case, the chance factor is indeed beyond the agent's control, since if he were to influence it, then it would fall under a different case---case B, in which causal factors including agent causation are considered.)

One might be tempted to object that such a presumably uncaused 'decision' *would* be attributable to me in some respect; for example, that my *failure* to control my behavior results from (i.e., is caused by) a general attitude on my part that leads me to allow myself to act impulsively.[28] But to the extent that such an attitudinal failure is a factor (as it may often be), the impulsive behavior does not fall under our case A---the case that the feature is uncaused. It would then fall under case B---the case that it is caused (in this instance, caused by the agent). Similarly, if the feature in question is an *act of Freeman's will,* it falls under 'caused by Freeman,' considered as part of case B.

B. FOR THE CASE THAT THE FEATURE IS CAUSED:

Either (1) the causal antecedent is something other than Freeman; or (2) it is some feature of Freeman or his actions which was already operative at the time when he chose to commit the act (for example, that he was of the opinion that he should commit the act, or that he failed to analyse the situation properly, or that he was an evil person and purposely chose to do the wrong thing).[29]

There is also a third possibility, that a combination of (1) and (2) could cause the feature; but if we consider both (1) and (2), we ipso facto account for their combination. To consider both cases:

1. FOR THE CASE THAT THE FEATURE IS CAUSED BY SOMETHING OTHER THAN FREEMAN:

The truth of our determinist thesis might appear automatically ensured in this case, but it is not. The sophisticated libertarian is not likely to overlook the possible objection that Freeman has had some say-so about whether he was ever going to put himself into the position to be affected by these external forces in this way, and that *in what way* he is affected depends as much on attributes of the character he brings with him to the situation (modes of experiencing, etc.) as it does on the external forces doing the affecting. In fact, Maurice Merleau-Ponty shows that it must be

> the organism itself [and its proper manner of offering itself to actions from the outside]---according to the proper nature of its receptors, the thresholds of its nerve centers and the movements of the

organs---which chooses the stimuli in the physical world to which it will be sensitive.[30]

Thus he points out that "The relations between the organism and its milieu are not relations of linear causality but of circular causality."[31] Such points as these are well-taken, particularly in that they show that living beings are not the passive, almost infinitely malleable creatures that some determinists take them to be. But the structures alluded to in this 'circular causality' fall under the heading of 'already-operative features of Freeman,' which will be dealt with in Case 2.

2. FOR THE CASE THAT THE FEATURE IS ATTRIBUTABLE TO SOME ALREADY-OPERATIVE FEATURE OF FREEMAN OR OF HIS ACTIONS:

This is the crucial case. If it cannot be demonstrated that this already-operative feature is itself attributable to outside factors beyond Freeman's control, then there will still be hope for libertarianism. To discover whether it is attributable to such factors, we must take a step backward in time, focus on the feature in *this* case under consideration (whatever property, previous actions, mental state, etc., or combination of such factors may have led Freeman to make the above decision), and go through a logical process similar to the one we have just been through, this time to decide whether *this* feature is attributable to factors beyond Freeman's control. For this purpose, we must consider two cases: Either (A') this previous feature now under consideration is not caused, or (B') it is caused:

A'. FOR THE CASE THAT IT IS NOT CAUSED:

As in case A, here too, if the feature is uncaused, then it was not caused to be the way it is by the agent, and therefore can be attributed only to chance, which is beyond the agent's control.

B'. FOR THE CASE THAT IT IS CAUSED:

Either (1') the causal antecedent was something other than Freeman; or (2') it was some previously operative feature of Freeman.

1'. FOR THE CASE THAT THE CAUSE WAS SOMETHING OTHER THAN FREEMAN

Determinism as we have defined it obviously holds good for this case as in case 1 above.

2'. FOR THE CASE THAT THE FEATURE IS ATTRIBUTABLE TO SOME ALREADY-OPERATIVE FEATURE OF FREEMAN:

This is the crucial case at this stage of the arguement just as case 2 was above. Now if it cannot be demonstrated that this already-operative feature is itself attributable to outside factors, then there will still be hope for libertarianism. To show that it is attributable to such factors we must take a *second* step backward in time, focus on the feature in *this* case under consideration (the attribute, previous action, mental state, state of the agent as a whole, etc., that led him to take the above decision) and go through a logical process similar to the ones we have been through in the above cases, this time to discover whether *this* feature is attributable to factors beyond Freeman's control. Toward this end, as one will anticipate, we must consider two possible cases.

By now the foresightful reader might understandably exclaim that we have merely succeeded in trapping ourselves in a vicious circle of considering causes of causes of causes, and so on *ad infinitum*. But not so! It must be remembered that we are still in the overall context of Case I, the case that Freeman began to exist at some time, T. And every time we take another step backward in our consideration of the sequence, we draw slightly closer to the final step we have to consider: the step that occurred at time T. When we reach this step in the consideration, we find a distinctly different situation, although it begins with the same 'chicken-or-egg' connotation; it will look like this:

Step N of our thought process---consideration of the feature of Freeman which remains to be considered after case N-1:

...To show that this already-operative feature is itself attributable to outside factors, we must take an *nth* step backward in time, focus on the feature under consideration in this case (case 2^{n-1}), *and go through a logical process similar to the one we have already been through n-1 times.* Either the feature in question was caused, or not:

A^n. FOR THE CASE THAT IT WAS NOT CAUSED

Determinism holds true here as in cases A, A', A", etc.

B^n. FOR THE CASE THAT IT WAS CAUSED

Either the causal antecedent was something other then Freeman, or it was some previous feature of Freeman:

1^n. FOR THE CASE THAT IT WAS SOMETHING OTHER THAN FREEMAN

Determination is true here as in cases 1, 1', 1", etc.

2^n. FOR THE CASE THAT IT IS ATTRIBUTABLE TO SOME PREVIOUS FEATURE OF FREEMAN

There can be no such case. For we are now considering time T, the time before which Freeman did not exist. Anything already operating at time T could not have been a feature of Freeman, because he did not yet exist.

Reflecting on what we have done so far, one will note that, for all cases subsumed under Case I, we have demonstrated the truth of the statement: Every decision a person makes is completely attributable to causal and/or chance factors over which the person does not have and has never had any control. Now we have to deal with all possible cases which are *not* subsumed under Case I, i.e., those in which Freeman did not begin to exist at any time, but has always existed (just in case such a thing might be possible).

II. FOR THE CASE THAT FREEMAN HAS ALWAYS EXISTED.

Whatever there is of Freeman that always was must be uncaused, since there could never have been any time at which it was caused to be what it was. So for this case, an argument can be constructed exactly like that for Case I, except that, instead of tracing all possible cases back to the time before which Freeeman did not exist, we would trace them to the time such that any features the present Freeman has in common with the Freeman of that time were never caused to be what they are--and thus were not caused to be what they are by Freeman. If he decides to choose against what he has always been, this new decision is only an expression of what he already was, since it was *that* Freeman who made the decision. Even in this case, the truth of the determinist thesis as we have defined it is borne out. Every decision Freeman makes is still attributable to factors beyond his control. In all possible cases, then, determinism (again, under our modified definition) is supported.

It is interesting to note that the above argument is neither purely a priori, nor is it merely empirical in the usual sense; that is, it makes no empirical claim or assumption that any particular thing or state of affairs exists. It does assume that *whatever* exists, exists in time (without, however, assuming one or another of the possible ontological conceptions of time, and without assuming that time is homogenous). This one assumption---the assumption that change takes place in the context of a 'before' and an 'after'---should easily be allowed, if for no other reason because the assumption that human actions take place through time is necessary before the freedom/determinism dispute can even arise. The theory of free actions is dependent on the postulation of time at least as much as the determinist position formulated here.

An important factor has tended to work to the disadvantage of the psychological-determinist outlook, often trapping it almost in the position of a philosophical straw man. Lacking a clear distinction between determinism and universal causasion on the one hand, and between determinism and logical fatalism on the other hand, the determinist side of the dispute has often had to bear the burden of establishing entire metaphysical and cosmological systems in order to support its claim. Libertarian aguments, by contrast, can be devised by reasoning about the evident data of immediate human experience. The determinist finds herself always lagging behind the opponent, constantly refuting arguments for the libertarian position while seldom able to advance much positive philosophical evidence for her own. But if she need not deny chance factors or postulate universal laws of nature in order to confute free will, then psychological determinism ceases to be a scienfic hypothesis based on the assumption (always remaining to be further verified) of universal causation, a postulate of common sense, or a hueristic assumption for psychology, and becomes a viable philosophical claim arguable in its own right, and on purely philosophical grounds.

The kind of psychological determinism I have advanced here leaves a number of unanswered questions. It would not appear to infringe on the individual's sense of moral responsibility (in the sense that he 'could have acted differently if he wanted to') as much as does the thesis that the agent could not possibly have chosen differently from the way he did; but it does seem a somewhat uneasy fit with some notions of moral blame, since it shows that a person's moral character, like the rest of his character, is derternimed by three factors---environment (factors external to Freeman that cause him to be the way he is), heredity (factors internal to Freeman which pre-existed him in a form prior to their being affected by the environment), and chance (which is a factor beyond Freeman's control in the sense of 'chance' we have employed). How compatible this kind of determinism might be with some other sort of human freedom besides the kind it contradicts (i.e., contra-causal freedom) would be a complex issue to resolve, but it obvoiusly does leave room for a distinction between the freedom from *presently* external forces on the one hand (such as societal mores and expectations, feared consequences, and the temptations of pleasure), and on the other hand the freedom (which we have denied here) from forces which at some remote time in the past had nothing to do with 'me', but which now form an integral part of what I am. This is a far cry from the 'puppet' portrait of man which is sometimes associated with the determinist position. In a sense, the view discussed here is a hard determinism (although devoid of assertions about universal causation or laws of nature) in that it leaves ablolutely no room for a contra-causal freedom.

But now we must examine to see more precisely what kind of free will it is that is *incompatible* with what has been said here, and what the ethical consequences of this incompatibility are.

2. *Ethical Implications*

(a) *Compatibilism and the word 'can'*

So far, we have spoken as though the kind of 'determinism' discussed in the previous section had been defined in such a way that it is incompatible with free will *by definition*. For this weak or modified determinism, unlike Laplacean or natural-scientific determinism, was defined as the thesis that 'every decision a person makes is completely attributable to causal and/or chance factors over which the person has (and has had) no control.' This thesis seems to directly contradict free will, if by free will we mean the thesis that some decisions are *not* attributable to causal and/or chance factors over which the person had no control. But there are many philosophers who either use 'free will' in a different sense, or who insist that, even though something may be completely attributable to factors beyond my control, it may at the same time, and without contradiction, be attributable to *me* in some meaningful sense as well. For this reason, 'soft determinism,' which holds both that determinism is *completely* true, and yet that the agent *could have* acted differently from the way she did (if she had wanted to), has always been a going option. Obviously, since the 'determinism' discussed in section (1) is a *weaker* form of determinism than the traditional Laplacean determinism in terms of which the compatibilism or 'soft determinism' controversy is *usually* framed, then it is at least as likely that our determinism is compatible with free will as it is that the stronger, Laplacean determinism is compatible with free will.

Yet it seems equally obvious that, for the purposes of ethical theory at least, any meaningful concept of free will that is *incompatible* with the traditional Laplacean determinism will also be incompatible with our modified or weaker form of determinism. For a *meaningful* concept of free will requires more than that a bodily movement should occur *merely by chance,* without being the *result* of the person's *decision* to, say, raise her hand; or that the decision to raise the hand occurs merely by chance, without resulting from the character or personality which the person making the decision already *has* (or perhaps *is)* at the moment when she makes the decision---thus trapping us back into the determinist reasoning of the last section. The decision must result from a previous condition of the agent's mind or character---not from pure chance---so that the question again arises as to whether the previous condition of the agent's mind ultimately resulted from factors beyond the agent's control or not.

Therefore if Laplacean determinism is incompatible with a *meaningful* concept of free will, then so is the weaker type of determinism we have developed here. For example, Peter van Inwagen argues that, if (Laplacean) determinism is true, then anyone who would choose to act differently from the way the laws of nature in conjunction with past events have predetermined her to act could do so only if she could render false either the laws of nature or the past.[32] Since van Inwagnen believes in free will, he therefore thinks he must reject determinism. (Alternatively, anyone who believes in determinism would have to reject free will.) Although van Inwagen's argument is framed in terms of Laplacean determinism, the same consequence would follow from our modified determinism if we add to his argument one qualification: In order for free will to be true, a person must be able to *purposely* (i.e., not just by accident) act differently from the way she has been predetermined to act. Therefore, in order for free will to be compatible with determinism, a person must render false either the past or the laws of nature. For, if the person is to *purposely* do something, then her choice to do it cannot result from pure chance, and therefore must result from a previous condition of her mind (or psyche, or character). But if the previous condition of her mind is the result of the laws of nature, past events, *and chance,* then the only way the person can act contrary to what these factors are going to predetermine her to do would be by rendering false this previous condition of her mind, which is to falsify (or change) the past. So adding the element of chance into the picture of the way conditions of the mind come about does not make it any easier to purposely act contrary to the laws of nature in conjunction with past events. The only modification we would have to make to the usual incompatibilist argument is that we must include some chance occurrences as some of the past events that have occurred. These chance occurrences, along with previously lawful occurrences and the laws of nature, will result in the agent's doing whatever she does if what she does is *purposeful* (and therefore if her decision is the result of a condition of her mind or character rather than occurring through pure chance and thus in a way completely uninfluenced by her mind or character).

Instead of defining determinism, as van Inwagen does, to imply that the conjunction of the total state of the universe and the laws of nature entail the present state of the universe, we have defined determinism to imply that the conjunction of the total state of the universe and the laws of nature entail the present state of the universe *except for those present events that result from pure chance.* Now, if the agent's choice is to be a *meaningful* instance of free will, it must result from the agent's will, and therefore cannot result from pure chance. So, again, if free will is incompatible with the traditional Laplacean determinism (as van Inwagen has argued), then it will also be incompatible with our modified determinism. In short, an agent can no more easily render false the laws of nature in conjunction with past events *and events that are the result of chance,* than she can render false the simpler conjunction of the laws of nature with past events.

The essence of the compatibilism dispute (as has been argued in more detail elsewhere)[33] hinges on the definition of the word 'can'. Compatibilists say that an agent 'can' do something even if it would have been necessary for either the past or the laws of nature to have been different in order for her to do it. Incompatibilists say that the agent 'cannot' do something if it would be necessary for either the past or the laws of nature to have been different in order for her to do it. Both are right, but in different senses of the word 'can'. The compatibilists are right to claim that it is not *logically* impossible that the past or the laws of nature be different from what they are, and therefore it is not logically impossible that the agent do something that would render false either these laws of nature or the past. But the incompatibilists are right to claim that it *is physically impossible* for the agent to render these things false. So the question, really, is which of these two senses of 'can' is the relevant one if we want the corresponding compatibilist or incompatibilist position to have non-trivial ethical implications.

The Appendix of this book provides a complete logical demonstration that, given the usage of 'can' in this physical sense, van Inwagen's argument for incompatibilism (with slight modifications to meet certain objections from his critics) is deductively valid. But it is not really necessary to go into that much technical detail in order to see that the disagreement between van Inwagen and his critics hinges on their different usages of 'can'. Clearly, van Inwagen is using 'can' in the *physical* sense, and the claim is being made, not as a logical impossibility, but as a part of the meaning of what *determinism* asserts, that it is an empirical or ontological fact that one cannot change the past or the laws of nature. I.e., it packs into determinism the essence of the claim that one 'cannot' render the past false; thus it is no surprise that determinism implies incompatibilism in this sense.

But now listen to the way 'can' is used by the critics of van Inwagen's argument. Terry Horgan, for example, focuses on the distinction between a 'divergence-miracle' and an 'altered-past' interpretation of compatibilism.[34] That is, some philosophers interpret counterfactual statements to posit that the past would have been the same as it was in the actual world, up until a point immediately prior to the time of the antecedent, at which point a 'divergence miracle' would have occurred to bring about the counterfactual. Others interpret counterfactuals to mean that the entire history of the universe would have to have been different in order for the counterfactual to have occurred in the way imagined. Compatibilists who assume the first type of analysis of counterfactuals are called by Horgan 'divergence-miracle' compatibilists; those who assume the second type of analysis are 'altered-past' compatibilists. Horgan argues that, according to the altered-past type of compatibilism, it is still possible that a person "can do something...which is such that, if he did it, then [some statement describing some past event] would have been false."[35] And according to divergence-miracle compatibilist, it is still possible that the person can do something which is such that, if he did it, then the laws of physics would have to have been different. But van Inwagen's response to the altered-past compatibilist will be precisely that the person *cannot* do such a thing. For, if we define 'can' in a way that is consistent with van Inwagen's usage, we will say that a person can do something if and only if it is within the person's power to do it *without* past events' having been different from what they in fact were, and *without* the laws of nature having been different from the way they were. In this sense, if determinism is assumed, then the person 'cannot' do anything but what he in fact does. And van Inwagen's response to the divergence-miracle compatibilist will be precisely that the person cannot do such a thing because, by this same definition of 'can', a person 'cannot' do anything that would require the laws of nature to be different from what they are. In this sense, if determinism is assumed, then a person cannot do anything but what he in fact does. (For a more detailed discussion of van Inwagen's usage of 'can', see Appendix.)

The response to Fischer's criticisms will be similar, and even more simple and obvious. Fischer says, "All that van Inwagen has established (trivially, I might add) is that one cannot...render a proposition about the past false. But it clearly *doesn't follow* that one cannot perform some act which is such that, if one were to perform it, the past would have been different from what it actually was."[36] But, if Fischer were using the definition of 'can' which we have assumed van Inwagen is using, then he could not make this claim. For, by this definition, if one were to perform some act such that, if one were to perform it, the past would have been different from what it actually was, then one would *be* rendering a proposition about the past false. For, by this definition of 'can', one cannot act differently from the way the previous history of the universe in conjunction with the laws of nature have predetermined one to act.

Similarly, Horgan says, "Essentially, all we are saying is that [a person] can do something that he is causally determined not to do; and it is no surprise to learn that the compatibilist is committed to *that*."[37] Obviously, the compatibilist's statement here also becomes false if van Inwagen uses the word 'can' to mean what we have claimed he must mean in order for his argument to withstand the criticisms. (Again, for more detailed discussion, see Appendix.) But at this point, Lewis, Fischer and Horgan might well proclaim in unison that, although van Inwagen's argument may be technically valid on this interpretation, it becomes *trivially* valid. Indeed, we have seen that Fischer has already accused van Inwagen of such a triviality, simply as a consequence of the way his definition of 'can' makes his conclusion true by definition.

Or, on the other hand, is it the *compatibilists* who are making a trivially true statement when they say that a person can do something even though the previous history of the universe or the laws of nature would have to have been different in order for her to do it? In order to make this statement, the compatibilist must define 'can' so that someone can do something even where the previous history of the universe combined with the laws of nature make it impossible for her to do it.

If we are going to argue, not about whether van Inwagen's argument is valid, but whether it is his definition of 'can' or the compatibilists' definition that leads to trivial results, then perhaps we need to see how each definition would affect the resolution of the supposed conflict between determinism and certain types of ethical claims. That is certainly one of the most important tests of whether an interpretation of 'could have acted otherwise' is trivial or not. If one of the main motivations (if not the main motivation) to preserve the logical possibility of a compatibility between determinism and free will is that it (or its denial) has non-trivial ethical consequences, then if van Inwagen's conclusion (given his definition of 'can') does have such non-trivial consequences, we can hardly regard it as trivial.

To be sure, there is also a type of 'compatibilism' that cannot be assessed in this way---the 'compatibilism' which asserts, as does Davidson, for example, that mechanistic and teleological explanations of the same action or event are compatible.[38] But, as has been shown at great length by a number of writers including the present one,[39] this type of compatibilism is not really relevant to whether 'compatibilism' in van Inwagen's sense is the case, because free will is not necessary for the Davidsonian 'compatibilism'. For Davidson, it is only necessary that I be able to act because of a conscious purpose as well as because of a set of physical causes; whether I 'could' have acted from *different* conscious purposes from the one I did act from is a separate issue (and the one we are interested in here, in fact).

The following discussion will therefore try to decide whether van Inwagen's definition of 'can' leads to a trivial sense in which people cannot act otherwise than the ways they have been predetermined to act. To do so, we must decide whether this statement, on this interpretation, has non-trivial ethical consequences, and whether a divergence-miracle or altered-past compatibilism can have any non-trivial ethical consequences.

(b) To the real ethical matters: the concept of 'ought'

Let's begin with the easiest aspect of the question. On the assumption that determinism, as we have interpreted it, is true, does this conclusion make a difference as to whether any notion of 'ought' per se is possible? It seems clear that there are certain concepts of 'ought' which are compatible with determinism, and certain concepts of 'ought' which are not. Those which are compatible with determinism seem to have the following feature in common with each other: 'I ought to do X' means that, under the given circumstances, 'it would be better' if I were to do X than if not. 'It would be better' can be defined to mean 'productive of better utilitarian consequences,' or 'more fair,' or 'more exemplary of virtuous character,' or 'tending more toward the actualization of consciousness,' etc., depending on whether one is a utilitarian, a deontologist, a personalist, an existentialist, etc. To say that I acted differently from the way I ought to have acted, by this kind of definition of 'ought,' may not imply that it was 'my fault' that I acted that way, nor does it necessarily imply that I am to be blamed, or held morally responsible, or judged to be deserving of punishment. Whether the statement that I ought not to have done something implies these other concepts depends on how they are defined; we shall return to them presently. But first, we should consider whether determinism negates all concepts of 'ought' per se in case freedom is incompatible with determinism in van Inwagen's sense, as argued in the previous section.

Everyone has heard the familiar argument to the effect that determinism negates all meaningful concepts of 'ought' because determinism implies that no one can ever act in any different way from the way she does act; and thus that, since ought implies can, it makes no sense to tell people that they ought to do something other than what they are going to do.[40] By 'makes no sense,' the proponent of this view may mean 'is meaningless,' or 'is false,' or sometimes something more like 'is pointless' or 'is a waste of time.'

If the conclusion is that telling people that they ever ought to have acted any differently from the way they did act is always to make a *false* statement, then this conclusion would indeed seem to follow, *if* one assumes that ought implies can in an appropriately strong sense of the word 'can'. For, although it is always *logically* possible that the person could have acted differently, even given determinism (because it is logically possible that either the laws of physics or the previous history of the universe *could* have been different), it is never *physically* possible the the person could have acted differently, given the previous history of the universe. Van Inwagen seems to use 'can' in the stronger, physical sense. So if ought implies 'can' in this strong sense, then the ought statement would certainly seem to become false if determinism is true. I.e., to say that I ought to do X implies that it is not physically impossible for me to do X.

It might appear to some that there is an important respect in which people *can* do what they are told they ought, even in van Inwagen's physical sense of 'can'. Consider a future-tense situation. Suppose we tell someone that she ought to do X, and suppose our convincing her that she ought to do X contributes to the causation of her choosing to do it. There is a sense of 'can' in which the person can do what we tell her to do in this case. Namely, if our convincing her to do it contributes to the causation of her doing it, then she can do it. Moreover, it is true in this case to say that she still has the power (before we tell her) to either do what she ought, or not to do it. That will depend on whether our telling her that she ought to do it convinces her to do it. This is the reason Ibn Khaldun believed in very strict criminal sentences although he also believed in complete determinism.[41] By threatening very harsh sentences, we are in effect doing the prospective offender a favor, because we are thereby making it more likely that he will make the right decision.

However, on closer inspection, it turns out that, given determinism, the person cannot act any differently even in this case from the way she does in fact act. For whether we tell her that she ought to do it has already been predetermined---among other things, by whether our own environment, heredity and luck resulted in our being adept enough at the use of reason to give a convincing argument. And whether she will accept this argument has already been determined by those environmental, hereditary and chance factors in the etiology of her character that either resulted in her being adept enough at the use of reason to accept our arguments, or resulted in her being too inept to do so.

So, at the point when we tell the person what she ought to do, it has ultimately already been predetermined whether she will do it or not, although we ourselves may be instrumental in bringing about the outcome, and although we do not yet know whether she has been predetermined to do it or not to do it, since we do not know all the facts, either about her environment, heredity and previous luck, or about our own.

Some will insist that it is not always ineptness in the use of reason that prevents a person from accepting a sound moral argument, but rather a malicious attitude. Or, again, she may be convinced that the argument is sound, but refuse to act accordingly out of malevolence or evil character. But whether the person is malevolent, malicious or evil has already been predetermined by her environment, heredity and previous luck; thus, whatever she decides to do, it is never the case that it would be physically possible for her to do otherwise, given the previous history of the universe. And, in this sense, she *cannot* do otherwise.

Such philosophers as Nowell-Smith and Schlick insist that it is only necessary that the person 'can' do what she ought in the sense that it is within her *power* to choose either to do it or not to do it.[42] But this view entails a sense of the word 'can' which really ends up lacking important consequences since it is such an exceedingly *weak* sense of 'can'. For, in order to be able to choose to do what she ought to do, the person must have been predetermined to be the kind of person who will make this kind of choice. And if she has not been predetermined to be the kind of person who will make this kind of choice, then it is not physically within her *power* to make this kind of choice. I.e., it is never physically within one's power to choose differently from the way one has been predetermined to choose, since this would entail either some previous fact or the laws of nature having been different from what they were---although it is true that the outcome of the situation may well depend on how one chooses.

Of course, there is logically nothing to preclude us from simply *defining* 'could have acted differently' to mean 'would have acted differently if one had chosen differently,' as Nowell-Smith does. But to stipulate such a definition as this is both trivial and misleading, in that by this definition it is sometimes true to say that someone can do something even though it is completely impossible for her to do it, given the previous history of the universe. To say that someone can do something even though it is completely impossible for her to do it given the previous history of the universe is to define the word 'can' in such a weak sense that to say that 'ought' needs only to imply 'can' in this exceedingly weak sense of 'can' is virtually tantamount to saying that 'ought' need not imply 'can' at all.

It is true that Nowell-Smith has a reason for preferring that 'ought' imply such a weak sense of 'can' rather than implying no sense of 'can' at all. This has to do with his concept of moral responsibility, which will be discussed later. But for the present, we are trying to determine, not whether determinism conflicts with moral responsibility, but whether it conflicts with 'ought' statements per se. Our conclusion is that, in order to maintain the meaning of 'ought' statements in the face of determinism, one must either define 'ought' in such a way that it does not imply 'can', or at least in such a way that it implies 'can' only in the sense that one 'has the option' to do what one ought. In Chapter Two, we saw that it is always false to say that one ought to do X if one will never have that option; for then X will never be the best option in any situation, thus one ought never to do X. But to require that one must have the option to choose X does not imply that one's choice has not been predetermined. Determinism entails that it is physically impossible for me to 'be able to' do X if I have been predetermined to choose not to; in this sense I *cannot* do it. I 'can' do it only in the weaker sense that I do 'have the option' to do it; whether I do it or not depends on a choice which I make, although which option I will choose has already been predetermined.

What is much more important for the compatibility of determinism and 'ought' than Nowell-Smith's argument is that there are senses of 'ought' in which 'ought' need not imply 'can' except in the very weak sense that one 'has the option' to do what one ought. If 'I ought to do X' means nothing more than 'Given the option, it would be better if I were to do X,' then it would be true to say that I ought to have done X even if I *could* not have done it in any sense of 'can' which would imply physical possibility. I.e., *it would have been better* if I had done it. So the argument that determinism makes *all* ought statements either false or meaningless is not sound. For if 'I ought to do X' is defined to mean 'it would be better if I were to do X, given the option,' then this statement may be true even if I cannot do X in any non-trivial sense.

But the real question, as far as the conflict between determinism and ought is concerned, is whether determinism renders ought statements pointless or a waste of time. We have already touched on the answer to this question. Even if whatever a person chooses to do will have been completely predetermined, it is not pointless or a waste of time to tell the person what she ought to do and why. For the soundness of our reasoning will be one of the determinants of the person's decision, to the extent that she has good reasoning ability (and perhaps good intentions as well, unless we can convince her to have good intentions). If the person may well do what she ought as the result of our telling her she ought to, whereas she would not have done so otherwise, then telling her what she ought to do can hardly be pointless or a waste of time. So, although it may be pointless to say 'You ought to do X but I know you cannot,' it is not pointless to say 'You ought to do X; I do not yet know whether you can, but my telling you that you ought to do it may well be one of the determining factors.' Nor is it pointless to say 'You ought to have done X, although you could not.' Such a statement is useful because it informs the person that the decision that she made was the wrong one, and this knowledge may affect her future behavior.

(c) The concept of 'desert'

But now for the more difficult aspects of the question. It is not really whether determinism conflicts with *all possible* senses of 'ought' that bothers moral philosophers, but rather whether it conflicts with *certain specific* concepts of 'ought'---especially those concepts which include a legitimate place for moral responsibility, guilt, blame, desert, and the assertion that it is someone's 'fault', in some non-trivial sense, if she is not morally virtuous (however one defines 'virtue'). Each of these concepts can be defined in different ways, some compatible with determinism, some incompatible.

Most work on the moral consequences of compatibilism and incompatibilism has centered on the question as to whether determinism leaves room for a meaningful concept of moral responsibility. But, for reasons that will become apparent, it will be easier if we postpone this question until we have first dealt with another question that usually lurks just beneath its surface: Does determinism leave room for any meaningful concept of *desert?* I.e., does it make sense to say (and can it ever be true to say) that anyone deserves anything, given that no one ever could have acted differently from the way he or she did?

When it comes to the concept of desert, the traditional compatibilist solution, used by Smart, Schlick, Nowell-Smith and others,[43] is of no use even if we grant a very weak sense of 'can'. For, even if we were to grant Nowell-Smith's argument that 'could have acted differently' means 'would have acted differently if one had chosen differently,' the argument is irrelevant to the issue of desert. We shall see presently that, by most concepts of desert that philosophers want to defend, to say that someone would have acted differently if she had chosen differently can never entail that she *deserves* punishment if it is also the case that she could not have chosen differently in the first place, though it *may* entail that she *ought* to be punished. Is an incompatibilist determinist (in van Inwagen's sense of incompatibilism) committed to the thesis that no one deserves anything, or that the concept of desert is meaningless? That depends, first of all, on what one *means* by 'desert' and, secondly, whether one is asserting that giving people what they deserve in one sense or another has *intrinsic* value, or only *extrinsic* value.

Part of the difficulty of defining desert is that philosophers who use the term often fail to define or analyse its meaning in a way that would communicate to those who question its meaning. E.g., Terry Pinkard, a contemporary 'liberal' theorist, is careful to distinguish between desert and entitlement as two different ways in which 'giving each her due' could be intended.[44] In the context of a careful analysis of entitlement, he appeals to our intuition to establish that a person does not necessarily deserve the same things that she is entitled to. Yet Pinkard never defines what he means by 'deserve'. Perhaps this is no significant problem for Pinkard, since his ultimate conclusions do not make assertions about what people deserve, though he does seem to imply that desert should be irrelevant to political decision-making, which is difficult to understand or question if one does not know what 'desert' means. Far more disconcerting are theories like von Hirsch's and Kellogg's, in which one of the most important claims is that people should get what they deserve, yet desert is never defined in any clear way.[45]

If we do attempt to define desert intelligibly, there are at least four ways to do it. The first of these four seems to be the most prevalent in philosophical discourse, and does not seem to superfluously duplicate other moral concepts (thus it is the one we shall end up using), but perhaps we should mention all four to avoid confusion among them. (1) To say that people should get what they deserve sometimes seems to mean that they should be rewarded proportionately to the moral virtue of their character or to the rightness of their actions. Or (2) it may mean that they should get what they have a right to receive. Or (3) it may mean, not that they should *necessarily* receive benefits proportional to merit in sense (1), but rather that the *society has a right* to impose on them what they merit in this sense (e.g., the society may be deemed to have a right to impose, say, some harsh criminal punishment, but perhaps *should* not do so unless doing so is beneficial). Still another possible sense of 'desert' that is sometimes used in ordinary language, though seldom in philosophical discourse is that (4) people 'deserve' whatever they ought to receive, all things considered.

Sense (4) will be ignored here, since it merely makes 'desert' into a cognate of the word 'ought', the import of determinism for which we have already discussed and will be discussing further. Since philosophers seldom actually use 'desert' in sense (3) either, but usually handle this concept with the term 'moral responsibility,' let's not call it 'desert'. Later, we shall see that one possible concept of 'responsibility' is what is really being described by this definition. Sense (2) of 'desert'--- that people should get what they have a *right* to receive---does not necessarily imply any proportion between virtue and reward. Nor does it necessarily conflict with determinism, unless one specifies what people have a right to receive in a way that conflicts with determinism. But it would seem that the only way to do this would be to insist on a proportion between virtue and reward---i.e., on 'desert' in sense (1). In a utilitarian theory which maintains that the society has a duty to care for the sick, for example, people would have a right to be cared for when sick, since duties and rights are correlative. And to make this claim in no way conflicts with determinism. Sense (2) of 'desert' thus really uses 'desert' as a synonym of 'rights' in the sense of entitlement, as in 'I have a right to be cared for when sick.' Since it is not necessary to use two terms for the same concept, we shall henceforth use only sense (1) of 'desert'---i.e., that people should be rewarded proportionately to their moral virtue or to the rightness of their actions.

What does determinism have to do with whether or not people should get what they deserve in this sense? That depends on whether we mean that their getting what they deserve has intrinsic or extrinsic value, and on what type of moral theory we are using (which might also include a theory of 'excuses'). If we mean that this proportion has *extrinsic* value, then, clearly, any ethical theory will have room for it, whether determinism is true or not. (i) A utilitarian, for example, will often find it useful to reward people in proportion to their moral virtue, because a society of virtuous people will often be a happier society on the whole and in the long run. (ii) A Rawlsian rational reflector in the original position may well prefer some such proportion, all else being equal, because it will allow him to get rewards, if it turns out that he has been predetermined to want them badly enough, by being morally virtuous. (iii) A personalist or virtue ethicist will regard such a proportion as extrinsically valuable because it tends to encourage moral virtue, which to such theorists has intrinsic value.

But if the question is whether such a proportion has *intrinsic* value, it would seem that no moral theory could maintain this in the face of determinism and van Inwagen's incompatibilism under our interpretation of his terms. For (i) a utilitarian cannot attribute intrinsic value to anything except whatever promotes the general welfare. So the proportion between rewards and desert can have only extrinsic value in this system. (ii) A deontic theory, whatever its basis, cannot require such a proportion if the proportion is unfair. But, if fairness has any meaning, then it would be unfair to penalize someone for something that is ultimately caused by factors beyond his control, *unless there is something to be gained by doing so.* E.g., a Rawlsian rational reflector in the original position who knows that determinism is true would not elect to punish people for things that they have been predetermined to do, unless there is something to be gained by doing so, because for all she knows she may be one of the ones who are predetermined to lack moral virtue and to decide to do immoral things. Thus a Rawlsian cannot consider a proportion between moral virtue and rewards to be intrinsically valuable, though he may sometimes find it to be extrinsically valuable.[46] Similar problems will be encountered by any contractualist justice theory. But any *noncontractualist* justice theory must include a doctrine of 'excuses', so that a man who climbs on a tower and shoots people at random because a brain tumor caused him to decide to do so will not be held to deserve punishment. But by the same reasoning, if all choices are caused by factors beyond the person's control, then they are all excusable, even if people 'can' act differently from the way they do in the *weak* sense of 'can' (which is the only sense in which any compatibilism could be left open to us given van Inwagen's argument).[47]

On the other hand, if a justice theorist penalizes someone because there *is* something to be gained by doing so, then he values the proportion between virtue and reward only extrinsically, not intrinsically. (iii) If we assume a personalist theory, then aside from the value of fairness and utility (which are usually included in personalist theories), a personalist might also argue, from an analysis of the structure of agency, that the consequences of an action are inseparable aspects of the action as such.[48] E.g., the action of deciding to compete in a sport includes, as part of the meaning which the agent attributes to his act, that if he performs less well than his competitors, he will not win the prize. If it were guaranteed that the person would receive the prize regardless of what he did, then he would not be making a genuine choice when he chose to do X rather than Y (since part of the meaning of the choice is that the two options are expected to have different consequences). But, a personalist might argue, a person who does not make real choices is not a person to as much of an extent as he would be if he did, even if it should be granted that the person's personality structure (and thus indirectly his choice) has been predetermined. A person whose character has been predetermined still has more value than a quasi-person with no character. Thus the correspondence between actions and consequences (and thus desert) has value because it facilitates the existence of genuine personhood, which has intrinsic value. Suppose we grant this argument. Its logical conclusion would be only that people's getting what they 'deserve' has *extrinsic* value when, if, and to the extent that allowing such an eventuality is the best method, under the circumstances, to facilitate personhood. If *not* giving people what they deserve (e.g., in cases of rehabilitation) accomplishes the same purpose better, then that is what the personalist would choose, and for the same reason. At least if determinism is true, then, personalism can attribute only extrinsic value to the proportion between rewards and merit.[49]

In general, we notice that no *reason* can be given why the proportion between desert and reward has value without either making this value into an extrinsic value, or conflicting with determinism. For the only reason that would make the value of the proportion an intrinsic value would be to say that it is somehow more fair for deontic reasons to maintain the proportion. But if determinism is true, then this cannot be prima facie more fair, since it penalizes people for having personality characteristics that ultimately are caused by factors that could not have been avoided. Even though the person could have avoided doing wrong if he had chosen differently, his choosing as he did could not have been avoided given that person's total environment, heredity, and luck, without violating the laws of physics. And one cannot violate the laws of physics. Most compatibilists will instinctively want to respond here that moral responsibility requires only that the person would have acted differently if he had chosen differently. But we are speaking here only of whether *desert* can have meaning as intrinsic value in the face of determinism. We have not yet gotten to moral responsibility. We shall see that whether a person can be meaningfully held responsible for his actions does not necessarily have anything to do with whether he *deserves* the corresponding rewards or punishments from the standpoint of any *intrinsic* value. If a man climbs up on a tower and shoots people at random because he has a brain tumor, it would be logically possible for compatibilists to give reasons as to why this person should be held morally responsible (though they probably would not want to make such a claim). After all, he *would* have acted differently if he had chosen differently. By contrast, it would *not* be logically possible for even a compatibilist to offer any reason as to why this man would *deserve* punishment in the sense of an intrinsic value attributed to any proportion between the punishment and the wrongness of the action (i.e., the extent to which the man ought not to have done what he did).

How can we be sure that a deontic theory of fairness (either a contractual or a non-contractual one) would be the *only* possible argument for a proportion between virtue or rightness and reward that would not make this proportion into an *extrinsic* value? Because, given any X, to say that this proportion is valuable because X has value is to say that X is the intrinsic value at stake, and the proportion is merely a way to promote X---unless it can be said that this proportion is an *instance of* X. Fairness theorists sometimes believe that this proportion is an *instance of* fairness (although, if determinism is true, they are incorrect in this belief). But a utilitarian cannot meaningfully claim that such a proportion is an *instance of* the general welfare or happiness; nor can a personalist meaningfully claim that it is an *instance of* virtuous moral character. Rather, a utilitarian may claim that this proportion *often tends to promote* the general welfare or happiness; the personalist may claim that it *tends to promote* good character. Similarly, a fairness theorist may, without contradicting determinism, claim that such a proportion tends to promote fairness, thus making it into an extrinsic value in a deontic theory. (For, as we have seen, a Rawlsian might believe, e.g., that a rational reflector in the original position would prefer to see people rewarded proportionately to their virtue, all else being equal, because such a proportion would increase the rational reflector's chances of getting the reward simply by increasing his own personal virtue or acting rightly.)

With regard to desert in sense (1), then, we must conclude that using it as a criterion never has intrinsic value, if determinism is true, but it often does have extrinsic value, regardless of what type of theory one believes in.

(d) The concept of 'responsibility'

In what sense, if any, can there be *moral responsibility* if determinism and our interpretation of incompatibilism are true? This depends on which ethical theory one believes in, and on what one means by responsibility. If we were to define 'X is responsible to do Y' to mean nothing more than 'X ought to do Y,' then we would merely be wasting the word by letting it function as an exact duplicate for the word 'ought'. The interesting question is whether there is a sense of 'responsibility' that does not duplicate the meaning of the terms we have already discussed. There seem to be two types of such definitions: There is Nowell-Smith's definition, discussed in (i) below; and there is a contractually-established sense of responsibility, discussed in (ii). Both these definitions of responsibility seem to conceptualize it in terms of whether a person can legitimately be 'held answerable' for fulfilling his obligations or failing to do so. By 'X is held answerable for Y' in this sense, we usually tend to mean that there may be conceivable or actual situations where it would be 'legitimate' (in some sense) for X to be forced to do Y or punished for not doing Y (perhaps leaving open the possibility that there may also be some situations where it would be better not to force or punish the person). If there is a meaningful concept of 'responsibility', defined along some such lines, then there will be logically possible cases in which it is not 'legitimate' to hold X responsible for doing Y, even though he ought to do (or have done) Y. In this way, the concept of responsibility can avoid merely duplicating the concept of 'ought'. For example, a man with a brain tumor may not be held responsible for his act of shooting people, although he ought not to have shot them. Of the two ways of reconciling such a notion of responsibility with determinism (and there are really two different senses of the term, corresponding to these two ways), which one we choose will end up depending in large part on which moral theory we choose.

We shall see that a utilitarian may choose between the two different senses of determinism-compatible responsibility, whereas only one of these two senses is available in relation to non-utilitarian values.

(i) For a pure utilitarian, Nowell-Smith's concept of responsibility would seem to be adequate. It is only necessary to hold that the person could have acted differently if she had wanted to, which does not entail free will. But the real question is whether utilitarianism even *needs* any such concept. If we tell people that they must take responsibility for their actions, in the sense that they will be rewarded or punished accordingly, we thereby have a good chance of entering into the causation of their decision-making process, and thus of causing them to choose the right action. Therefore, it is better to hold people responsible for their actions than not to do so. Unfortunately, some people will in this way be forced to accept responsibility for things which ultimately could not have been avoided. To the extent that such situations promote unhappiness, utilitarianism implies that they ought to be avoided. But to the extent that the criminal's (undeserved) unhappiness is conducive to maximal general happiness, it is not to be avoided. To object to this point because it leads to unfairness is simply to object to utilitarianism per se, for fairness is not an intrinsic value in utilitarianism, though it often is an extrinsic value. But, given this concept of responsibility, determinism does not present utilitarianism with any additional problems which it did not already have for completely different reasons.

But the Nowell-Smith notion of compatibilism, while it does not conflict with utilitarianism, is really superfluous for such a moral system anyway, because, in *any* instance where it produces better consequences to force or punish a person (whether the person *can* do what she ought or not), it would be legitimate for a utilitarian to force or punish her. It just happens that it probably will never produce better consequences to punish someone unless she 'can' obey the rule in question, using 'can' in the context of Ibn Khaldun's point that it is not a waste of time to tell the person what she ought to do, since our telling her may be one of the determinants of whether she 'can' do it. I.e., it may not have become completely determinate whether the person is going to obey the rule until she finds out that she is going to be punished if she refuses.

(Absent the threat of punishment or condemnation, it has not yet been determined that she will do what she is going to do.) It is only in this sense that it makes any difference to utilitarianism whether the person 'can' do what she ought, whether she 'could have' done it if she does not, and whether she 'could have' not done it if she does. But, in principle, if it ever *did* produce better utilitarian consequences to punish someone for an act she 'could' not avoid (even in Nowell-Smith's weak sense and even given Ibn Khaldun's point), a utilitarian would have to do so. So, for utilitarianism, no compatibilism is needed whatever, not even the Nowell-Smith variety. Certainly, no notion of free will is needed.

On the other hand, if utilitarianism is *not* the correct moral philosophy, then such a response to the determinism problem is not adequate to resolve the issue of moral responsibility. For then the question would remain as to whether anyone, even a supposedly democratically constituted government, has a *right* to hold people morally responsible to obey certain rules simply because doing so produces *better consequences,* on the whole, than not holding people responsible to obey these rules. For the question arises whether it is *fair,* in any given case, to hold someone responsible for events that could not have been avoided, regardless of the utilitarian consequences of holding the person responsible.

(ii) To defend a concept of moral responsibility in a non-utilitarian value system in the face of determinism and incompatibilism, one needs a contractualist defense. According to the contractualist (as explained more fully elsewhere),[50] the relationship between the society and the individual who is responsible to obey either the formal or informal rules of the society (which are binding only to the extent that they are just) is like the relationship between a creditor and his contractual debtor. If the debtor promises to pay the debt, but then becomes unable to do so, the creditor has the *right* to take the actions stipulated in the contract, such as repossessing property, even though it is not the debtor's 'fault' that she is unable to pay. The debtor is responsible to honor the terms of the contract because she agreed to them. By agreeing to the terms of the contract, she accepted the risk that, when the time came to honor them, she might not be able to do so and therefore would have to suffer the consequences. There is a sense in which the society has more of a right to hold a person responsible to honor such a just contract than to hold her responsible to honor an agreement that is not just, or that she never would have agreed to honor unless she had had unequal bargaining power, or she had been deceived into agreeing to terms that were presented misleadingly, etc. Ultimately, it might turn out that the important question is what would have been stipulated in an ideal, hypothetical contract rather than in any real one.

It is beyond our scope here to elaborate such a social contract concept. The point is that, in this sense, it is not necessary to believe in free will or compatibilism in order to have a concept of moral responsibility, i.e., that the society has a right to hold people answerable for their actions in the sense that it is legitimate to force or punish them under certain conditions, but not legitimate under other conditions. This concept of moral responsibility is sufficient for the purposes of either a utilitarian or a non-utilitarian moral system. Of course, it is true that determinism is incompatible with some types of moral theories---those that require an intrinsic value for desert criteria, or a more stringent notion of responsibility, or a concept of the will which requires that it be free. But the type of compatibilism that would define 'can' in such a way as to avoid van Inwagen's conclusion---a compatibilism which would have to use the weak, Nowell-Smith sense of 'can'---would be inadequate to save any of these moral theories from the untenability that results from their conflict with determinism. For we have seen that, if determinism is true, then no intrinsic value for desert criteria can be defended. The Nowell-Smith concept of responsibility, far from accommodating a broader range of moral theories, really accommodates a narrower range---the purely consequentialist ones---but, for these theories, it is superfluous anyway. As for the concept of 'ought', only those concepts of 'ought' which do not necessarily imply 'can' in a strong sense remain viable if determinism is true.

To sum up: Van Inwagen's assertion that a person cannot perform an action if predetermined not to do so is not trivial, because it has important ethical consequences. It enables us to eliminate all those theories which entail concepts of 'ought' that must necessarily imply 'can' in the strong sense, yet leaves us to choose from among a range of utilitarian, deontic, personalist and other theories whose 'oughts' do not necessarily imply 'can', but imply only that one 'has the option' to do what one ought. It also eliminates all theories which require a more stringent concept of responsibility than contractualism can justify. And it enables us to eliminate theories in which giving people what they deserve has intrinsic value.

On the other hand, the statement that people 'can do what they have been predetermined *not* to do'---which must be made if one is to disagree with van Inwagen's incompatibilism---requires a sense of 'can' that makes *this* statement trivial, at least if we judge from the fact that it has no ethical consequences whatever. Such a statement is not *necessary* if we are to allow any concept of 'ought' which does not directly conflict with determinism; it is not *sufficient* to establish any concept of 'ought' which *does* conflict with determinism. Similarly, such a statement also is not *necessary* if we are to allow a concept of 'responsibility' adequate for all theories other than those which directly conflict with determinism; yet it is not *sufficient* if we are to allow any concept of 'responsibility' that *does* conflict with determinism.

Finally, such a statement is not *sufficient* to ground the thesis that it is intrinsically valuable for people to get what they deserve; and it is not *necessary* in order to ground the thesis that giving people what they deserve is extrinsically valuable, regardless of which type of moral theory one subscribes to. If a statement of the compatibilist thesis is neither necessary nor sufficient for any of these purposes, it would seem that it is useless as far as the realm of ethics is concerned. Nor is such a statement necessary in order to support the compatibility of mechanistic and purposeful explanations of actions. We must therefore conclude that it is not van Inwagen's incompatibilism that is trivial; rather, the type of compatibilism that defines 'can' in a weak enough way to avoid van Inwagen's conclusion is trivial.

Since determinism, as we have defined it, is true, and since this determinism conflicts with many moral theories but not with some others, it will inevitably play a crucial role in the overall comparative-coherence strategy outlined in Chapter Two. Specifically, determinism is one of the key factual or ontological statements with which a moral theory must be consistent in order to survive the elimination of all those theories which are not factually adequate. In the next two chapters, we shall see more precisely which kinds of theories must be eliminated because of this kind of consideration, and how to carry out comparative-coherence analyses with respect to those which remain logically possible.

NOTES

[1] David Schaefer, *Justice or Tyranny? A Critique of John Rawls' "Theory of Justice"* (Port Washington: Kennikat Press, 1979); Tibor Machan, "Social Contract As a Basis of Norms: A Critique" (see Chapter One, note 4); Wojciech Sadurski, "Contractarianism and Intuition" (see Chapter One, note 4); Jeremy Waldron, "Theoretical Foundations of Liberalism," *Philosophical Quarterly* 37 (1987), 127-50.

[2] Michael Sandel, *Liberalism and the Limits of Justice* (New York: Cambridge University Press, 1982); *Liberalism and Its Critics* (New York: New York University Press, 1984); "Morality and the Liberal Ideal," *The New Republic,* May 7, 1984, 15-17; Agnes Heller, *Beyond Justice* (Oxford: Basil Blackwell, 1987); Michael Walzer, *Spheres of Justice* (New York: Basic Books, 1983); Roberto Unger, *Knowledge and Politics* (New York: Free Press, 1975).

[3] Rawls, *A Theory of Justice,* 311.

[4] Rawls, *A Theory of Justice,* 100.

[5] R. D. Ellis, "Fairness and the Etiology of Criminal Behavior," *Philosophy and Social Criticism* 13 (1987), 175-194.

[6] George Gale, "Some Metaphysical Perplexities in Contemporary Physics," *International Philosophical Quarterly* 24 (1986), 393-402; P.

C. W. Davies and J. R. Brown, *The Ghost in the Atom* (Cambridge: Cambridge University Press, 1980).

[7]J. M. Jauch, *Are Quanta Real? A Galilean Dialogue* (Bloomington: Indiana University Press, 1973).

[8]A. Aspect, J. Dalibard and G. Roger, *Physical Review Letters* 39 (1982), 1804; see also notes 6 and 7 above.

[9]C. S. Peirce, "The Doctrine of Determinism Re-examined," Charles Hartshorne and Paul Weiss, eds., *Collected Papers of Charles Sanders Peirce* (Cambridge: Harvard University Press, 1982).

[10]Searle, *Minds, Brains and Science*, 87.

[11]G. H. von Wright, *Explanation and Understanding* (Ithaca: Cornell University Press, 1971), 74ff. See also *Causality and Determinism* (New York: Columbia University Press, 1974), 100ff.

[12]Searle, 88.

[13]Searle, 88.

[14]Michael Simon, "Action and Dialectics," *Philosophy and Phenomenological Research* 39 (1979), 468-69.

[15]Thomas Talbott, "Indeterminism and Chance Occurrences," *The Personalist* 60 (1979), 253-261.

[16]A possibility which A. C. Danto denies in *What Philosophy Is* (New York: Harper and Row, 1968), where he suggests that the truth or falsity of any statement having empirical content cannot be the proper concern of philosophy but that such claims must be relegated to the inductive techniques of the particular sciences.

[17]Richard Taylor, "Fatalism," *The Philosophical Review* 71 (1962), 56-66; "Fatalism and Ability," *Analysis* 24 (1962), 25-27; "A Note on Fatalism," *The Philosophical Review* 72 (1963), 497-99; "Comment," *The Journal of Philosophy* 61 (1964), 305-07; *Metaphysics* (Englewood Cliffs, N.J.: Prentice-Hall, 1963), 54-69.

[18]R. L. Franklin, *Freewill and Determinism* (London: Routledge, 1968), 334-40; Ledger Wood, "The Free Will Controversy," Mandelbaum, Gramlich and Anderson, eds., *Philosophic Problems* (New York: Macmillan, 1975), 308; Robert Young, *Freedom, Responsibility and God* (New York: Harper and Row, 1975), 19-38; John Turk Saunders, "Professor Taylor on Fatalism," *Analysis* 23 (1962), 1-2; Bruce Aune, "Fatalism and Professor Taylor," *The Philosophical Review* 72 (1963), 96; Richard

THE ETIOLOGY OF PERSONALITY 141

293-95; John Turk Saunders, "Fatalism and Ordinary Language," *The Journal of Philosophy* 62 (1965), 211-22; Charles D. Brown, "Fallacies in Taylor's 'Fatalism'," *The Journal of Philosophy* 62 (1965), 349-53.

[19] Kieth Lehrer, *Freedom and Determinism* (New York: Random House, 1966), 175-202.

[20] Frederick S. Perls, *Ego Hunger and Aggression* (New York: Random House, 1969), 209.

[21] As in William Davis, *The Freewill Question* (The Hague: Nijhoff, 1971), 9; John Hospers, *An Introduction to Philosophical Analysis* (Englewood Cliffs, N.J.: Prentice-Hall, 1932).

[22] Except for the additional stipulation that the chance and/or causal factors must be *beyond the agent's control* if this kind of psychological determinism is to be true, the present formulation of it resembles the point of view of those who argue that attributability to mere chance does not make an act free---e.g., R. E. Hobart, "Free Will as Involving Determinism and Inconceivable without It," *Mind,* 1934, 2-27. Some problems with Hobart's formulation have been pointed out by Philippa Foot, "Free Will as Involving Determinism," *Philosophical Review* 66 (1957), 439-50; also by J. J. C. Smart, "Free Will, Praise and Blame," *Mind,* 1961, 291-306, where Smart formulates his own version. (Smart, of course, is the principle target of attack in the Talbott article discussed above.) A different formulation of the idea that attributability to chance does not make for freedom has been given by E. D'Angelo, *The Problem of Freedom and Determinism* (New York: Columbia, 1968), 14ff. D'Angelo's point seems to have been greeted with undeservedly harsh criticism. He argues that if the self is not caused by some event, then it is either uncaused or self-caused. If uncaused, it reduces to mere chance. If self-caused, it must exist prior in time to itself. D'Angelo's view has been largely disregarded on the basis that it assumes that a cause must always exist prior to its effect. This is the essential objection raised by Robert Young in *Freedom, Responsibility and God* (see note 18), 123. But this objection really carries little weight at all, for if a cause is simultaneous with its effect, we can keep tracing the chain of causes until eventually we reach the end of the series of simultaneous causes, and the last item in this series would have to be either caused by something previous to itself, or attributable to mere chance. With this amendment, D'Angelo's argument seems to remain basically sound. However, D'Angelo's way of stating the case entails problems better avoided---problems such as precisely clarifying the ontological status of 'cause', 'the self', and 'self-causation'. Also, it is not clear how D'Angelo could answer the Talbott objection, which can be raised against him as easily as against Smart.

[23] William J. Earle, "Do Feelings Cause Actions?" *Philosophy and Phenomenological Research* 35 (1975), 540-48.

[24] For example, Hobart (see note 18).

[25] The Kantian objection that existence is not a predicate is not really applicable here. Such 'existence' predicates as 'to exist as a decision making entity' and 'to exist as the person one is' are not pure or mere existence predicates, but are genuine predicates which say more about the subject than simply that it exists.

[26] The law of excluded middle has been challenged in those cases where the terms of the argument have no meaning; if we grant, however, that 'cause' has some meaning or other, then we do not need to state what this meaning is (or even be able to state it) in order to be entitled to use the law of excluded middle with 'cause' as the predicate in question.

[27] Someone may charge that this reference to 'entities' and 'features' hypostatizes a logical relation into a metaphysical relation. This objection would be cogent only if our usage of 'entity' implied that an 'entity' cannot also in turn be a feature of some more basic 'entity'. This, however, I do not mean to imply. By 'entity' I only mean something which is capable of assuming the role of content for forms and relationships. That something functions as a content for a form or relatinship does not mean that its own ontological status might not in turn be that of a form or relationship characterizing some other, perhaps more basic content. Any form or relation can also be one of several contents which together make up a higher-order form or relation. Thus terms like 'content' and 'entity' need not imply any metaphysical concept of a simplest-possible-substance, material stuff, or anything of that sort.

[28] This is essentially the argument Rollo May, *Power and Innocence* (New York: Norton, 1972), 205-11, uses in his discussion of Mellville's *Billy Budd*. According to May, Billy Budd's 'innocence', in the sense that he is ignorant of the circumstances that make his actions wrong, does not relieve him of the moral responsibility for the wrongness of those actions. May says that if it is within Billy Budd's power to *find out* that what he is doing is wrong, then he is guilty of a sin of ommission in not finding out. This argument can also be traced in its essential structure to St. Augustine's *On Free Choice of the Will* (New York: Bobbs-Merrill, 1964), Book Three, Chapter XXIV, 143ff.

[29] The objection that a cause need not precede its effect is refuted in note 22.

[30] Merleau-Ponty, *The Structure of Behavior* (Boston: Beacon, 1967), 13.

[31] Merleau-Ponty, *The Structure of Behavior*, 15.

[32] Peter van Inwagen, "The Incompatibility of Free Will and Determinism," *Philosophical Studies* 27 (1975), 185-99; *An Essay on Free*

Will (Oxford, 1984); "Reply to Narveson," *Philosophical Studies* 32 (1977), 93.

[33]John Martin Fischer, "Van Inwagen on Free Will," *Philosophical Quarterly* 36 (1986), 252-60; Terrence Horgan, "Compatibilism and the Consequent Argument," *Philosophical Studies* 47 (1985), 339-56; Richard Foley, "Compatibilism and Control Over the Past," *Analysis* 39 (1979), 70-74; John Martin Fischer, "Incompatibilism," *Philosophical Studies* 43 (1983), 130-31; David Lewis, "Are We Free to Break the Laws?" *Theoria* 47 (1981), 113-121.

[34]Horgan, 342-43.

[35]Horgan, 343.

[36]Fischer, "Van Inwagen on Free Will," 255.

[37]Horgan, 348.

[38]Donald Davidson, "Mental Events," L. Foster and J. W. Swanson, eds., *Experience and Theory* (Amherst: University of Massachusetts Press, 1970); "Actions, Reasons, and Causes," *Journal of Philosophy* 60, 686.

[39]Ellis, *An Ontology of Consciousness.*

[40]E.g., see Hospers, *An Introduction to Philosophical Analysis,* Chapter 5; Paul Edwards, "Hard and Soft Determinism," Sidney Hook, ed., *Determinism and Freedom* (New York: Macmillan, 1958); Kant, *A Critique of Practical Reason,* 30.

[41]Ibn-Khaldun, *The Muqaddimah,* abridged, trans. F. Rosenthal (Princeton: Princeton University Press, 1969).

[42]Patrickd Nowell-Smith, "Free Will and Moral Responsibility," *Mind* 57 (1948), 45-61; Moritz Schlick, *Problems of Ethics* (Englewood Cliffs: Prentice Hall, 1939), Chapter 7.

[43]Smart, *Ethics, Persuasion and Truth* (London: Routledge & Kegan Paul, 1984); see also note 42.

[44]Terry Pinkard, *Democratic Liberalism and Social Union* (Philadelphia: Temple University Press, 1987).

[45]Andrew von Hirsch, *Doing Justice: The Choice of Punishments* (New York: Hill & Wang, 1976); Frederic Kellogg, "From Retribution to 'Desert'," *Criminology* 15 (1977), 179-92.

[46]James Sterba develops this point in *The Demands of Justice* (Notre Dame: University of Notre Dame Press, 1980).

[47]See note 40; see also the *Ethics* special issue on excuses, January, 1986.

[48]George Sher, *Desert* (Princeton University Press, 1987), esp. Chapter 3.

[49]I have discussed this issue more extensively in "The Moral Significance of Hard Toil: Critique of a Common Intuition," *Philosophical Forum* 21 (1990), 343-58.

[50]R. D. Ellis, "Fairness and the Etiology of Criminal Behavior," (see note 5); also *Theories of Criminal Justice: A Critical Reappraisal* (Wolfeboro, N.H.: Longwood Academic, 1989).

PART III

ELIMINATIONS AND COMPARISONS OF THEORIES

CHAPTER FIVE

ETHICAL QUESTIONS WITH DEFINITE RESOLUTIONS

We have seen that the answer to the determinism question immediately dictates the answers to some moral questions, and delimits and circumscribes a range of answers to others. For example, the value of the proportionality between rewards and merit can be only an extrinsic value ---which of course is far from saying that it has no value. We shall now find that the two psychological facts discussed in Part II, taken together and used in the way indicated in Part I, can help to provide the answers, or at least delimit the range of possible answers, to a number of other major ethical questions. In some cases, the thesis of the value of consciousness, which was established in Chapter Two, will lead directly to a range of options about what ought to be done, while the psychological facts involved allow us to definitively conclude that certain 'oughts' are true. In other cases, the combination of these facts only renders some normative theories more coherent than others. In still other cases, these same facts allow us to completely eliminate certain untenable classes of theories from the coherence analyses altogether.

First, let's quickly survey the most important questions of ethics to which any metaethical inquiry is directly relevant. The following list can serve as a guide. The first two questions are susceptible to definite resolution and will be discussed in this chapter. The third and fourth questions seem to be susceptible only to comparative-coherence resolutions, which are only probable and always theoretically subject to revision; these will be discussed in Chapter Six. The questions are:

1. Qualitative value questions: (a) What ought people to do? (b) What kinds of things have value? (c) Is there anything that ought to be done besides promote value?

2. Questions about the source of values: (a) How does 'valuable' in the ethical sense relate to 'valued' in the psychological sense? (b) How do people *acquire* their values, and to what extent does this acquisition entail ethical relativism? (c) Ought people to be inculcated with certain values as opposed to others, and how would such an ought relate to the value of 'freedom'?

3. Questions of value priority: (a) If there are different values, on what basis are priority questions resolved? (b) How should values be distributed? (c) What is the relative priority between the maximization of value for all individuals on the one hand, and on the other hand the most just distribution of value?

4. Quantitative questions about duties and oughts: (a) To what extent ought people to channel their resources into promoting value? (b) To what extent are people *obligated* to channel their resources into promoting value? (c) To what extent ought one, and to what extent is one obligated, to give non-egoistic (in the narrow sense) values priority over egoistic ones?

Understanding the sense of these questions requires an understanding of certain key terms with respect to which we have not yet committed ourselves to any specific definitions. Before proceeding any further, let's see if we can specify the meanings of these terms in such a way that all the important questions can be asked and discussed intelligibly.

1. *Definitions*

(a) Problems in defining ethical terms

It may seem odd that a book on ethics has gotten this far without committing itself to precise definitions of the key moral terms. After all, most philosophers (or at least analytic philosophers) usually begin by defining their terms, and then proceed to make statements using these terms and to defend those statements. This kind of method may work well in many contexts, but it does not work so well in ethics. The reason is that, in ethics at least, the definitions of terms seem almost inevitably to have substantive claims packed into them, claims which could be meaningfully questioned if some of the terms had been defined differently, but which cannot be meaningfully questioned if one accepts the combination of definitions offered. For example, Mill may define 'I ought to do X' to mean 'X is more productive of the good than any other alternative,' but an open question can be posed against him: Is it not *meaningful* (though

ETHICAL QUESTIONS WITH DEFINITE RESOLUTIONS 147

perhaps false in Mill's opinion) to say that I ought to do X even though Y would produce more good than X? Similarly, 'good' itself may be defined by Mill to mean 'desirable to someone,' but against this definition it can be asked: Is it really *meaningless* to say that X is bad even though many people desire it, or that it is good even though no one desires it? Such open questions can be posed against almost any system of definitions ---unless, as Moore points out, there are 'moral intuitions' with reference to which the terms can be *ostensively* defined. As far as moral intuitions themselves are concerned, however, we have seen that there are plenty of reasons to doubt their truth or authenticity.

This problem becomes all the more baffling when we remind ourselves of the simple point, discussed in Chapter One, that it is meaningless and misguided to quibble over the 'true' meaning of a word. If someone wants to let a given sound denote a given meaning, there is theoretically no real reason why she should not, provided that she remains clear and consistent in this usage. The problem is that ethical theories tend to become incommensurable with each other in this way. If different moral theorists are to debate over what people 'ought' to do, then they must be able to do so using one sense or the other of 'ought'. It might therefore appear that the broadest or most inclusive definition possible would best suit this purpose---a definition so broad as to be invulnerable to any open question. But when the definition becomes broad enough to be invulnerable to any open question, it can be understood only in terms of the 'intuition' of 'moral qualities,' which then badly stacks the deck against theories opposing this way of discovering moral truth, and thus of understanding what moral terms mean.

In case anyone should think we have falsely limited these alternatives, perhaps it will help to recall Moore's argument on this point.[1] For Moore, the entire appeal of intuitionism rests on the necessity to define any system of terms by appeal to at least one 'simple' or 'ultimate' term which people already understand without having it defined to them. In any definition of any word, he says, the sense of the word is indicated by giving other words whose meaning is simpler. For example, in defining the word 'horse', we make references to 'legs', 'eyes', etc., which are simpler parts of the complex thing we are defining. If we are then asked to define 'eyes', we cite still simpler, more basic components that go together to make up the 'eye', such as 'nerve', 'ability to perceive color,' etc. But, says Moore, if we continue this process indefinitely, defining each term in terms of more simple terms, then we shall sooner or later reach some ultimately simple term which cannot be defined in any simpler terms. We may, for example, define 'color' as that which 'red', 'blue', 'yellow', etc., have in common with each other. But when asked to define 'yellow', all we can do is show the questioner several examples of yellow things, saying 'Look and see! This quality, which you experience in each of these objects, is yellow.' Only by directly and immediately *experiencing* 'yellow' can a person understand what the word 'yellow' means. All Witgensteinians, of course, are now thoroughly familiar with this point.[2]

Just as this is true in the physical realm, Moore also maintains it is true in the ethical realm. If we ask what the word 'right' means, Moore will tell us that 'right' is that quality of an action which characterizes it as productive of the greatest possible good under the given circumstances. When asked what 'good' means, however, Moore tells us that he cannot define the word 'good' because, just as the series of definitions leading to an understanding of the word 'horse' had to stop somewhere, with some most simple term in the series, so must the series of definitions leading to an understanding of the word 'right' end somewhere, with whatever the simplest, most irreducible term in its series might be. In this case, Moore thinks that the most simple term in the series, the one with which we must stop asking for any further definitions, is the word 'good'. If a person does not already know, through her own experience, what 'good' means, no one can tell her. Of course, this is not to deny that there is a philosophically trivial sense in which the term may be defined; if a Frenchman says that he does not understand what we mean by the word 'good', we may tell him that it means the same as the French word *bon*. But, in the important sense, if the Frenchman has never experienced the actual phenomenon that we mean by both 'bon' and 'good', we can never explain it to him, let alone prove or demonstrate to him that this or that particular thing is in fact 'good'. To prove that 'good' is such an ultimately simple term which is indefinable except through direct intuition, Moore offers his famous 'open question argument':

> Whoever will attentively consider with himself what is actually before his mind when he asks the question 'Is pleasure (or whatever it may be) after all good?' can easily satisfy himself that he is not merely wondering whether pleasure is pleasant.[3]

On the basis of the open question argument, Moore concluded that the word 'good' is just one of those words which cannot be understood in any other way than by experiencing the phenomenon to which the word refers. To define it in any other way is to commit the naturalistic fallacy, because, against any definition of 'good' as 'so-and-so', the 'open question' can still be asked, 'But is so-and-so good?' If this question still has any meaning, then 'good' and 'so-and-so' cannot mean the same thing by definition. One may *assert*, of course, that everything which is good is also pleasant; nonetheless, this does not imply that 'good' *means* 'pleasant'.

In spite of the wide influence of Moore's branding as a 'naturalistic fallacy' any attempt to define moral terms using non-moral terms, his reasoning is not now generally regarded as conclusive. Werkmeister points out that Moore's sense of the word 'natural' is ambiguous when he says that morals terms must not be defined in terms of 'natural' terms. The only clarification Moore gives on this point is to say that every 'natural' property of a natural object could exist by itself in time, whereas 'non-natural' properties cannot so exist. But by this definition, the color yellow would not be a natural property, since it cannot exist by itself in time. Since the word 'natural' remains unclear, so does Moore's assertion that 'good' is a 'non-natural' property of objects. What kind of property is a non-natural property?[4]

Perhaps more important, there are those who deny that the naturalistic fallacy *is* a fallacy. They insist that, when they say 'Only pleasure is good,' they are not simply giving a definition of 'good'; rather, they are stating that two things are *identical* which people had not formerly recognized as identical. But this is no more a fallacy than to assert that 'Clark Kent is Superman.' Suppose, they would insist, that someone makes the statement, 'Clark Kent is Superman.' Should we accuse the speaker of committing a fallacy on the basis that he must be *defining* Clark Kent as Superman, in which case his statement 'Clark Kent is Superman' would mean nothing more than 'Clark Kent is Clark Kent'? One hardly thinks so. Obviously, 'Clark Kent is Superman' has a definite meaning, especially if the equation asserted is news to everyone. Moreover, 'Clark Kent is Superman' means more than just 'Clark Kent is present whenever Superman is present.' It is not as though Clark Kent and Superman are two separate people who always go around together. The statement asserts that they are *the same* person. Similarly, many naturalists would argue that the assertion that 'Only pleasure is good' is a meaningful statement which does not merely assert that 'Only pleasure is pleasurable.' They deny, in other words, that their equation of pleasure with the good is a mere definition of the word 'good' to mean 'pleasure'. Richard Brandt, the rule utilitarian, for example, is carefully explicit in affirming that his equation of the terms is no mere definition, but rather an assertion.[5] J. O. Urmson even goes so far as to assert that Mill was not equating pleasure and good by definition either.[6] It follows from this type of defense against the naturalistic fallacy critique that, as far as the open question argument is concerned, to ask 'Is Clark Kent Superman?' may be to ask a meaningful question even if Clark Kent and Superman are in reality the same person. 'Clark Kent' and 'Superman' may refer to the same person seen from different points of view, or merely at different times without considering that they might be the same person. Ralph Barton Perry thus insists that it is possible to clarify our understanding of words further and that, on reflection, we may realize that what we *really* mean by a certain word is not, after all, what we *thought* we meant.[7]

The naturalists also have another answer to the open question argument. Suppose a naturalist does define 'good' to mean 'whatever is pleasurable.' Moore then attacks such a definition by means of the open question argument by asserting that one can still ask the question 'But is pleasure good?' and still be asking a question that means more than simply 'But is pleasure pleasurable?' But, against this move, some naturalists (though not all of them) respond that 'But is pleasure good?' *is* a meaningless question which asks nothing more than 'But is pleasure pleasurable?' The (alleged) fact that the question 'Is pleasure good?' means nothing more than 'Is pleasure pleasant' is the *reason why* this type of naturalist believes that 'good' can mean nothing other than 'pleasurable' in the first place. F. C. Sharp, for example, takes this type of position in support of his naturalistic conclusion on the issue.[8] So the controversy really reduces to a disagreement about whether the 'good' can mean anything other than 'pleasure' in the first place. The naturalists experience the phenomenon to which the word 'good' always applies as being the same phenomenon to which the word 'pleasure' applies. If Moore wants to say that the phenomenon to which the word 'good' applies can possibly be anything else, then the naturalists insist that Moore tell them what this phenomenon is. *But that is just what Moore has said cannot possibly be done,* because 'good' is one of those ultimately simple terms which cannot possibly be defined, except by means of directly and immediately *experiencing* that to which it refers.

Moore concludes that, if the word 'good' is to mean anything at all, then we must assume that people have a special *moral sense* which tells them what the word means, just as they have a visual sense that tells them what the word 'yellow' means. This moral intuition, then, must be the only possible source of ethical truths. Those who cannot have moral intuitions, because of some deficiency in their makeup, can perhaps be helped by means of psychological treatment, but they can never be helped by having the truth of moral statements *demonstrated* to them, because such statements by their very nature are incapable of any kind of demonstration except through direct intuition.

Against this consequence of More's position, John Mothershead levels the following criticism:

> Throughout the history of ideas intuition has been relied upon to support prejudices, and the reliance upon it of contemporary quacks is notorious. No doubt there are perfectly honest people who take themselves so seriously that their hunches or guesses do in fact come to them with the stamp of truth engraved upon them. What most people experience as 'seeming true' is for them certainty. Despite their evident sincerity, one can only suppose them to lack either education, humility, or both.[9]

To this objection may be added the many other objections given of intuitionism, and of Moore's specific way of applying it, in Chapter One. The result is that *definition through the intuition of moral qualities leads to ungrounded beliefs about substantive normative claims.* On the other hand, Moore seems correct in his claim that any non-ostensive (i.e., non-experiential, non-phenomenological) definition leaves itself open, in principle, to some open question or other. Even if I believe that every instance of 'goodness' is an instance of 'going to Mecca,' for example, someone can still reasonably ask, 'But is it not *meaningful* (though perhaps false) to assert that X is good even though X does not take one to Mecca?'

The real problem here is that Moore's entire argument rests on a confusion about the way words are defined. Suppose someone begins to work an algebra problem by saying, 'Let's let X mean the number of apples, and let

ETHICAL QUESTIONS WITH DEFINITE RESOLUTIONS

Y mean the number of bananas.' To be sure, someone could raise an 'open question' about this system of definitions by asking, 'But would it not be *meaningful* (though perhaps false) to say that some number is equal to X without being equal to the number of apples?' Certainly, some number could be equal to X without being equal to the number of apples if the system of definitions had been set up in such a way that X was not *defined* as the number of apples to begin with. Since, as we saw earlier (in Chapter One), anyone can define any term to mean whatever she wants it to mean, as long as doing so facilitates communication, it follows that the real open question is not whether it is 'correct' or 'incorrect' to define 'X' to mean 'the number of apples,' but rather whether the system of definitions allows everything to be said that needs to be said, and everything to be asked that needs to be asked. For example, if there were reason to believe that there are not only apples and bananas, but also oranges involved in the problem, then it would be reasonable to challenge the system of definitions on the grounds that it precludes our being able to talk about the number of oranges. But if there is no reason to believe that there are any oranges involved in the problem, then to raise such an 'open question' would be ridiculous quibbling. Similarly, if there were any reason to believe that rewarding people according to their 'desert' has intrinsic value, for example, then it would be important to challenge any system of definitions which would exclude such an intrinsic value by definition. But since, as we saw in the last chapter, determinism rules out the possibility of such an intrinsic value in any meaningful sense, then it would be ridiculous quibbling to object to some system of definitions on the grounds that it does not facilitate the assertion that there is any such intrinsic value. Certainly, there may be other systems of definition in which it is meaningful to say that the proportion between rewards and 'desert' has intrinsic value (though the statement would be a false one). But the fact that there are other possible systems of definitions is no indictment of the one in question.

On the other hand, it is also important to remember that any system of definitions must include at lest one term which is defined ostensively, i.e., whose meaning can be experienced by means of experiencing the phenomenon to which the term refers, whether the phenomenon be an empirical object, an emotion, or an idea. Otherwise, no one would clearly understand what system of phenomena the system of terms is supposed to refer to. The dilemma that is really posed by Moore's argument is this: If a term is to be defined ostensively, is there any way to do so without referring to the direct intuition of *the moral truth?* The definition of a unicorn, for example, may refer to other immediate experiences which we have had of other objects, whose meanings are then used to build up the concept of 'unicorn'; but the having of these other experiences does not prejudice our judgment as to whether any unicorns *in fact exist.*

There is only one workable resolution for this problem. We must begin by letting everyone use words to mean whatever she wants them to mean. We must then stipulate that, when the time comes for different theorists to debate the merits of their theories, each theorist must be willing to translate her theory into terms whose meanings are broad enough to render both theories commensurable for discussion---*but only if reasons can be given for believing that the opposing theory is likely to be true.* The reason for this last qualification is that the ultimate purpose of the communication to be established is to find out which theory is most likely to be true. Thus there is no purpose to be served by requiring, say, a utilitarian to broaden her sense of the word 'ought' to include the meanings which competing theories attach to the word 'ought' *unless* some evidence can be offered in favor of the competing theory. This demand for evidence serves to limit the applicability of 'open question arguments' as a result of the following chain of inferences: If no reason can be given why I ought to act according to theory X, then, no matter *what* 'ought' might mean, it will be self-contradictory to believe that I ought to act contrary to the way I believe I ought to act. But if there are better reasons for believing theory Y than theory X, then if I am honest with myself I must admit that I believe that it is correspondingly more *likely* that I ought to act according to theory Y. In the extreme case, if there are no reasons whatever to believe in X, then it would be self-contradictory to believe that I ought to act according to X rather than Y. Thus to believe X, under these circumstances, is to believe something which is self-contradictory. And there is no need to define our terms in such a way as to allow us to express theories the belief in which would be self-contradictory. If I believe that it is good to go to Mecca under a certain conception of 'good' such that 'good' is defined to mean 'P', and can offer evidence for this belief, then it is pointless quibbling for someone to ask, 'But is it not at least *meaningful* to say that going to Mecca is not good even though going to Mecca is P?'---unless, that is, there is some *reason to believe* that going to Mecca is not good in the different sense of 'good' being suggested.

To consider an analogous definitional problem in a non-moral example, suppose a biologist defines 'primate' as 'a mammal of a species such that (a) its skeletal structure is of such a character that with only slight evolutionary modification it could walk upright, and (b) it has an opposable thumb.' And suppose that the same biologist elaborates a complete system of classification in which there is no mention of any species which has feature (a) but not (b) or vice versa. And then suppose some critic asks, 'But what would you say about a species that has feature (a) but not (b)? Should such a species not be considered a primate species, since it is closer to the primates than to any other category? So then must you not broaden your definition to include as primates those which have feature (a) but not (b)?' Obviously, the answer is: No, there is no *need* to do so, unless evidence can be adduced that there *are* or *may be* beings with feature (a) but not (b). Absent any such evidence, the proposed system of definitions is perfectly adequate to communicate everything that needs to be said on the subject, which is the purpose of defining one's terms.

As long as this purpose is accomplished, one may define any word to mean whatever one wants it to mean. (Note also that the original system of definitions would be on even more solid ground if it had already been proven somehow that it is logically or ontologically *impossible* for a species to have (a) without (b) or vice versa. Analogously, a system of ethical definitions is on very solid ground if it has already been proven that moral claims not expressible by this system of definitions are logically or ontologically impossible---as has been done, for example, with regard to the thesis of an intrinsic value for a proportion between welfare and 'desert'.)

The importance of this point for ethical-definitional purposes is that it enables us, in principle at least, to close all open questions at the point beyond which there is no substantial evidence to support any of the theoretical possibilities left out of account by closing the open question. For example, there would be no need to respond to Moore's open question in defending a utilitarian definition of moral terms unless there were some reason to believe that a non-utilitarian value system might be the correct one. As it happens, there *are* reasons to believe this: Namely, it is possible to erect a non-utilitarian value system whose coherence is at least as impressive as that of utilitarianism. There are also specific arguments that can be adduced for specific theories, and there are some problems that can be raised against the coherence of utilitarianism. Thus some non-utilitarian value systems qualify as at least minimally coherent theories, and for this reason we must have a vocabulary of terms whose meanings are comprehensive enough to talk about them. But if these theories were not at least minimally coherent, there would be no need to define our terms comprehensively enough to talk about them. And in this case the open question would have no force. For example, we saw in Chapter Two, section 1, that, if the moral terms are defined in an appropriate way, it is true to say that I always ought to do what I prudentially ought unless there is some plausible non-prudential ought statement that would conflict with the prudential ought.

Besides the danger of packing incommensurable theoretical claims into different systems of definitions of moral terms, another problem in defining moral terms is the same as in defining any other terms: If the system of terms is to avoid circularity, then the meaning of at least one of the terms must be defined ostensively. In the context of moral theory, however, the danger is that an ostensive definition of any moral term will lead either (1) to an appeal to intuit some moral quality, or (2) to an automatic subjective-emotivism, or (3) to some other arbitrary equation of moral and non-moral terms. Thus one might define 'good' as 'approved of' (i.e., emotively) or as 'that which I intuit as having a certain quality which can be understood only by experiencing it' (thus letting the intuition play the ostensive role), or as 'agreed to by the majority of the people in a given society' (thus arbitrarily equating moral terms with some non-moral terms).

Someone may object that the claim that at least one term must be defined ostensively is controversial. Some hermeneutic philosophers and deconstructionists, for example, insist that one understands a term only by seeing the total context of terms with which the term in question interrelates.[10] But the purpose of deconstructionism is precisely to enable us to enter into the at-first-hopeless circularity of a system of terms by enabling us to more *concretely experience* what the meanings might have been *to* those who used them. This in itself is an attempt to approximate *ostensive* understandings of the terms in a phenomenological way. The process of 'deconstructing' the apparent meanings of the terms is just a specific case of phenomenological reduction through imaginative variation. We try to imagine whether the terms could have had different meanings if their users had understood the cultural context in a different way, and whether they could have any meaning at all outside of any cultural context whatever. The most important difference between deconstructionism and phenomenology is that deconstructionism insists that no phenomenological reduction can ever be complete, and therefore that the meanings of terms can never be as precise or as clear as we would like to believe they are; i.e., they would never have any meaning outside of some cultural context. But the inference that deconstructionists frequently draw from this point---that ethical relativism of the cultural-relativist genre is the correct approach to ethics[11]---is not a valid one. For some systems of definitions are more clear than others, precisely *because* they more closely approximate an immediate *ostensive* rootedness than others; and, given a relatively clear system of definitions, some ethical judgments are more likely to be true than others. Indeed, as we have seen, some are obviously completely untrue.

Both the need for at least one ostensive term and the need to withstand open questions without falling into intuitionism can be addressed effectively and simultaneously in only one way. The system of terms must have at least one ostensively-defined element, but the resulting theory must be able to defend itself against any open question argument arising from any other minimally coherent theoretical possibility supportable by genuine evidence or argument. What the outcome of the comparison between such a pair of rival theories will amount to is either (1) acceptance of the theory which, all in all, is more likely to be true, and rejection of the other, or (2) acceptance of the claims of both theories, but with priority given to the normative claims of the more probable theory in proportion to the probabilities of the two theories. To accomplish (2) may mean expanding one or both theories' definitions of certain terms, or introducing new, more inclusively defined terms, in order to make the two theories commensurable.

Now it is possible to define the main moral terms in such a way that (i) one of them is defined ostensively, and (ii) the only theories not describable using the definitions in question are those which have already become untenable or less than minimally coherent in light of logical, factual and ontological considerations. Such definitions might be called 'adequately comprehensive' definitions.

An adequately comprehensive definition is comprehensive enough to allow any question which needs to be asked, and to leave open questions which need to be left open. It will not necessarily be so comprehensive as to facilitate the communication of ethical statements which cannot possibly be true, nor will it necessarily be so comprehensive as to leave open questions for which a positive answer is insupportable by any evidence or argument. The following system of adequately comprehensive definitions should allow communication with regard to the main ethical concepts for which metaethical questions are especially relevant.

(b) Adequately comprehensive definitions of key terms

An ostensive definition of any concept begins, either explicitly or implicitly, with a direct phenomenological reference to a subjective experience. We then, either formally or informally, 'purify' the sense of what we mean. For example, we might at first think of 'good' as meaning 'valued by someone' or 'desired by someone.' But when we think of people's 'desire for' or 'valuing of' heroin, e.g., we realize that by 'good' we did not really originally mean just *anything* that anyone might desire or value, for the heroin is in some other sense 'undesirable' and 'disvaluable' to the person in question. When we refine this sense, we may then think of 'good' as 'desired or valued on the whole and in the long run.' But then we reflect on the fact that heroin would not be 'good' for the person even if she did desire it in the long run---say, if she preferred to survive the ten-year average life expectancy of a heroin addict, stealing to support the habit, rather than to live a longer life devoid of the pleasure of heroin. We then realize that by 'good' we really originally meant something more like that which the person *would* desire or value if she were well-informed about all her options, honest with herself, and were not 'unduly influenced' by bad habits which have already been formed but would not have been formed if the agent had known what was 'good' for her in the first place.

The ostensive definition of 'intrinsic good,' then (if 'good' is the term we choose as our ostensive term), phenomenologically reduced, ends up meaning something like 'whatever could be intrinsically desired or valued by a well-informed and authentic (i.e., self-honest) subject.' This definition of 'good', in fact, will be used in the analyses that follow. Its ostensiveness is guaranteed by our ability to *directly experience* what it means to desire or value something. But such a definition is capable of leaving open the questions that need to be left open. It does not insist that anything that anyone values has value (which would close off the possibility of non-relativistic systems), or that the aggregate good is to be calculated simply by adding up in a quantitative way the goods for all individuals (which would close off systems that give fair distribution priority over maximizing the quantity of individual goods in existence); also, 'subject' is here taken to mean 'conscious being' and therefore does not preclude goods which are valuable for animals.

There are of course other ways to define 'good' (one may, after all, define any word however one likes), but the meaning just described---

whatever word one uses to denote it---is essential to ethical inquiry and (I hope to show) can adequately serve the purpose of discussing any at-least-minimally-coherent ethical theory. Because the aggregate good is not equivalent by definition with the mathematical sum of all individual goods (since an aggregate is not always the mere sum of its parts), it will serve our purposes to simply treat 'good' and 'valuable' as synonyms, distinguishing between 'value for individuals' and 'aggregate value' just as we have done for the two types of 'goods'. This equation tends to save confusion since the words 'valued' and 'valuable' tend to be associated with each other in so many ways (though, as we have defined them, they are by no means equivalent).

To be sure, open question arguments can be raised against this definition of 'good' or 'valuable'. Is it not at least possible that something that could never be desired by any well-informed, authentic subject might be 'good' in a different or broader sense of the concept 'good', which therefore ought to be taken into account? But the answer to this open question argument is that there is no need to take into account any such broadened or different notion of 'good' unless the person using the word in this way can say something supportable with some kind of evidence or argument. And the only ways to support theories using concepts of 'good' which are not framed in one way or another in terms of what is or could be 'good *for* someone' are untenable because of determinism. We have seen already, for example, that the thesis that a 'proportion between welfare and well-doing' such as the one Kant advocates cannot be intrinsically good if determinism is true (though it might be extrinsically good). More will be said on this point.

There can, of course, as hinted above, be a concept of 'aggregate good' distinguishable from the mere sum of individual goods. Many concepts lend themselves to having statements made about aggregates of instances of them that could not be made about single instances of them. For example, we can say things about aggregates of subatomic particles that cannot be said about individual particles. The question whether an aggregate good is reducible to the mathematical sum of individual goods is a question which must be and is left open by the above ostensive definition. The reason for this is that it is possible that a well-informed and authentic subject, if altruistically motivated by a universal empathy, might well value a given distribution of valuable things independently of the value of the things themselves. More specifically, such a subject might find that, when individuals who value various things organize themselves into 'societies' (a term as yet to be formally defined), it is a valuable thing for such a society to 'obligate' itself (another term as yet to be defined) toward the various individuals in ways that are fundamentally the same for each individual; that, therefore, aggregate value maximization, in order to reflect this sameness of obligation, is not determined by the arithmetic sum of individual values.

When the values of different individuals conflict with each other, some favoring one distribution policy and some favoring another, then the

ETHICAL QUESTIONS WITH DEFINITE RESOLUTIONS 157

question as to which policy is aggregately best cannot be closed by definition. Nonetheless, we shall see that no policy which promotes no individual value whatever for *anyone* can possibly qualify as aggregately valuable by the definition being used here. For no well-informed, authentic subject motivated by a universal empathy could possibly value such a policy. And we have seen that the ideally authentic subject would have to be so motivated in order to optimize his consciousness.

Questions of quantitative comparison are also left open. If we define 'intrinsic good' to mean 'whatever could be intrinsically valued by some well-informed and authentic subject,' it does not necessarily follow that something which can be valued by more such subjects is better than someing which can be valued by fewer; or that something more strongly valued is better than something more weakly valued. No such quantitative judgment necessarily follows, because we have not yet devised a way to quantify or mathematicize value, whether individual or aggregate. Some concepts, such as maleness or femaleness, do not lend themselves to quantification. Others, like competence at some skill, may be quantified in a variety of different ways. It may turn out that whatever is more valued is more valuable, but this question cannot be closed by definition. It may turn out, for example, that things which are valued in a way compatible with the greatest aggregate value (which may not be the mathematical sum of individual values) are more valuable than things which are valued in ways incompatible with the greatest aggregate value.

After at least one term has been defined ostensively, the others may be defined in any way that facilitates communication, allows to be said whatever needs to be said, and does not close questions that need to be asked. I shall use the expression 'one ought, prima facie, to do X' to mean 'It would be aggregately prima facie good if one were to do X, given the option.' 'One ought actually to do X' will then mean 'It would be aggregately best, all things considered, if one were to do X, given the option.' (Remember that what is 'aggregately best' has been defined in such a way that it may or may not be determined by the mere sum of individual goods.) By adding 'given the option' onto the ends of these definitions, we arbitrarily stipulate that 'ought' in our sense implies that one has the option. It would be possible to omit this stipulation (as does Smart), but we have already seen that such a definition would not facilitate any better communication, and if anything would make it more difficult. The definition just given would be inadequate if there could be some meaningful sense of 'ought' in which one ought to do anything other than what it is aggregately best for one to do. But we shall see that no such thesis can possibly be true. The only systems which would deny that one ought to do what is aggregately best are (1) *egoistic* systems, and (2) systems to which I shall refer as (a) *'rule-bound'* systems and (b) *'retributive'* systems. Regarding egoism, a *purely* egoistic system would indeed deny that I ever ought to do what is best for subjects other than myself (except for the extrinsic purpose of indirectly benefiting myself). This system is untenable, as we have seen, because, if I am the least bit motivated to benefit others (which Chapter Three showed I am), then I am motivated to submit myself to an Aristotelian training program which will bring my own desires as much into harmony with what is best for others as I possibly can. Thus there are things which it is meaningful to say I ought to do other than benefit myself. As for the egoistic oughts which are included in *partially* egoistic systems (i.e., those which say that one *sometimes* ought to benefit oneself), they do not require any other definition of 'ought' than the one just explained, since by benefiting myself I am contributing to the aggregate good, while at the same time I am benefiting others to the maximum extent to which this ostensibly partially-egoistic nature would allow. This, however, is all that any system can require in the way of non-egoistic oughts, since it would be pointless to tell people to do what their essential nature would compel them not to do. As for 'retributive' and 'rule-bound' systems, we shall see in section (2) below that the former are incompatible with determinism, whereas the latter cannot be supported with any evidence.

Of course, 'One ought to do what is aggregately best' does not imply that 'One ought to promote the greatest possible quantity of *individual* goods,' since 'aggregate good' is not equated by definition with 'the maximum amount of individual goods.' This, again, is a *distributive* and *quantitative* question which should not be closed by definition of the qualities involved. Also, in equating 'One ought (insofar as possible) to do X' with 'X is aggregately best,' we avoid the expression 'X is productive of good consequences.' To do X may not produce any consequences at all, but may be good in its own right. Or it may be good because it inevitably results from a good emotional quality. These questions are left open by the definition.

By the word 'society', I shall mean a group of individuals who interrelate *qua* conscious beings in any way whatever. The *extent* to which something is a 'society' in this sense will be taken as a variable which is proportional by definition to the extent to which the individuals interrelate qua conscious beings. Any conscious beings who are in any way aware of each other's existence do interrelate qua conscious beings, at least to a fair extent. Thus all humankind is a society to a fair extent. However, the members of more closely interrelated groups, such as nation-states in contemporary history, constitute societies to still greater extents.

The importance of the word 'society' for our purposes is that we need it in order to define the concepts of moral and legal rights. These rights may be negative or positive. I have a positive moral right to X to the extent that a society to which I belong ought, if possible, to provide me with X. I have a negative moral right to X to the extent that the society ought to prevent people from depriving me of X. I have the corresponding legal rights if a society to which I belong agrees, in some meaningful sense, to do what it ought to do in these respects by legal means.

The words 'duty' and 'obligation', which I shall take as synonymous, will be used as follows: 'I have a duty to do X' means that someone has a right for me to do X.

Since individuals belong to 'societies' to the extent that they interrelate qua conscious beings, there are respects in which I as an individual have duties toward other individuals with whom I interrelate, since at that point I have to a certain extent constituted a 'society' with that individual. Obligation therefore admits of degrees. I may be more obligated toward someone with whom I interrelate societally in a more real sense than with others. If obligation admits of degrees in this way, it follows that so do rights. People in Ethiopia have a stronger prima facie right to be fed when starving by other Ethiopians and by the Ethiopian government than by 'distant' peoples and governments (i.e., those with whom they do not interrelate in as real a sense). But since all conscious beings interrelate to some extent, the Ethiopians have a weaker prima facie right to have their needs met by distant peoples and governments as well. (Needless to say, the refusal of the Ethiopian government to meet its stronger obligation toward its people does not erase my weaker obligation toward them.)

What is the point of defining rights and obligations in terms of 'societies'? The point is that this method captures a distinction (and one that many people seem to draw) between what one *ought* to do and what one is *obligated* to do. It is possible that there are instances where I *ought* to do something but am not *obligated* to do it---e.g., I *ought* to drive downtown, find a homeless person and find him a place to sleep, in the sense that it would be good if I were to do so, at least prima facie. But I am not obligated to do so. It is true, of course, that I do have a general obligation to help all people, since I belong to societies with them in real senses. (If nothing else, I am generally aware of their existence.) But it is also true that I am doing things in general to fulfill this general obligation---giving money to charities, paying taxes, voting for policies that would require these taxes and would provide benefits to those who need them, etc. So it can be argued that there can be circumstances in which my *obligation* to the person who is probably freezing in the streets downtown at this very moment has been discharged as conscientiously as could be required, yet I still *ought* to do something extra or supererogatory because *it would be good* if I were to do so. On the other hand, it would also be good if I were to stay here and continue writing this book. Which action would be *better* is a quantitative and distributive question for which we have not, up to this point, formulated principles that would be adequate.

It is imaginable that there could be conflict situations in which a supererogative ought outweighs an obligatory one. For example, Wagner was not obligated to write his great music, but to facilitate doing so he violated many obligations---notably, the obligation to repay debts to his friends, and the obligation to respect the feelings of his first wife, who strongly would have preferred that he materially support her in a more adequate way. Whether or not one can ever be 'justified' in such actions (i.e., whether one ever 'ought' to act in such a way) is a question which at this point in our inquiry remains open.

We should hasten to acknowledge that a slight difficulty will at first glance appear to arise in defining duties and obligations in the way we just have. If the society ought to, for example, collect more taxes than it does, someone may ask whether it then follows that I am morally obligated to donate these additional funds to the government, even though I know that no one else is going to. In order to formulate a practically applicable answer to this kind of question, we must distinguish between two very different kinds of cases for which the question could be asked: Case (I): The society ought to require any given person to do X regardless of whether others do X or fail to do it. Case (II): The society ought to require everyone to do X, but ought not to require that one person do X unless it can succeed in getting a reasonable number of others to do so. In case (I), there would seem to be a strong presumption (which we shall later confirm) that I am obligated to do X. In case (II), on the other hand, I am obligated to do what the society ought to require me to do, i.e., to do X *if* the society can succeed in getting a reasonable number of others to do X. In both cases, it remains true that I am obligated to do what, in that case, the society ought to require me to do.

Thus it might well be argued that the society ought to require me not to commit murder regardless of how many others do so; if so, then I am morally obligated to refrain from murder regardless of whether any formal law prohibits it. (For the question is not what the society *does* require of me, but rather what the society *ought if possible* to require of me.) By contrast, it can also be argued that the society ought *not* to require me to pay taxes which no others under similar circumstances are required to pay, or which they in fact cannot be induced to pay (for we shall see later that this would be unfair); therefore I am not morally obligated under such circumstances to pay such taxes. In some cases, of course, it may be that I *ought* to do certain things even though I am not obligated to do them.

Another apparent problem with this way of defining duties and obligations is that it might initially seem to leave no room for situations in which we have duties toward people arising from the peculiarities of particular circumstances in relation to which the larger society, for one reason or another, ought not to legislate. For example, if I am a fairly good swimmer, it can well be argued that I not only *ought,* but further still have a *duty* or *obligation* to save a drowning person. Yet perhaps the society ought not to require people to save drowning people because in such cases it would be impossible to establish negligence in any reliable way. The argument for this duty, nonetheless, hinges on the idea that no amount of supererogatory good that I might accomplish can ever compensate for the wrong that I have done by neglecting what I ought to have done in this one particular case. One does not compensate for murdering one person by, say, donating enough money to UNICEF to save ten starving children. Thus the responsibility to the drowning person is no mere 'ought', on the same level with the responsibility to give money to UNICEF. Rather, it is a duty or obligation.

But the reason I am obligated, and not only ought, to save the drowning person is that, in the instant when she and I come into interrelation with each other, the two of us form a 'society' in the sense used here. I.e., we relate in a very real sense as conscious beings. And in such a relationship, it would be good, if it were possible, for both people to be *required* to do what they ought in relation to each other. Thus this 'society' of conscious beings *ought if possible* to require me to do what I ought, even though in fact it does not; therefore, I have a duty toward the other member of the society. This is why I sometimes have stronger duties toward those with whom I interrelate in real senses than toward those I do not know or with whom I do not interrelate in as substantial a way.

Another complicating factor in this type of situation is that there may be times when the society prima facie ought to provide certain rights or require certain duties of its members, yet a more important prima facie ought implies that it ought *not* to provide these rights or require these duties. For example, it may be that the society prima facie ought to prosecute a certain type of offender, yet at the same time, in the interest of fairness, it prima facie ought *not* to prosecute a given offender if it has for one reason or another refrained from prosecuting all previous such offenders in similar circumstances. What the society *actually* ought (if possible) to do is determined by the correct balance or decision between these conflicting prima facie oughts. People's actual moral rights and duties are then determined by what a society to which they belong actually ought to provide for them and require of them (if possible).

Further possible objections to these definitions will be considered as we progress.

The words 'right' and 'wrong' are notoriously ambiguous. Some say that a person has acted wrongly if she failed to do what she ought; others, if she failed to do her duty; still others recognize no distinction between these two alternatives. I shall say that a person acts 'rightly' if she does what, all things considered, she 'ought', and wrongly if she does not. This is a purely arbitrary terminological choice.

Another important moral word is the word 'fair'. This word applies specifically to the distribution of values or valuable things (taking 'things' to include intangible 'things' such as opportunities, consideration before the law, etc.). A distribution of value or valuable things is 'fair' if it is a distribution that prima facie ought to be promoted for reasons other than maximizing the *amount* of individual good (individual good, again, meaning that which can be valued by well-informed and authentic subjects, and not *necessarily* what *is* valued). Fairness comes into play if and to the extent that mathematically maximizing the amount of individual good is not necessarily what ought to be done, i.e. the best thing to do.

The system of definitions just outlined may not be the only adequately comprehensive one that could be developed. But it does seem to satisfy the requirements for a workable system of definitions which neither appeals to 'moral intuitions' nor closes off important questions by definition.

Now that we have some definitions to work with, we can attempt to lay a metaethical foundation for answering the four important general questions raised at the opening of this chapter. The remainder of this chapter and the next one will be devoted to this endeavor.

2. Qualitative Value Questions

Given this system of definitions, the first two of our four important general questions are answered more easily than are the third and fourth. The first general question, again, is:

1. Qualitative value questions: (a) What ought people to do? (b) What kinds of things have value? (c) Is there anything that ought to be done besides promote value?

As discussed in Chapter Two, and in accordance with the system of definitions just outlined, I use the expression 'promote value' in a broad, inclusive sense. If a pure utilitarian like Smart believes that maximizing happiness is the only intrinsic value, then he believes that maximizing happiness 'promotes value,' and that one ought to promote value in this way. If a Rawlsian, on the other hand, believes that fairness in the distribution of happiness has intrinsic value, then he believes that to promote a fair distribution system is to promote value. According to this usage of 'promote value,' the bone of contention between utilitarians and Rawlsians is not whether or not one should promote value, but whether a world characterized by fairness in the distribution of goods has more value than a world not characterized by such fairness.

If 'promote value' is defined in such a way as to include either maximizing individual goods or promoting fairness, then all three aspects of question (1) have really already been answered by our previous discussions, and it remains only to pull these answers together. Because the answer to (c) is negative, (a) and (b) can be collapsed into one question. I.e., it is not the case that one ever ought to do anything other than promote value, either in terms of maximizing individual good or in terms of promoting the aggregate good (which, in some theories, will include fairness in the distribution of individual goods). The *priority* ordering of these different kinds of 'value promotions' is not settled by this statement, but is postponed to our question (3) in the next chapter.

The reason it is not the case that one ever *ought* to do anything other than promote value is that it can never be intrinsically *valuable* to do anything other than promote value. Since we have defined 'I ought to do X' to mean 'It is aggregately best that I do X,' and 'valable' as a synonym for 'good', it becomes true by definition that I ought to do only those things which promote value. The real question is whether 'ought' has been defined in a too restrictive way, i.e., whether legitimate open questions can be raised against this definition.

According to the analysis in section 1(a) above, a definition can be rejected on the basis of an open question argument only if some more inclusive definition facilitates the communication of assertions for which some legitimate evidence or argument can be offered. For, after all, it is legitimate to define one's terms in any way one pleases, provided that the system of definitions in question facilitates communication and discussion of all conflicting views on the subject that need to be considered. But we saw that there is no need to broaden our definitions in order to include possible assertions which are not at least minimally probable. And it requires only a slight extension of the discussion of determinism and incompatibilism to see that any assertion that we ought to do anything other than promote value ultimately ends up either contradicting determinism by resorting to the thesis that the use of 'desert' criteria for rewards and punishments ought to be promoted for its own sake rather than for the sake of something else; or else asserting that certain rules ought to be followed for which no reason can be stated whatever, as the following analysis will show.

Suppose someone asserts that people ought to do some type of action, X, even though X does not result in the actualization of any value, i.e., result in either individual good or aggregate good, either well-being or some preferable distribution of well-being. Such a theory would perforce envision possible situations in which X ought to be done even though to do so reduces the amount of aggregate value or increases the amount of aggregate disvalue. This feature is characteristic either of a *retributive* system of ethics, or of what I am calling a *rule-bound* system. In a retributive system, 'justice' ought to be done in the sense of giving people what they 'deserve' even if everyone involved is the worse off for it, and even if fairness in the distribution of benefits is not thereby increased. In a rule-bound system, the rules ought to be obeyed even if everyone involved is the worse off for it, and even if fairness in the distribution of benefits is not thereby increased.

Technically, a retributive system is just one particular type of rule-bound system, and in practice most rule-bound systems tend to be retributive ones, or at least to have a retributive component. Since there are some arguments against retributive systems that do not apply to other types of rule-bound systems, however, I shall consider them as two different types of systems.

We should note that theories which would advocate reducing the total amount of *individual* good in order to promote a greater amount of *aggregate* good count as systems which would 'promote value' as this expression has been defined. For to sacrifice the maximization of (individual) goods for the sake of the maximization of *fairness* is, according to the above system of definitions, to maximize the *aggregate good* (or aggregate value), with fairness counting as a type of aggregate good or value.

Then what kinds of theories *would* advocate anything other than 'promoting value' in this sense? It would seem that the only theories that do this would be those which either advocate a 'retributive justice' which cannot be reduced to 'distributive justice,' or advocate obedience to rules whose purpose is neither to distribute nor maximize individual goods, i.e., either a retributive system or a rule-bound one. The difference between Rawls and Kant is illustrative in this regard. For Rawls, rewards and punishments, benefits and burdens, are to be distributed on the basis of the hypothetical preferences of the person in the original position. The reason this person's perspective is regarded as so special is that here we have a person whose essential *motive* is to *maximize value*. But, by not letting her know who she is, we trick her into wanting to maximize aggregate value rather than individual value; this aggregate value, Rawls believes, consists in a certain specific type of compromise between distributive fairness for individual value and the quasi-utilitarian maximization of individual value. I.e., this specific compromise is the one Rawls believes will best promote *aggregate* value, defined by him as 'fairness' per se. A social system which purposely acted in such a way as to reduce the well-being of everyone below an amount compatible with fair distribution (in Rawls' sense of 'fair') could never be advocated by Rawls' system. It is essentially an aggregate-value-maximizing system, with fairness in distribution counted as a very important type of aggregate value which enjoys priority over other types.

A Kantian, on the other hand, could conceivably advocate (and I personally think Kant himself did advocate)[12] in certain types of situations doing an action which would actually reduce the total amount of *aggregate* value (again, defined to include fair distribution and/or maximization of individual goods). For example, if it were known that the assassination of some particularly horrible tyrant---say, Hitler---would on the whole result in both a greater sum of individual goods and a more fair distribution of those goods, whereas refusing to assassinate the tyrant would result in both a smaller sum of individual goods and a less fair overall distribution of those goods (some of the goods in question being life itself for some people), many Kantians still would not allow themselves to carry out the assassination. Indeed, even if refusal to assassinate the tyrant were to result in the tyrant's causing the death of millions of innocent people, many Kantians would still refuse. For they would not be able to will that others assassinate *them* under similar cumstances. In this respect, the Kantian system is 'rule-bound'. The

Kantian system is also *retributive* in advocating a 'proportion between welfare and well-doing...even if nothing further results from it.'[13]

This retributive element in Kant's thinking, of course, is untenable, as we have already seen, because of determinism. There can never be any legitimate *reason* to insist on giving people what they 'deserve' in the sense of a 'proportion between welfare and well-doing' except where that *reason* becomes the intrinsic value for the sake of which the proportion between welfare and well-doing serves as an *extrinsic* value. (Again, there can be many instances of this latter case.)

As for the rule-bound nature of the Kantian or any other interpretation of a quasi-inviolable 'moral law,' it would seem that Kant's system can be treated as paradigmatic for this type of system. Kant clearly proposes to offer a system of moral rules which are at once demonstrable rather than arbitrary, and at the same time not hypothetical, i.e., not dependent for their validity on any prudential goal-orientation. Thus the system promises to be genuinely non-consequentialist in nature. Kant argues that, if there is going to turn out to be any demonstrably binding categorical imperative in ethics, by contrast to a hypothetical imperative, then its bindingness must not be based on any psychological theory of human nature, or on any assumption about what kinds of goals people may have in life. These could only lead to hypothetical imperatives which a person might choose to follow if she found that doing so served her purposes, or which a group might follow if doing so served its purposes. Such considerations could never ground a categorical imperative, which would be universally binding and equally applicable to all people in all circumstances. The requirement for a categorical rather than a hypothetical imperative thus seems quite a tall order. It implies that the rightness of obeying the imperative cannot depend on the consequences of such obedience. Rather, the duty involved would be so necessary and universally binding that we must 'do our duty, even if the sky falls.' The question arises, if we are not to demonstrate the bindingness of duties and the rightness of acting according to these duties on the basis of the goodness of the *consequences* of so acting, then how *can* we demonstrate them?

Kant believes that only *one* such principle is capable of qualifying as a categorical imperative, although the principle can be stated in various ways and has far-reaching implications. The one universally binding categorical imperative which does not depend for its validity on any consequences is: 'Act only according to that maxim by which you can at the same time will that it should become a universal law.' I.e., do nothing which you could not consistently be willing for everyone to do in similar circumstances. It is the *inconsistency* of willing the universalization of a maxim that makes it unallowable, not our mere *emotional preference* that it not be universalized. Many a classical musician would have difficulty being willing for everyone to play rock music, but this consideration does not make 'Do not play rock' a valid and binding rule of conduct. 'Don't tell deliberate falsehoods,' on the other hand, is supposed to qualify as a binding duty because, if we were to will that everyone should tell falsehoods, then we would thereby will a state of affairs in which no one would take anyone else's word for anything, which would defeat our purpose in telling the falsehoods we wish to tell; we would therefore wish something which, when universalized, would be self-contradictory, or at least inconsistent in some very strong sense.

Perhaps a more clearly self-contradictory example would be a situation in which there are five pieces of pie to be divided among five people. Before taking the second piece, Kant insists that we ask ourselves, 'Would I be willing for everyone to take two pieces?' Obviously, we could not possibly will this, for to do so would be to will a self-contradiction. Under the circumstances, everyone cannot possibly have two pieces.

But how does Kant *demonstrate* that we should act according to no maxim that is not universalizable in this sense, and that his principle therefore qualifies as a valid and universally binding categorical imperative? It seems that moral experience is a type of experience for which synthetic a priori concepts are needed. Kant admits that we cannot deductively *prove* that there is any such thing as moral responsibility. Our experience of 'moral responsibility' may be a mere illusion. But, Kant says, we must *assume* that morality is real. The necessity for this assumption is one of the most difficult points in Kant's theory. He simply says that, if we ask ourselves whether we would be willing to allow that the world we live in might be devoid of any objectively valid moral principles, we would find such a notion so repugnant, and so foreign to the sense of our everyday experience, that we *must* elect to live *as if* there were moral principles.[14] But, if we once accept that there is a moral law, that there is a categorical imperative, then it is not difficult to demonstrate exactly how such a law would have to be formulated. Only one imperative can possibly be categorical without becoming completely arbitrary: Act according to no rule which you could not consistently will be to a universal guide to human conduct.

Why is this the only possible categorical imperative? Because it is the only one which is neither (a) an arbitrary rule subject to disagreement among people with different *emotional preferences,* such as 'No one should dance on Sunday'; nor (b) hypothetical rather than categorical in nature. It escapes the arbitrary and subjective nature of principles based on mere intuition or emotion because of its purely *formal* nature.[15] I.e., it rules out *only* those types of actions the universalization of which would entail willing a logical inconsistency, and it *demands* only those types of actions the refraining from which would entail a similar inconsistency. Of course, we are not compelled to accept the supposition that there *is* a moral law. But, again, Kant thinks that life with *no* concept of genuine moral value whatever---which would be the only other alternative to the categorical imperative---would be unacceptable. Moreover, if we decide that there is no moral law whatever, we thereby render ourselves incapable of making any sense of the phenomenon of moral experience. If we want a theory of morals (and apparently we do need one; even the hardened criminal fills his speech

ETHICAL QUESTIONS WITH DEFINITE RESOLUTIONS

with the assignment of moral blame, although he places this blame elsewhere than in himself), then we must accept the categorical imperative.

However, Kant also emphasizes that an act is not really morally right unless it is performed for the right reason--i.e., out of respect for the moral law. The act is not right if it is done by accident, or in spite of an unsuccessful attempt to avoid doing it. It must be done willingly. Otherwise, it would be motivated by mere prudence and therefore would be guided only by a hypothetical imperative, not the categorical imperative. Morality, for Kant, is the realm in which people do not merely obey the laws of nature in an involuntary sense, but also have the power to act 'according to a conception' of law. Reason itself, in some sense, intervenes in nature, causing actions to occur which would not occur if there were only beings which obey laws of nature involuntarily and not also rational beings. A rational being, in Kant's sense, has the power to avoid self-contradiction, whether explicit or implied in actions, even if one's drives and impulses might otherwise have driven one to behave less rationally. We therefore have the power (or freedom) to voluntarily regulate our actions according to the dictates of reason.

Since one must thus act contrary to impulses, Kant must therefore also believe that it would be impossible for people to act according to the categorical imperative unless we also had free will. If our actions were all determined by desires and impulses, then we could only act according to hypothetical imperatives. Thus, without free will, morality as Kant conceives it would be impossible.

We now know, however, that this demand for such a radical free will is a demand for the impossible, and indicates that there must be something fundamentally wrong with Kant's system. Perhaps he has scoffed too quickly at consequentialist systems; perhaps if he had been forced to take them more seriously he could have reconciled himself to the notion that life is at least worth living, after all, even if a consequentialist system is the best we can do.

Since the failure of Kant's system is so paradigmatic of the failure of rule-bound systems generally (as I shall attempt to show), it is instructive to consider the reasons for this failure. One criticism of Kant which technically is not legitimate does at least serve to move us very quickly and effectively into the problematic area of the system. Mill suggests that Kant fails, "almost grotesquely," to show that there would be any contradiction involved in the universalization of the most immoral imaginable rules of conduct, but shows instead that *undesirable consequences* would follow from the universalization of such rules.[16] This criticism is not valid as it stands because the categorical imperative does not prohibit actions the universalization of which would have undesirable consequences; it prohibits only those actions the universalization of which would be self-defeating because they would involve willing a self-contradictory or inherently impossible state of affairs. For example, to will that everyone should take more than an equal share of a pie would be to will a mathematical impossibility.

Yet it may be that Kant gets out of this problem only by creating worse ones. Suppose, for example, that we tell a Mafia hit-man not to commit murder unless he can will without inconsistency that everyone try to kill other people whenever they think they can get away with it. The hit-man could reply something to this effect: Certainly I can will without inconsistency that anyone who can get away with killing others may do so. For I have provided my own protection against being murdered, as is everyone's responsibility. And, while I realize that my willing the universalization of this kind of action may well involve a certain *risk* that, in spite of all my efforts to protect myself, someone will nonetheless succeed in murdering me, the benefits of killing people are worth the risk.

While we may consider the hit-man's risk an unwise one to take, it does not seem to involve any self-contradiction, inconsistency or self-defeatingness. It would seem to follow, then, that if inconsistency is required in order to prohibit a rule of action, then Kant's categorical imperative does not prohibit murder, the most vicious of all crimes. Kant might insist here, of course, that what he means is that if I were to will that everyone else should not only *attempt* to commit murder, but also *succeed* in doing so, *then* I would be involved in inconsistency. But this does not seem to be the case. Suppose I am getting ready to kill someone whom I hate very much---whom I hate so much that I would be willing to die in order to ensure his death. Then my willing the universalization of murder would not be to will something which makes my action self-defeating purely from the standpoint of whether the action accomplishes its goal. Moreover, even if everyone *succeeded* in committing murder, this would still not necessarily entail that I would be one of the victims. It would simply involve me in an even greater *degree* of risk than if everyone only attempted to commit murder.

The Kantian might then respond that, while the universalization of murder would not render my act of murder impossible, it would at least defeat *other* purposes which I have, such as staying alive. But in that case, Kant becomes vulnerable to Mill's original criticism, namely that an action is prohibited only if its consequences would be undesirable on utilitarian grounds, i.e., would defeat my *purposes* in life. This answer, then, is not available to Kant.

Suppose, to further generalize this criticism, that someone says that he does not believe it is anyone's responsibility to help anyone in times of trouble; that no one has a duty to support relief programs for the unemployed, the aged, the disabled, etc. In fact, let's go to the absolute extreme and imagine that our Scrooge does not believe in helping anyone under any circumstances. Let's say he justifies this belief on the basis that it is each person's responsibility to save money, have insurance policies, etc., to cover such possibilities. Suppose further that Scrooge has made all possible such provisions for himself in case of hardship.

Then would there be anything self-contradictory, self-defeating or inconsistent in his being willing to universalize such an attitude? Granted, he is taking the risk that he himself may need help someday. But, considering all the preparations he has made for such a contingency, the risk is small. Thus his unhelpful attitude, when generalized, would not seem self-defeating. What is inconsistent or self-contradictory about being willing to take a risk?

Kant's categorical imperative therefore seems to be too lenient, because it seems to allow a number of behaviors which most people would be inclined to consider immoral; it would seem to allow them simply because their universalization would not entail any inconsistency. Extending the same criticism to the issue of rights, a corresponding problem can be detected. Since the categorical imperative is not adequate to rule out all the behaviors we would like to regard as immoral, such as refusing to help others and murdering, then it also establishes too few corresponding rights, such as the right to expect help in old age or disability, and such as the right not to be murdered.

Furthermore, as Frankena points out, those duties which *can* be established by means of the categorical imperative seem to be too strictly universal.[17] For example, the duty not to lie seems immune to the above criticisms because the categorical imperative would imply that the universalization of lying behavior would be self-defeating since one's own lies would not be believed. But this would then imply that one should *never* lie, which seems counterintuitive. When the Gestapo comes to the door looking for Jews, is the moral course of action to tell the truth? This would seem to be what Kant's theory implies, *unless* we try to make room for exceptions in ways that Kant himself did not do. For example, we might say that the telling of lies in certain specific types of exceptional cases could be universalized without becoming self-defeating. There would be nothing self-defeating about being willing for everyone to lie in cases where it is necessary to help someone. Thus we could have our universal rule of conduct be 'Never lie except to help someone.' Such a move would not make the rule hypothetical, as we noted at the beginning of our discussion of Kant. It is possible to qualify the rule without making it hypothetical.

But then other problems arise. If we allow one type of exception to be stipulated, we inadvertently drag in numerous others by the same token. Suppose we let the rule say, 'Never lie except to trick someone after having told the truth enough times in a row that your lie becomes believable.' This could be universalized without becoming self-defeating. Or we could say, 'Only lie 10% of the time,' or 'Only lie when you can be reasonably sure the lie won't be detected.' These are the kinds of principles most criminals follow when dealing with each other, after all, so why should there be any inconsistency in their being willing for the rest of us to follow them as well? In fact, Scheler thinks that if we went on long enough with these kinds of examples, we could show that there are no actual rules of conduct that strictly follow from the categorical imperative at all.[18] The principle is too formal to have material consequences.

Once we carry the criticism to this extreme, it might seem for a moment that, at least in some instances, Kant is defensible. Take the example of five people dividing five pieces of pie among themselves. Barring certain specific circumstances (such as the case in which all five people will starve unless one of them survives by eating the whole pie), there seems no way that one person can will without logical inconsistency the universalization of the rule, 'Everyone can take a second piece.' The problem is that each *can* consistently will the rule, 'Everyone can *try* to take a second piece if she wants to.'

Another problem with the categorical imperative is that it seems unclear whether it means not to do something which *everyone* should not do, or not to do something which *anyone who pleased* should not do. Smart's objection against rule utilitarianism would appear to apply to Kant's reasoning here.[19] If the categorical imperative means that we should not do something we could not will that *everyone* should do, then it would seem to have strange consequences. For example, no one should become a philosophy teacher because if everyone became a philosophy teacher, everyone would starve, thus defeating the purpose of teaching philosophy. But if we mean not to do something which *anyone who pleased* should not do, then the categorical imperative would allow that it is all right for me to teach philosophy since, if everyone *who pleased* taught philosophy, no problem would eventuate. It is a safe bet that few if any others will please. By the same token, it would become all right to lie if we happen to know that not very many people are going to want to lie, all right to murder if we know that not very many people will want to commit murder, etc. For then it would follow that the universalization of the rule of conduct to cover all those who find themselves wanting to engage in the immoral behavior would entail no inconsistency; the number of lies told would then not defeat my purpose in lying, the number of deaths would not greatly increase my chances of being murdered, etc.

So far, we have touched on the kinds of problems that arise in attempting to apply the categorical imperative to particular kinds of cases, finding that some vicious behaviors seem to be allowable by it, and some desirable ones prohibited by it (such as lying to the Gestapo to protect Jews); it does not seem to establish enough duties to support enough corresponding rights for must people's tastes, whereas it does seem to establish some duties that should not be established as universals. These observations do not exhaust the criticisms that have been raised along these same lines, but merely summarize the logic of some of the more obvious ones. But now let's take one further step, and we shall find that the failure of Kant's system was inevitable for reasons that essentially will plague all rule-bound systems.

Kant is at great lengths to emphasize that an action is not really right unless motivated by respect for the moral law. If I do the proper thing by chance, simply in the normal course of following my emotions and inclinations, then I am acting in order to accomplish a consequence toward which my psychological constitution impels me---for example, seeking happiness. In such a case, I follow mere prudence, or a hypothetical imperative. Only when following the categorical imperative, however, would I act morally. This happens only when my motivation is respect for the moral law. The objection that is raised against this notion is that this feeling of 'respect' seems to be a psychological state or emotion, like any other emotion. As such, it would be capable of motivating my behavior only if it were stronger than other motives which also happened to be present at the same time. But in this case, I would be obeying my strong- er impulse even when obeying the categorical imperative. It would then follow, if we assume Kant's principle that the *motive* is what counts, that I cannot follow the motive of respect for the moral law unless it happens to be present and happens to be stronger than other motives. It would be no more possible to voluntarily produce a strong feeling of respect than a strong feeling of sympathy for my neighbor (which Hume had suggested as an adequate motivation for moral behavior, for example) or a strong feeling of pleasure in helping others. But Kant denies that these emotions can be produced at will. If they could be produced at will, then acting according to them would not so obviously imply acting according to a merely hypothetical imperative, as Kant has initially assumed; or Kant might choose the other absurd alternative, that even acting out of respect for the moral law is acting according to a hypothetical imperative, in which case it is impossible ever to act according to a categorical imperative.

Kant's answer to this objection, of which he was somewhat aware, is that, in order for morality to be possible, man must have free will. Thus we can freely choose to act out of respect for the moral law rather than out of any other emotion. One question that arises here is quite obvious: Even if we grant free will, why is it necessary to act out of respect for the moral law and for no other reason? Could we not act out of benevolent feelings which we had also freely chosen to have? Why does Kant limit freedom just to the one emotion of respect for the moral law? If there is freedom, then why can we not freely will to love our fellow creatures, for example, and then act out of this emotion? This objection, in the final analysis, leads to confusion about what Kant is really saying, and leads some to wonder whether he himself knew.

But a more pressing problem is the problem of the possibility of a free will per se. Indeed, we saw earlier the magnitude of this problem. Kant seems to be requiring a contra-causal freedom here. But we have seen that any contracausal event would not be a result of an agent's will, so that the type of determinism we ended up with in the last chapter would rule out the kind of free will Kant seems to need in order for actions to be motivated by categorical rather than hypothetical imperatives. There simply is no free will of the kind Kant insists on.

Kant, of course, is explicit in his denial that morality would be possible without free will, since it would be meaningless to blame someone for committing an action which he was predetermined to commit. But determinists object (as we have seen) that not morality per se becomes impossible if determinism is true, but merely Kant's particular brand of morality. Kant overgeneralizes here, they say, by mistaking the notion of blame, which is only a small and dispensable part of morality, for the whole of morality. They maintain that it *does* make sense to say that people *should* do this or that type of action, if and only if *it would be better* if they did. But whether or not it would be better if they did has nothing to do with whether free will is true. Kant, of course, disagrees strongly with such a conception of morality. But his disagreement only serves to invite another criticism: Is Kant's conception of morality really the only one possible, as he brashly claims it is?

The reason Kant offers us for accepting the notion of a moral law in the first place seems to be twofold. (1) We would not be willing to live in a world with no moral principles whatever. (2) We have a moral experience, an 'experience of obligation' which must be explained in some way or other. But argument (1) seems to involve an equivocation, because, having gotten us to agree that we must have *some* conception of morality, he proceeds to demonstrate that only a categorical imperative can qualify as a moral principle *in the true sense* of the word 'moral'. But is the true sense of the word 'moral'---that is, what Kant regards as the true sense---the *only* sense that would satisfy the condition which we have agreed must be met, i.e., that there must be *some* conception of morality? Why could utilitarianism not satisfy us here? Would anyone really be unwilling to live in a world governed by, let us say, rule-utilitarianism? Or how about the Christian principle of universal love for one's fellow humans? Would we be unwilling to live in a world governed by it? Or by a Rawlsian concept of distributive justice (which requires no free will)?

Regarding argument (2), critics charge that no such theory as the categorical imperative is necessary to explain the 'experience of obligation' that we all have. It is simply an experience which tells us that we know, in a given situation, what the right and wrong thing to do is, and that we 'should' do the right thing. But this can be explained just as effectively on the basis of any other system of morality as it can by assuming Kant's theory. Moreover, many psychologists, and some philosophers (such as Aristotle) would say that it can be explained purely in terms of psychological principles; it is explainable without the assumption of a non-natural moral law. In fact, as discussed above, a 'feeling of obligation' would be perfectly conceivable even if determinism were true.

What is the ultimate cause of the failure of Kant's system? It is simply that the task he sets himself is impossible to begin with. He wants to discover some rule which it would be logically inconsistent for any rational subject to disobey, without letting the reason for the inconsistency depend on any motives of any subject. The problem is that, if no subject had any motives of any kind, then it would be a matter of indifference whether anyone obeyed any rules at all. The tenability of any such inquiry as ethics depends not only on the possibility of there being conscious beings in the universe, but on there being conscious *and emotional* beings---'emotional' in the sense of caring about something, even if only the search for something to care about, or even if only the value such beings place on continuing to exist or have placed on their existence in the past.

Any system which is 'rule-bound' in the sense we have been using will fail for the same reason. One might be able to *arbitrarily* assert that X ought to be done even if harmful to everyone and not conducive to a valuable distribution system. But one cannot *demonstrably* make such assertions, even in the modest sense of being able to adduce some modicum of evidence to support them. Such theories therefore lie outside the realm of minimally-coherent theories and must be eliminated, as must 'retributive' theories which claim that the proportion between welfare and well-doing ought to be promoted even if not beneficial---for such a theory is no more probable than its own contradiction, and indeed less so.

If 'retributive' and 'rule-bound' theories are eliminated, we are then left only with those possible theories which assert either that the sum total of individual values ought to be promoted, or that aggregate value, including the value of a 'fair distribution' of individual values, ought to be promoted. But there is nothing that ought to be done other than promote value of one sort or another. The question as to what the priority of these different kinds of values ought to be, of course, is part of our third important general question and will be deferred to the next chapter.

We are now in a position to assert with absolute certainty that there are two types of prima facie intrinsic values, and that these values, prima facie, ought to be promoted. The first has already been demonstrated; the second will be demonstrated in subsection (b) below. Since rule-bound and retributive theories have been rejected as less than minimally-coherent, it will then follow that people ought to act in such ways as to promote those values whose value can be demonstrated, without worrying about whether some non-consequentialist principle or other might take priority over the moral consequences of actions.

(a) Individual values

We saw in Chapter Two that the existence of an optimal amount of consciousness in those beings capable of consciousness inevitably has value, and that the goods necessary to this optimal conscious existence also have value. There is no need to recapitulate that reasoning here. Since the avoidance of pain, or at least severe pain, is one of the necessary conditions for this purpose, it also has value. Pleasure also has some value, though we saw in Chapter Three that if 'pleasure' is defined in a meaningful way it normally has less value than the optimal intensity of consciousness. All of these points concerning individual values are now well established. What remains to be resolved is whether aggregate value can be reduced to the mere sum of individual values, or whether there is aggregate value as distinguishable from this mere sum. We shall now see that the latter is the case.

(b) Aggregate value

We have seen that it is prima facie the case that one ought to promote the conscious existence (and, to a lesser extent, the happiness or pleasure, and certainly the absence of excruciating pain) of each individual capable of such existence. (It is understood, of course, that some beings are 'capable' of consciousness only to a negligible extent; an unfertilized egg has the 'potential' to become conscious in the same negligible sense, normally, in which I have the 'potential' to become an airplane, i.e., if the atoms of my body were appropriately rearranged and added to.) It follows that we ought to distribute the 'goods' necessary for the purpose of developing optimal consciousness in any given conscious being to as much of an extent as in any other. The real question is whether it makes any difference whether we divide, say, 100 units of such goods in some 'fair' proportion between two people, or whether we let one of the two individuals have all 100 units while the other has none. On the surface, it seems that, if our purpose were merely to maximize individual value, it would make no difference how the goods were to be distributed, as long as the total *amount* of these goods is maximized. However, this surface impression rests on a confusion about the way 'goods' are to be quantified.

In the case of an individual, there seems to be a sense in which it would be either irrational or inauthentic to incur, say, a 50% risk of losing very necessary goods in exchange for a 50% chance of gaining even much larger amounts of very 'superfluous' or 'non-essential' gratification. Such preferences seem to be obvious phenomenological data, and are regarded as completely non-controversial by many authors.[20] Pareto, for example, refers to a principle of 'diminishing utility of marginal goods,' meaning that the same good diminishes in value as the person who possesses it acquires more and more additional goods. The reason is that, given $10, a poor person is more likely to use it to buy essential or necessary goods, such as a meal, than is a rich person, who will more likely use it to buy frivolities for which no reasonable person would trade a meal when hungry. There seem to be certain types of 'necessary' or 'essential' goods which it would not be rational to trade for any amount whatever (or at least very large amounts) of 'non-necessary' or 'superfluous' goods. Goods which have equal *exchange values* on the open market may therefore have different 'use values' in different circumstances, depending on how 'necessary' or 'non-necessary' they are for the user. The same principle is a key assumption for Rawls. Why is it 'irra-

ETHICAL QUESTIONS WITH DEFINITE RESOLUTIONS 175

tional' for the person in the original position to risk abject misery or poverty in exchange for a chance to be filthy rich? The reason is the same as the reason a rational gambler would never bet his right arm on a hand of cards, no matter what the stakes. There are certain necessary or essential goods the permanent loss of which results in greater disvalue than the positive value of *any* amount of non-necessary goods could ever add up to (or at least greater than *comparatively much larger* amounts of non-necessary goods as measured in terms of their exchange value).

If the aggregate good were measured by the same standards as individual goods, and if the individual good for one person is considered no more or less aggregately good than the same amount of individual good for another, then it would follow that a greater amount of pain for one person ought not to be exchanged for a lesser amount of pleasure for someone else. This is the standard assumption of the traditional utilitarian calculus as reflected in typical cost-benefit analyses. But if we add to this principle the principle of the priority of necessary goods, it follows that one person's necessary goods should not be sacrificed in exchange for an 'equivalent amount' (as measured in exchange value) of non-necessary goods for someone else. This complication results in a very different kind of utilitarian calculus from cost-benefit analysis.

First we must note that, in reality, the distinction between necessary and non-necessary goods is not a sharp one. Instead, the extent to which a given good under given circumstances is 'necessary' is a matter of degree. Some goods are more 'necessary' than others. This means that, at all points along the continuum from 'very necessary' to 'very unnecessary' goods, a distinction must be accommodated between 'use value' and 'exchange value.' This distinction prevents the aggregate good from being equal to the mere sum of individual goods (as measured in exchange values), for the following reason: In the context of aggregate value measurement, it is possible to distinguish between 'use value' and 'exchange value,' whereas in the context of value for one individual no such distinction arises. The exchange value of a good is determined by the amount of other goods which all members of the given market, on average (in some sense), would be willing to exchange for the good in question. Suppose all exchange values are measured on a scale from 1 to 10, and suppose that for any given individual the 'minimal standard' below which one would not risk falling is 2. Any given individual will thus consider the difference between 1 and 2 to be far more important than the difference between 7 and 8. As one ascends the scale, a difference of 'one' is less and less important. However, in terms of *exchange* value, people on the average are willing to pay just one unit for any difference of one unit.[6]

For example, a given type of car may be worth less, in terms of individual *use value,* when used as a family's second car than when used as some other family's primary car. But the *exchange value* is simply the average amount of money that *people in general* could be induced to exchange for the car. The fact that for one family the car may be a necessary good whereas for another it is a non-necessary good figures into its use value, but not its exchange value. The concept of exchange value recognizes no distinction between necessary and non-necessary goods in the sense we have been discussing.

As a result, $10 worth of exchange value may have more use value to a poor person than to a rich person. The same 'amount' of goods, when measured in exchange value, is worth more or less, depending on how necessary or non-necessary the goods are to the person using them. When we consider that the extent to which goods may be 'necessary' or 'non-necessary' is a matter of degree, we realize that the aggregate value of goods cannot be accurately assigned merely by demanding that there be a 'minimal standard' below which people are not allowed to drop. Rather, it is necessary that the difference between 'necessity' and 'non-necessity' be recognized, to the extent that it exists, throughout the entire scale of values from top to bottom. In other words, the measurement of the aggregate value of goods must be done in terms of their use value rather than their exchange value. This will mean, in sum, that a good with a given exchange value has more use value to one person than to another; and that, therefore, one person ought to have that same good to a greater extent than another person ought to have it. Even if the 'good' in question is an intrinsic value, such as happiness or well-being, the same point still applies in principle, although it is difficult to measure such parameters. The difference between one unit of happiness and two must be regarded as more important than the difference between seven and eight. For no rational gambler would consider these two differences as having equal importance in her own life, and would not as willingly risk the former as the latter.

If the person who ought to have a certain good to a lesser extent has it, whereas someone who ought to have it to a greater extent does not have it, it follows that goods are not distributed (prima facie) as they ought to be distributed. There is obviously a quasi-Rawlsian sense of 'fairness', then, which hinges on the difference between necessary and non-necessary goods, which in turn gives rise to the difference between use value and exchange value. In this quasi-Rawlsian sense, we can say that 'fairness' is the condition in which all goods are had by those who ought to have them. But this is exactly the same as a condition in which existing goods are distributed so as to *maximize use value* (by contrast to exchange value). I.e., those who have the most pressing use for any given $100 *have* the $100, and those who have the least pressing use for any given $100 do not have it. And the distribution of all $100 units of goods is accordingly in proportion to the pressingness with which people need the goods (i.e., have a use for them). The primary difference between this kind of value system and that of Rawls would seem to be that this value system (let's call it 'use-value utilitarianism') treats the extent to which goods are necessary as a *variable,* rather than attempting to define a 'least advantaged' class of people as defined by some 'minimal standard.' We shall explore this issue more fully later.

ETHICAL QUESTIONS WITH DEFINITE RESOLUTIONS 177

This 'use-value utilitarianism' would also be quasi-Rawlsian in that deviations from the distribution of goods in proportion to people's needs (i.e., use for the goods) would be justified if such deviations led to an increase in the total quantity of *use* value (by contrast to exchange value) and if this additional use value is distributed 'fairly' according to the same criterion, i.e., if the goods so produced are distributed in proportion to their use value to all people rather than according to their exchange value. This criterion creates an internal conflict, of course, which we must consider in a moment.

There is therefore one concept of 'fairness' which can be summarized by the injunction 'Maximize use value!' The only essential difference between this system and utilitarianism is that utilitarians tend to think in terms of maximizing exchange values. If instead they were to maximize use value, they would end up agreeing that a type of 'fairness' (essentially, a quasi-Rawlsian type of fairness) in the distribution of goods has *intrinsic* value, not merely extrinsic value. (We also saw in Chapter Three that utilitarianism is incorrect in assuming that happiness is the only individual good, but that is beside our point here.)

The reader may by this time have thought to insist, 'Aha! But there is a contradiction here!' To be sure, the injunction 'Maximize use value!' *does* engender a fundamental moral conflict. On the one hand, it implies that we ought to distribute the valuable goods in existence according to their use value rather than their exchange value---i.e., allotting goods to each person in proportion to her need for them. On the other hand, the same injunction, 'Maximize use value!' implies that we ought to *increase* the quantity of valuable goods which *do* exist (as measured by their use-value). But there are some situations in which certain inequalities in the distribution of use values can facilitate the creation of a greater quantity of use value. *To the extent* that capitalist economic relations (which lead to distributive inequality by definition) are useful in creating greater and greater quantities of valuable things (capitalism, of course, is *sometimes* counterproductive to this end), we can say that the entire capitalist period of the history of mankind dramatizes more than anything else the conflict between these two principles. It is the classic conflict between distributive justice on the one hand, and on the other hand traditional utilitarianism---although utilitarianism has been grossly misunderstood by its own advocates because they see themselves as recommending the maximization of *exchange* value rather than of use value.

This 'use-value utilitarianism' is obviously dramatically different from the more traditional 'exchange-value utilitarianism' in its ability to accommodate justice concerns. We shall see in the next chapter that the Rawlsian type of 'fairness' corresponds essentially to the same 'fairness' implied by use-value utilitarianism. Rawls' argument from the distinction between necessary and non-necessary goods in decision theory is perfectly analogous to the use-value-utilitarian argument that goods ought to be distributed according to their use value rather than according to their exchange value---which, all else being equal, is tantamount to distributing goods on the basis of need.

However, there is still another, more radical, and in a sense less equivocal notion of fairness which can also be advocated on the basis of some of the reasoning presented earlier. I say 'less equivocal' because, if we use the definition of 'fairness' provided in the last section, the distribution of goods according to their use value is fair only in an equivocal sense. 'Fairness', in the sense defined above, refers to a distribution that prima facie ought to be promoted for reasons other than maximizing the amount of individual good. If we understand 'maximizing the amount of individual good' to mean maximizing these individual goods as measured in *exchange value,* then the distribution according to use value would indeed qualify as a kind of 'fairness' by this definition. But if we understand 'maximizing the amount of individual good' to mean maximizing these individual goods as measured in *use value,* then there is no 'fairness' which ought to be promoted for reasons other than maximizing the amount of individual good. However, in either event, there is a more radical concept of fairness that must be contrasted against this one, which can be summarized as follows.

Suppose Smith and Jones have the same amount of goods as measured in use value. And suppose the society is forced to choose between Policy A, which would not change anything, and Policy B, which would create additional goods, but for some reason could do so only on the condition that Smith would retain ownership of the total amount of additional goods, and that Jones would be slightly inconvenienced, thus creating an unequal distribution of goods. Given these options, use-value utilitarianism must unequivocally favor Policy B, assuming that Jones' inconvenience is slight enough, since Policy B promotes a greater amount of use value than Policy A. Of course, a use-value utilitarian would prefer that the additional goods be created and then distributed 'fairly' (i.e., in such a way as to maximize their use value, thus distributing them to those who most need them), but we are assuming in our example that this option is not available.

The more radical concept of fairness, however, which I shall call the 'genuinely deontic' concept of fairness, would not automatically endorse a policy which maximizes use value irrespective of the way the newly-created use value is to be distributed. It would argue that fairness in the distribution of goods is prima facie valuable regardless of whether such fairness serves to maximize the amount of use value in existence or not; that this prima facie value could even, in some instances, take priority over the value of maximizing use value. Such a position insists that each person has a prima facie 'right' to be treated fairly. This right derives from the fact that a society functions in certain crucial respects analogously to the way it would function if there were a 'social contract.'

We have defined a 'society' as any group of people who interrelate qua conscious beings in any way whatever, noting that some groups interrelate

ETHICAL QUESTIONS WITH DEFINITE RESOLUTIONS

to greater extents than others, and thus constitute 'societies' to greater extents than others. One example of a way in which conscious beings may interrelate more closely than if they were merely aware of each other's existence is the case in which people form a legitimate social contract. A 'legitimate' social contract is one which rational and authentic people would have chosen to enter if they had had an equal bargaining position with the other parties in the contract. This must be granted because no contract can be considered a true contract at all if someone would enter it only at the point of a gun or under duress. No existing government, of course, is a perfectly legitimate contract, but some more closely approximate legitimacy than others. To the extent that such a social contract exists among a group of people, the society as a whole has promised each individual that it will promote that person's interests, all else being equal. It cannot be assumed that this promise can never be overridden by some conflicting and more important value; but, prima facie, the society ought to keep the agreement which it has made with each individual, since it is better to have a legitimate social contract than not to have one. This being the case, each individual has positive rights corresponding to the fact that the society ought to keep certain aspects of the agreement, and negative rights corresponding with other aspects. (Even if there were no social contract, of course, people would have certain rights corresponding with what the society as a whole ought to do, but if there is a social contract, these rights become more extensive, as we shall see.)

The society is thus obligated, with respect to each individual, to promote that individual's welfare as agreed. Since the contract is a legitimate one only to the extent that it is one which people would have chosen to enter into under conditions of equal bargaining power (as established above), it follows that the society has an *equal* obligation to respect the terms of each contract with each individual. Thus it is prima facie obligated to promote all individuals' welfare equally, and therefore prima facie ought to distribute any benefits over whose distribution it has control on an equal basis. For, if it does not distribute all benefits equally, all else being equal, then it has not fulfilled the conditions of each contract with each individual to an equal extent. Therefore, the society ought to promote the consciousness and well-being of all members equally, and thus ought to distribute goods in such a way as to accomplish this objective. We must also consider in this context that the value of goods must be measured in terms of use value, not exchange value. So to promote the consciousness and well-being of all members equally does not mean contributing equal exchange values to all, but instead means contributing equal *use* values to all---which is tantamount to contributing to each according to her need, since the needy have more use for any given quantity of exchange value, on average, than do the well-to-do.

If the society is to promote the well-being of all members equally, then, when it comes to goods whose distribution the society has the ability to control, it ought to distribute them equally, all else being equal. It follows that, if the society has the ability (i.e., the power) to redistribute Smith's excess goods to the needy Jones, it ought to do so, all else being equal. For these are indeed goods whose distribution the society has the ability to control.

By the definition of the words 'right' and 'duty', we can say that, if the society *ought* to distribute goods with its power in a certain way, then everyone in the society has a prima facie right to have goods distributed in that way. Therefore everyone also has a prima facie duty not to interfere with their being distributed in that way.

These prima facie rights and duties apply only to the extent that all else is equal. But if there are also valid reasons to follow the use-value-utilitarian principle, 'Maximize use value' (and we have seen that there are), then there will be many instances where the intrinsic value of *maximizing* use value conflicts with the intrinsic value of *distributing* use values equally. Some correct balance between the two principles would then have to be found.

We have already seen that the society also ought to maximize use value. Now we see that the maximization of use value may sometimes conflict with the genuinely deontic concept of fairness, which is more radical in some conceivable instances than the use-value-utilitarian conception of fairness. If the argument in support of the deontic concept of fairness is sound, and to the extent that such social contracts are approximated in some really-existing society, there is a genuinely *normative* conflict between the principle that the society ought prima facie to promote deontically fair distribution on the one hand, and on the other hand the principle that the society ought prima facie to maximize use value. But if the deontic argument is *not* sound, or if such social contracts are not at all approximated in real societies, then there is still a conflict between fairness (i.e., use-value utilitarian fairness) in the distribution of existing goods on the one hand, and on the other hand creating additional goods; however, we shall see in the next chapter that it can be argued that this conflict is not a genuinely *normative* one. Since the principle of distributing existing goods according to use value and the principle of maximizing the creation of additional goods *both* flow from the *one basic* principle---that use value ought to be maximized ---it follows that the conflict can be resolved simply by calculating which particular balance between the two principles is most likely to maximize use value on the whole and in the long run. We might not be able to complete such a calculation with any degree of precision, but it appears, at least on the face of it, that in principle such a calculation is possible and is the basis on which such conflicts within use-value utilitarianism should be resolved.

It seems, however, that the argument in support of the deontic concept of fairness *is* sound. Only the extent to which it is applicable to particular, really-existing societies is in doubt. Moreover, it seems that, at least to some extent, it is applicable to really existing societies. If so, then the society prima facie ought to promote deontic

ETHICAL QUESTIONS WITH DEFINITE RESOLUTIONS

fairness, yet at the same time it prima facie ought to promote the use-value-utilitarian maximization of individual values. These two conflicting normative principles are radically independent of each other, yet are both demonstrably true. The minimum number of first principles that a coherent normative theory can contain is therefore two, and any theory which posits a rule for the resolution of the conflicts between these two principles will contain three first principles. Under no circumstances can a minimally coherent theory contain only one first principle, for to do so would be to deny one of the independent and demonstrably true first principles just mentioned.

How such conflicts might be resolved is the main question of the next chapter, which deals with quantitative and distributive problems. No definitive solution can be given, because the verification of the normative assumptions needed to resolve conflicts such as the one just described must rely on coherence comparisons of theories, not deductive proofs. But coherence comparisons by their very nature can result only in probabilistic conclusions which in principle are subject to further revision.

We *can*, however, conclude at this point that there are three intrinsic prima facie values:

(1) The existence of conscious beings to an optimal extent.

(2) The avoidance of intense pain and the promotion of pleasure or happiness.

(3) Fairness in the distribution of the goods necessary to fully conscious existence and conducive to appropriate positioning along the pleasure-pain continuum or continua, to the extent that goods serve these purposes, i.e., to the extent that things *are* goods (for 'goods', after all, have been defined as those things which do serve these purposes).

Before moving on to the third and fourth of the four major general questions which were posed at the beginning of this chapter---these remaining questions being those which involve quantitative and distributive problems---,we must quickly address the second major question, the one involving problems about the source of values.

3. *Questions About the Source of Values*

a) How does 'valuable' in the ethical sense relate to 'valued' in the psychological sense? (b) How do people acquire their values, and to what extent does this acquisition entail ethical relativism? (c) Ought people to be inculcated with certain values as opposed to others, and how would such an ought relate to the value of 'freedom'?

As far as the mere definitions of the terms are concerned, the most that can be said tautologically about the relation between 'valuable' and 'valued' is that X can be prima facie intrinsically valuable only to the extent that some possible well-informed, authentic subject *could* intrinsically value X. We can also say as a result of the argument developed in Chapter Two that, if there were no well-informed, authentic subjects who valued anything, there would still be 'values' in the sense that it would still be true to say that it would be better if there *were* some subjects. In this sense, it is possible that there could be value even if no one valued anything. It is similarly possible that there could be values which are different from any of the ones that any actually existing subjects actually value. This could be true, for example, if none of the subjects were well-informed enough or authentic enough to value the things that they would value if well-informed and authentic. It could also be true if, although the subjects were well-informed and authentic, they had not yet had the time or opportunity to execute their Aristotelian training programs. For example, if the conditions of survival were extremely bleak and conducive to fierce competition rather than cooperation, and if under these conditions conscious beings were predominantly egoistic (which even in primitive cultures they do not seem to be), morality would for the most part simply remain impossible until conditions could be improved to some minimal extent. Yet, even in such circumstances, it would be true to say that it would be better if conditions were conducive to this outcome, and that this outcome ought to be promoted insofar as possible. In this sense, such an outcome would be valuable, though a value which had not yet been fulfilled.

How do we know what would be valued by a well-informed and authentic subject, given that probably no one is perfectly well-informed and authentic? It seems inevitable that the best we can do to ensure well-informedness is to make as conscientious an effort as we can to collect the relevant information, or in some instances to imagine what the valuational result would be *if* we had all the relevant information. Similarly, the best we can do to ensure authenticity is to make as conscientious an effort as we can (given the inauthenticity present in us) to perform as complete a phenomenological reduction as we can with regard to our possible and actual motives qua authentic subjects. I have described at some length the complexity of this problem,[21] but it should not really be necessary from the *metaethical* standpoint to go into the details of the process. The important point for present purposes is that we ought to proceed on the basis of the best information we can get, in the sense discussed in Chapter Two, section 1, and we ought not purposely to proceed contrary to the best information we can get.

Since not everything that is valuable is valued, nor is everything that is valued valuable, we can easily conclude that a pure ethical relativism is not only unwarranted, but untenable. For it assumes that anything that is valued by one person is as worthy of the title 'valuable' as anything valued by any other person. Racism thus becomes as legitimate a value as tolerance, and pushpin is as good as poetry. We have seen ample evidence already to show that this is not the case. *Some* values, of course, even legitimate ones, may be completely culturally relative and others partly relative. For example, communitarians emphasize that it may be a good thing, from the standpoint of optimizing people's consciousness through a 'sense of community' (which promotes empathy), that people who share the same community also share some values of a nature which must be considered, from any objective standpoint, completely arbitrary.[22] Strictly speaking, however, the objects of these culturally-relative values are only extrinsically valuable. They serve to promote the intrinsic value of optimal consciousness, but do so no better than some different, even apparently contradictory value could have done in the context of a different culture. As Ralph Linton suggests, the same intrinsic value *must* be promoted by means of different extrinsic values if environmental conditions differ.[23] For example, Arab Bedouins value seven layers of clothing in order to keep cool, whereas many native South American Indians value nudity for the same purpose.

It is true, of course, that people do acquire their values through the 'deterministic' (in our modified sense) interaction of heredity, environment, and luck. As we saw, however, (C. S. Lewis notwithstanding)[24] the fact that someone is predetermined to believe or value something does not render the belief or value incorrect. If it did, then, of course, the conclusion that a computer reaches when it states that 2 + 2 = 4 would have to be deemed untrue because predetermined. '2 + 2 = 4' will remain as true if I have been predetermined to believe that it is true as it would be if I were predetermined to believe that it is false.

Nor does such determinism imply any ethical relativism. Different people will of course have to be excused for different moral errors which result from different life histories. Primarily for this reason, I have argued elsewhere that punishment can have only a preventive purpose.[25] As a normative question, this issue is really beyond our scope here, but it should be easy to see why this implication would follow from determinism. Nonetheless, the fact that people's values tend to be largely predetermined by the community in which they grow to maturity (most Nebraskans are traditionally Republicans) implies that the community has a prima facie responsibility, in some sense, to promote the development of certain kinds of values over others, since people's values do not come out of the clear blue. If it would be better, prima facie, for people to value tolerance than racism, then, by the definitions of 'ought' and 'duty' we have been using, the community not only ought prima facie to try to cause people to learn to value tolerance, but in fact has a prima facie duty to do so.

A problem arises when we notice that the prima facie value of inculcating desirable values may conflict with the prima facie value of 'freedom' in the sense of 'freedom from.' Even a person whose personality structure has been predetermined is still free from many factors which are presently external to him, and there are reasons to believe that this freedom has value. One reason is that it is dangerous in a real-political sense to allow any government, even a good government, the power to indoctrinate people. It is simply too likely that the government or its indoctrination ministry may fall into malicious, self-serving, or ignorant hands. For the same reason, societal indoctrination of a less formal nature is in principle just as likely to produce harm. The world has seen well enough how much harm can be inflicted by a morally indoctrinated but otherwise competent nation.

But there is a more basic reason for the value of 'freedom from.' It is the one described by phenomenologists like Gendlin,[26] who emphasize that consciousness, in order to unfold authentically (and therefore to *be* conscious to an optimal extent) needs to *become* or *unfold* in a unique pattern which the individual consciousness can only discern through a very intimate self-understanding. For an outside agent to enter the process, even as a personally concerned teacher, advisor or counselor, requires the utmost delicacy, lest the person's authentically-motivated pattern be eschewed because of the temptation of the easy but ultimately destructive path being offered (i.e., destructive to conscious development because inauthentic).

To determine how the conflict between these two prima facie values should be resolved, we need a basis on which to answer the quantitative and distributive questions about ethics. The same is required in order to resolve any other problem involving conflicts and priorities among various values. The next chapter will attempt to address these kinds of questions, which, as already indicated, are more difficult than the ones considered so far.

NOTES

[1]G. E. Moore, *Principia Ethica* (Cambridge: Cambridge University Press, 1903).

[2]This point is evident throughout Witgenstein, as throughout most of the analytic philosophers discussed above. In fact, it is one of the main reasons for the demand for operational definitions in science.

[3]Moore, 16.

[4]W. H. Werkmeister, *Theories of Ethics* (Lincoln: Johnsen, 1961).

[5]Richard Brandt, "Some Merits of One Form of Rule-Utilitarianism," in Thomas Hearn, ed., *Studies in Utilitarianism* (New York: Appleton-Cenury-Croft, 1971).

ETHICAL QUESTIONS WITH DEFINITE RESOLUTIONS

[6] J. O. Urmson, "The Interpretation of the Moral Philosophy of J. S. Mill," *Philosophical Quarterly* 3 (1953), 33-39.

[7] Ralph Barton Perry, *Realms of Value* (Cambridge: Harvard University Press, 1954).

[8] F. C. Sharp, *Ethics* (New York: Century, 1928).

[9] John Mothershead, *Ethics* (New York: Holt, 1960), 206.

[10] E.g., see Gadamer, Ihde, Bernstein, Foucault, or Lyotard.

[11] Hubert Dreyfus and Paul Rabinow, *Michel Foucault: Beyond Structuralism and Hermeneutics* (Chicago: University of Chicago Press, 1982).

[12] The passage in *Critique of Practical Reason,* p. 40, about the man who deserves a "right good beating...even if nothing further results from it" well illustrates this aspect of Kant's thinking.

[13] See note 12.

[14] E.g., *Critique of Practical Reason,* p. 72.

[15] Scheler, *Formalism in Ethics and Non-formal Ethics of Values.*

[16] J. S. Mill, *Utilitarianism* (New York: Dutton, 1931), 3-4.

[17] William Frankena, *Ethics* (Englewood Cliffs, N.J.: Prentice-Hall, 1963), 25-28.

[18] Scheler, *Formalism in Ethics.*

[19] J. J. C. Smart, "Extreme and Restricted Utilitarianism," *Philosophical Quarterly* 6 (1956), 344-54.

[20] Vilfredo Pareto, *Manual of Political Economy* (New York: Augustus Kelley, 1971); William Jaffe, "Pareto Translated: A Review Article," *Journal of Economic Literature,* December, 1972; Heinz Kohler, *Welfare and Planning* (Huntington, N.Y.: Robert E. Krieger, 1979), Chapter 2.

[21] Ellis, *An Ontology of Consciousness.*

[22] See Chapter Four, note 2.

[23] Ralph Linton, "The Problem of Universal Values," R. F. Spencer, ed., *Method and Perespective in Anthropology* (Minneapolis: University of Minnesota Press, 1954), 145-68.

[24]C. S. Lewis, "Answers to Questions on Christianity," Walter Hooper, ed., *God in the Deck* (Grand Rapids, Michigan: Eerdmans, 1970), 52ff.

[25]Ellis, *Theories of Criminal Justice;* "Fairness and the Etiology of Criminal Behavior"; "General Assistance and Crime Rates in the U. S.," *Policy Studies Review* 7 (1987), 291-303.

[26]Gendlin, *Experiencing and the Creation of Meaning; Focusing.*

CHAPTER SIX

ETHICAL QUESTIONS REQUIRING COMPARATIVE-COHERENCE RESOLUTIONS

Chapter Five established that there are certain basic principles of ethics which are definitely true. These principles must therefore be incorporated into any coherent system. Let's call these principles the 'minimal' principles of ethics. It may be possible for some viable system to *add to* these minimal principles, but none can *deny* any of them.

The minimal system just alluded to exhibits a major defect which detracts from its coherence, and may well make it less coherent than some other systems which would include the minimal principles but also add to them. The minimal system is *incomplete* in an important respect. It essentially posits two conflicting first principles: (1) Existing goods should be distributed according to their use value rather than their exchange value, which would result in fairness in the sense of essentially equal distribution of 'goods' as we have defined them; moreover, to the extent that a social contract exists, the society is prima facie responsible to distribute goods equitably according to use value (thus, for practical purposes, according to need) *regardless* of whether doing so increases the total quantity of use value in existence. At the same time, however, (2) new goods should be created so as to increase the total amount of use value in existence, which leads in many instances to very unequal distributions of goods. But the minimal system offers no criterion according to which the conflicts between these two principles can be resolved. Since both minimal principles are definitively *true,* however, the result is that the most coherent possible system of ethics will include at least two conflicting principles. And, all else being equal, a system which does not simply leave this conflict unresolved is more coherent than one which does. We must therefore explore the range of possible conflict resolution principles which arguably could be used to complete the system. And, in order to do so, we must consider systems which can only be compared with respect to their relative coherence, the result being that a more coherent system is more likely to be true than a less coherent system (for we now know that there is *some* true ethical system, through we might not be able to discover very precisely what it is).

This sixth chapter will therefore attempt to do several things. First, we shall see that, once the mathematicization of use-value utilitarianism is worked out, the Rawlsian and other approaches which emphasize decision theory in social policy represent special cases of use-value utilitarianism. Secondly, neither Rawls' *'maximin'* rule nor any other unique mathematical solution can definitively resolve the internal conflict within use-value utilitarianism between the creation of additional use values (which often tends to necessitate inequality) and the distribution of existing goods according to their use value (which tends to promote equality). Moreover, even when this internal conflict has been resolved as well as it can be, there still remains the more radical conflict between use-value utilitarianism per se on the one hand, and on the other hand the genuinely deontic concept of fairness. We shall see that there can be no one fundamental and provable principle from which the value of both deontic fairness and the maximization of use value could be logically deduced. If there were, a definitive, unique resolution for the conflict might be possible at least in principle. As it is, there is no definitive, unique resolution, and we must be content with the most probably correct, i.e., the most coherent, resolution.

We must therefore explore the possibility that non-minimal coherent systems can be established as more coherent than others, though not as certain as the minimal principles themselves. It may well be that a non-minimal system can be more coherent than the minimal system, because a non-minimal system can offer the possibility of resolving such conflicts (though without absolute certainty), and thus of achieving a greater degree of completeness than the minimal system. There can be no hope of completing such a vast project within the scope of this book. I shall try only to point the general direction which such an inquiry must take.

1. *The Inevitability of Moral Conflict*

No coherent ethical system can deny the reality of conflicts between the values whose existence were demonstrated in the last chapter. It must therefore confront the question: On what basis do we decide on the *amount* of value that different things have, assign the order of priority of values, and determine the right way to distribute these valuable things? Many theories try to avoid some of these questions by keeping our attention focused elsewhere. For example, systems of 'respect for persons' ethics sometimes try to evade the distributive question by insisting that the principle of respect for persons must *never* be violated. But to insist on the inviolability of this principle is to dodge the question of distribution just as surely as a utilitarian would dodge it if he were to say that the principle that everyone should be made as happy as possible must never be violated. For the question remains as to how we are to distribute respect for persons in those instances where those goods and rights due to people as a result of the principle of respect for persons *conflict* with each other.[1]

Similarly, communitarianism often tries to sidestep the distribution question by insisting that the values themselves result from the ethos transmitted by the community and its culture, and that the community should thus distribute goods according to the principles of the 'community values' which the community has already inculcated in its individuals.[2] But, like Rousseau in his exaltation of the 'general will,' they forget that the 'community' consists of majorities and minorities on various issues, and of individuals whose rights and interests will always conflict with each other to greater or lesser extents.[3]

In addition to the need for ethical theories to address the types of questions just mentioned, there is also the need that these questions be made mathematically or quasi-mathematically commensurable with each other. I.e., we must decide what is to happen when the maximization of whatever it is that is valuable conflicts with the principle according to which the valuable things are to be distributed. What happens if a fair distribution system causes the production system to grind to a halt? The values posited by the principles of value-maximization and 'fair' distribution (in either the deontic or the use-value-utilitarian sense) must somehow be measured against each other so that their relative priority in various contexts can be determined.

One way to accomplish this purpose is to regard fairness in distribution as simply one value among other values, as did Moore.[4] We can then assign a certain value to fairness, devise a way to measure the amount of fairness or unfairness that is engendered by an action or policy, and compare this negative or positive quantity with the negative or positive amounts of other types of value that are produced by the same action or policy. But, in the first place, the amount of fairness that is considered to be equal in value to a given amount of human welfare or 'happiness' seems of necessity to be a completely arbitrary decision in this system. And, in the second place, this strategy often leads to a kind of infinite regress. For, if fairness becomes a quantity that can be measured, then the question arises whether we should maximize the *amount* of fairness that can be produced in a given situation, or *distribute* the fairness as fairly as possible. For example, suppose that many impoverished people are being deprived of their right to receive welfare benefits because of insufficient resources to administer the programs effectively. By simplifying procedures, we could increase the number of applications being processed, thus decreasing the number of people who are in effect being deprived of their right to receive the benefits. But the price to be paid for this simplification of the procedure is that each case is a little more likely to be decided in an unfair way; computations are less precise and based on less complete information, so that the amount that each person receives is likely to be less fair. Anyone who refuses to admit that such conflicts occur simply has never worked in a welfare department or studied the way such operations function. Such conflicts occur literally thousands of times per day, and the entire system is completely permeated with them, even down to its computer software and hardware.[5] The philosophical import of this point is that, if fairness becomes just another commodity to be produced and distributed, *a la* Moore, then fairness itself becomes subservient to a larger, quasi-utilitarian calculus in which, in principle as well as in practice, great quantities of fairness can be sacrificed in favor of even greater quantities of general welfare---which quantities, again, seem also to be incommensurable with each other.

Rawlsians try to resolve this dilemma by means of game theory. But the raging controversies as to whether this or that decision principle should be used, and whether a given decision principle leads to this or that social policy, betray the fact that, no matter how a decision principle for the person in the original position is formulated, the dilemma remains.[6] For example, to insist that there must be a mathematically determined 'minimum standard' below which *no one* is allowed to fall is, first of all, to ignore the complexity of the way the actual world inevitably operates. The entire federal and state budgets could be spent administering the welfare system more effectively, yet some unfair denials of applications would fail to be caught. Given smaller expenditures, more unfair denials will slip through.

There is no escaping the reality of such trade-offs. Moreover, when we begin to mathematicize these concepts in the next section, we shall see that, if the minimal standard is set low enough so that any rational and self-interested person in the original position would be absolutely unwilling to risk falling below that particular standard for the sake of a good chance for *any* amount of gain whatever, then such a low standard can hardly masquerade as a guarantee of fair distribution in any meaningful sense. Similar problems arise if we interpret the 'maximin' principle, not as insisting on a 'minimal standard,' but simply as insisting that each decision must favor the 'least advantaged' position.

Now some might think---or at least hope---that conflicts between opposing normative principles can be resolved by showing that each of the two principles can be deduced from some other principle, which would then become the true first principle of the system. Such an overarching first principle would not only imply that the other two principles ought to be followed when there is no conflict; it would also allow a determination as to which one should take priority when there *is* conflict. In the case of the two conflicting principles of use-value utilitarianism, for example, it seems that the one overarching principle from which both are deduced---'Maximize use value!'---should be able in principle (if not easily in practice) to resolve the conflict.

There are two problems with this hoped-for solution. In the case of use-value utilitarianism, the problem is that the one first principle does not allow the inference of one *unique* solution to the conflict, as we shall see. In the case of conflicts between principles each of which is *independently provable* (e.g., the conflict between use-value maximization and deontic fairness), the problem is worse still. It is simply that, even if a single overarching principle could be found, and even if it could be independently proven, the fact would remain that both of the original conflicting principles can each also be independently proven *without reference to the overarching principle.* Thus, to the extent that the overarching principle prescribes that each of the two independently-provable but conflicting principles should give up or compromise its fundamental value assertion in any situation, the overarching principle itself conflicts with each of the originally-conflicting principles, yet has no legitimate claim to take priority over either of them. Instead of resolving the conflict, it creates new conflicts between itself and each of them.

A possible third alternative beyond utilitarian and deontological distribution systems has been gaining favor recently, an alternative which would like to undercut the very basis of the utilitarian/deontology dichotomy. It is variously labeled as 'perfectionism', 'developmentalism', 'self-actualizationism', and 'personalism'.[7] But, although such developmental approaches try to undercut the distinction on which distributive choices are based, essentially the same kind of question can be posed to these systems in their own terms: I.e., if something like human self-development is taken as the most important intrinsic value, then the question arises whether opportunities conducive to its generation should be aggregately maximized, or whether opportunities conducive to a lesser total quantity of self-development, but more *fairly distributed,* should be encouraged. Not only does this question pose a problem for developmental theories; it is also a problem for justice theories like Rawls' to the extent that these theories also must assume, as does Rawls, that the rational reflector in the original position will want to see opportunities for self-development incorporated into the social contract both because self-development is likely to be a desirable good for most individuals, and also because the effective functioning of the society crucially depends on the sense of community that will naturally be enhanced by the self-development of individuals, given the 'laws of moral psychology.'

If we survey the goods that were established earlier as definitely valuable, we find that these values conflict with each other in four fundamental ways. Some of these conflicts can be resolved empirically or through phenomenological reflection; others are irreducibly normative conflicts and require normative principles for their resolution. The four inevitable moral conflicts can be summarized as follows:

First, there is a conflict within each individual between happiness-maximization and conscious development. The resolution of this conflict is in principle available to phenomenological reflection. As such, it need not concern us in detail here.[8] We should note, however, that it is obvious (as discussed in Chapter Four) that, at low values for happiness (i.e., extreme misery), increasing happiness takes priority over the value of conscious development. At high values for happiness (i.e., when the value of frivolous, non-necessary pleasures are at stake), the value of conscious development tends to take priority. The point at which these two curves meet is a matter for phenomenological investigation.

Secondly, as we have clearly seen, there is a conflict within use-value utilitarianism between creating additional value and distributing the existing value fairly. The next section will be devoted primarily to the attempt to resolve this type of conflict. Although it will appear at first as though this conflict can have a unique and completely empirically (or phenomenologically) determinable resolution, without positing any additional *normative* conflict-resolution principle, such an empirical resolution proves very elusive, probabilistic, and indeterminate in its own right.

The third type of moral conflict is perhaps the most crucial of all. Even if the conflict within use-value utilitarianism can be resolved, that resolution must still be balanced against the conflicting value posited by the genuinely deontic concept of fairness. And the resolution of *this* conflict must be unquestionably normative in character.

The fourth conflict is the conflict between optimizing the consciousness and well-being of those who already exist, and optimizing the consciousness and well-being of those who do not yet exist, or exist only potentially. We have established so far that the most fundamental principle of value theory is that the existence of conscious beings has value. It would therefore seem that, all else being equal, if and to the extent that we want to maximize use value, we ought to create additional conscious beings in the future. Moreover, since the well-being of conscious beings has intrinsic value, to the extent that beings are conscious or have the potential to become conscious, and since these future possible beings have the potential to become conscious, then the actualization of the conscious beings---by way of bringing them into existence---has intrinsic value. But it is well known that the well-being of future peoples can conflict with that of existing beings.[9] And, in principle, the very *creation* of a maximal number of additional beings can impinge on both the welfare and the conscious self-development of those who already exist.[10] This conflict, then, is a really complex one which includes as facets within it all three of the other conflicts just mentioned.

We have said that the resolution of the first of these four conflicts depends in principle on empirical evidence and/or phenomenological reflection. Now a use-value utilitarian might very well argue that the second conflict also---the conflict between use-value creation and distribution---can be resolved empirically because its resolution is simply to appeal to the ultimate principle from which both conflicting principles are derived: 'Maximize use value!' If, for example, a given policy---call it Policy A---creates enough goods that, given the distribution system stipulated in the policy, it brings about a greater total quantity of use value than Policy B, then it ought to be preferred over Policy B even if B would distribute goods more in accordance with their use value than A. This principle, in fact, is the very essence of utilitarianism.

But there is still a problem with this resolution. Essentially, it is that, once Policy A has been carried out, it is still true that, given any 10 units of use value, it is as much the case that John ought to have them as that Bill ought to have them. Furthermore, if John has more, then it would increase the use value of some of John's goods if we were to redistribute them to Bill. Thus we ought to redistribute them to Bill. But we must also remember that, if John had known in advance that we were going to redistribute some of his goods to Bill, then he would not have had as much incentive to produce them in the first place. So, first of all, we must work out a delicate formula to determine how much of John's goods to distribute to Bill, and how much to let him keep. And then we must decide whether the government ought to actually do what it has promised John it would do. If so, then we seem to be advocating some kind of 'social contract' concept, which would then tend to necessitate an obligation on the part of the government or society to distribute goods on an equitable basis according to need, independently of whether doing so increases the total quantity of use value in existence, as we saw in the last chapter. Another problem is that, in theory, we should be able to simply calculate which policy will create the greatest amount of use value 'on the whole and in the long run.' But, in practice, there is no way to know how far into the 'long run' we should calculate our present actions, especially since there will inevitably be a point beyond which all our present calculations are going to be completely inaccurate.

Another complication arises from the importance of the interrelations between this conflict and the others---especially the conflict within each individual between happiness and conscious development. The problem is that, as soon as John realizes that he can enjoy his additional benefits only at the expense of Bill's suffering (in some hypothetical cases), he must cut off empathy with Bill qua conscious being. This attitude in turn reduces John's capacity for conscious existence. So, even if he benefits from the additional goods in the sense of getting enjoyment out of them, he is also harmed in that his consciousness is reduced in other respects, so that his total consciousness may well be reduced even though his enjoyment has increased. He must therefore do something to increase his empathy with Bill, which can be accomplished only by erasing some of the inequitable distribution as between them. Moreover, he cannot simply *give* some of his goods to Bill, for the effect of a relationship of dependency between the two men will counteract their empathy with each other qua conscious beings. To the extent that Bill and John relate to each other qua conscious beings (i.e., belong to the same 'society' as defined above), there is a certain extent to which neither of them can progress in the prospering of his pleasure and consciousness unless he tries his best to drag the whole society with him into this prosperity. And part of this attempt consists in resisting unequal distributions of goods, all else being equal.

So there is a certain tendency for any policy which distributes goods unequally to harm both the victim *and* the beneficiary of the inequality. And this tendency will always partially counteract the beneficial consequences of any policy whose purpose is to increase benefits at the expense of a resulting unfair distribution.

Suppose, for example, that John and Bill have finished dinner and are to share a pie for dessert. Since both people are well-fed and content, the pie is a very non-necessary good. Now suppose John has a coupon which would enable him to exchange the pie for a three-month supply of pies, but only if he is able to exchange the *whole* pie. In addition, suppose he will have no opportunity to share his extra pies with Bill, who is leaving town that night. If John therefore takes the whole pie (thus distributing it unequally), the total amount of pleasure to be gained from the pie will be increased. On the other hand, because John has cut off his universal empathy by taking Bill's share, he has reduced his overall consciousness, though his pleasure is of course increased. Since the degree of consciousness one can experience is more important than the degree of pleasure one can experience, John must choose to forego the extra pies and instead simply share the one pie equally with Bill. It is important to note that, in this case, the true *use* value of the one pie shared equally is greater than the use value of the three-month supply of pies shared unequally, even though the three-month supply has far greater *exchange* value.

It is often asserted that utilitarianism is the most coherent possible system because it has only one first principle. Since there can be no reasonable system which does not value the general welfare to some extent, it would follow that any system which values other things besides the general welfare can do so only by positing more than one first principle. But number of first principles is one of the important determinants of the coherence of ethical systems. And as far as other criteria for coherence are concerned, utilitarianism is on at least as firm a foundation, since the thing that it asserts as valuable---human happiness or well-being---is at least as plausible a value as any other.

We have seen, however, that it is possible to distinguish between utilitarianism in its usual sense, which advocates maximizing *exchange* value, and on the other hand a type of system which would advocate maximizing use value. Exchange-value utilitarianisms are completely untenable because they equivocate the concept of 'value'. While the thesis that human happiness or well-being has intrinsic value may be a plausible one (at least if we count self-actualization as a type of 'well-being'), it is plausible only if the value in question is measured in terms of use value. For a car which is used as a family's second car does not promote as much well-being as the same car would promote if it were used as a family's first car. Exchange-value utilitarianisms ignore the distinction between necessary and non-necessary goods, and thus make the mistake of thinking that human happiness or well-being can be measured in terms of exchange values.

By contrast, if a utilitarian system were to advocate the maximization of use value, the result would be that, as we have seen, the two corollaries of this principle tend to conflict with each other, and some further principle is needed to resolve the conflict.

In reality, we shall find that the attempt to establish a use-value utilitarianism would therefore result in three basic principles: (1) The principle that existing goods should be distributed according to their use value, which would result in fairness in the sense of equal distribution of use value; (2) The principle that new goods should be created so as to increase the total amount of use value in existence, which leads in many instances to unequal distributions of use value; and (3) some conflict-resolution principle to resolve the conflicts that arise between (1) and (2). Since the only viable utilitarianism would be a use-value utilitarianism, this means that the most coherent possible utilitarian system would have not one but three first principles---the same number that many deontic systems have.

Utilitarianism thus has no privileged status when it comes to number of first principles. Moreover, we shall see increasingly in this chapter that use-value utilitarianism has another problem. Its implications conflict to some extent with the implications of the 'genuinely deontic' concept of fairness which we saw in the last chapter definitely ought to be taken into consideration.

Since both use-value utilitarian maximization of value and deontic fairness are definitively true yet conflicting principles, the minimum number of principles in any coherent system is two, and the minimal system of ethics is the one that contains these two independent principles but lacks a resolution principle for them.

Before we can do justice to the problem of how to resolve the internal conflict within use-value utilitarianism, we must inevitably consider the project of *mathematicizing* a system for calculating and coordinating use values. The subtleties which will ultimately determine which resolution is most coherent depend crucially on making essentially mathematical comparisons. Moreover, recent philosophers have in effect attempted such mathematical solutions in the form of decision theory. Also, the conflict between use-value utilitarianism per se and the deontic concept of fairness seems to require some sort of mathematical resolution. When we ask 'What is the proper balance between X and Y in various contexts?' we are in effect asking for a mathematical formula, even if the ideal of a mathematical solution can be only very approximately and probabilistically realized.

2. The Mathematicization of Value

Now let's see if we can mathematicize, first, a method for the purely *use-value utilitarian* calculation of moral decisions. If this is possible, we might then be able to mathematicize a deontic-fairness decision principle which would be commensurable with it, finally arriving at one ultimate, composite decision principle. We shall see, however, that no unique solution is possible in the comparative quantification of necessary and less-necessary goods. If not, then there also can be no unique solution to the problem as to which ultimate decision principle is the correct one. The result is that comparative-coherence must be our guide in evaluating proposed decision principles.

First, let's try to construct a mathematicization of use-value utilitarianism per se. Suppose we rank goods as very necessary, moderately necessary, or very unnecessary. Since the relationship between use value and exchange value depends on the extent to which goods are 'necessary', it is possible that we can then compute their use value by multiplying their exchange values by 3, 2, and 1, corresponding respectively to 'very necessary', 'moderately necessary', and 'very unnecessary.'

Now suppose Policy A would create 2,000 units of exchange value, which would be distributed equally among 100 people. Each person would have 10 units at necessity factor 3 (i.e., very necessary) and 10 units at necessity factor 2 (moderately necessary). Each person's 20 units of exchange value are thus worth 50 units of use value. The total amount of use value in existence in this case is thus 50 X 100 = 5,000 units of use value.

And suppose Policy B would create 5,000 units of exchange value, which would be distributed equally among 99 of the people, leaving the 100th person with none. Each of the 99 people would then have approximately 51 units of exchange value. The first 10 of these units, let's assume, would be at necessity factor 3, and the remaining 41 are at necessity factor 2. The total use value is thus (30 + 82) X 99 = 11,088 units of use value. This amount of use value clearly exceeds the 5,000 units of use value promoted by Policy A. Thus Policy B, which reduces one person to abject misery for the sake of giving everyone else in the society some relatively unnecessary goods, should be preferred over Policy A according to a use-value utilitarian who uses this system of calculation.

Obviously, *something has gone wrong* in this calculation! A natural question which arises about it is this: Why does the use-value utilitarian concept of *'fairness'*, which should result from distributing goods according to use value (i.e., according to need) end up getting such a comparatively low priority in this analysis? The problem is that the way we have constructed the *measurement scale* for the 'necessity factor' corresponding to goods at various levels of necessity is completely *arbitrary*. In fact, we would have ended up with a different outcome if, instead of assigning the numbers 3, 2, and 1 to the three levels of necessity, we had assigned the numbers, say, 10, 5, and 1, or 20, 10, and 1.

In reality, the only correct way to ascertain the true proportion between necessary and non-necessary goods is to ask this kind of question: If I were deliberating under well-informed and authentic conditions, what would be the amount of pleasure for the enjoyment of which I permanently would be willing to lose my only means of transportation to work? Here we are asking how much relatively non-necessary benefit I would trade for an extremely necessary one (my only means of transportation to work, even if it consists of an old jalopy with very little exchange value). Of course, there is no such amount; mathematically, then, the amount of pleasure that would be exchanged for transportation to work is virtually infinite. In terms of 'necessity factors,' the necessity factor for a given exchange value's worth of one's only means of transportation to work is almost infinite, i.e., is always greater than the necessity factor associated with the exchange value of any given amount of very unnecessary goods such as, say, recreational motorboats. If we assign a necessity factor of 2 to the enjoyment of motorboats, so that 5 units of exchange value for motor boats equals 10 units of use value, then the use value of 5 units of someone's only means of transportation is almost infinitely greater than this amount.

I say *almost* infinitely greater' because the necessity factor for no good can be literally infinite. If it could, then it would be mathematically impossible to compare the value of saving one person from being tortured to death with the value of saving thousands---just the kind of decision that Resistance groups had to make during World War II. This problem, however, is a common one in mathematical relationships involving infinity, and is not of primary concern to us here. As George Gamow explains, it is sometimes necessary to recognize different levels of 'infinitude', some 'larger' than others.[11] For example, the number of infinitesimal points in an inch is infinite, but the number of such points in two inches is twice as great, and the number of such points in the universe is of a different order altogether.

The important point is that, no matter how much very-necessary or even moderately-necessary pleasure can be enjoyed by no matter how many people, the value of the necessity factor for someone's only means of transportation must be defined in such a way that no amount of such enjoyment can ever exceed one instance of necessary transportation. The 'intuition' that tells us that any system which allowed such trade-offs would be a fundamentally unjust system is simply the phenomenological experience of the fact that we ourselves would experience the value of necessary transportation as exceeding the value of any given quantity of very non-necessary pleasures.

But when we begin to consider less extreme examples, we find that there are still an infinite number of ways that we could assign the relative quantities of the necessity factors of various goods. Moreover, however we do assign these quantities, we will end up advocating a system which incorporates a greater or lesser amount of unfairness for the sake of maximizing some not-so-necessary goods. For we cannot define the scale in such a way that some given amount of any given good has more use value than *any conceivable* amount of the next-less-necessary good in the hierarchy.

What we are really asking, then, is a very similar question to the one Rawls asks himself: What decision principle would a rational (i.e., well-informed and authentic) person use in comparing the relative merits of less necessary with more necessary goods? Rawls chooses the 'maximin' rule; but we shall see that it is not at all clear why someone in the original position must necessarily prefer this rule over other decision rules which would also tend to give necessary goods priority over less necessary ones to some extent.

Once we grant that some goods are more 'necessary' than others, it becomes entirely possible that some goods are virtually 'absolutely necessary'---that there are some goods such that a well-informed and authentic person would not be willing to incur *any* risk of losing them for the sake of gaining *any* amount of non-necessary goods. Not only is it possible that there are such absolutely necessary goods, but whether there are or not is, in theory at least, a *factual* question, not a normative question. But the answer to this factual question has normative consequences. The existence of virtually absolutely necessary goods would imply a theory of justice at least very similar to the one Rawls has developed. In fact, it is probably true to say that much of the appeal of Rawls' theory derives precisely from the fact that he seems to enable us to answer normative questions by means of answering factual questions (i.e., by ascertaining what a person in 'reflective equilibrium' would *prefer).*

Now let's see if we can refine the mathematicization of use value in such a way as to accommodate these kinds of issues. In the process, we shall also see that the Rawlsian system of distributive justice is really only a special case of use-value utilitarianism. Suppose a society consists of four families, A, B, C and D. Family A has three cars, B and C have two each, and D has only one. Obviously, a use-value utilitarian would say that an economic growth policy which would create an additional car and give it to family D would be better (all else being equal) than a merely redistributive policy which would simply give one of A's cars to D, thus making the number of cars equal. For D would be as well off as a result of the growth policy as of the redistributive policy, whereas A would be *better* off as a result of the redistributive policy. The total amount of use value would be increased more by the growth policy than the redistributive one. Although A's third car has less use value than anyone's first and second cars, it still has some value. On the other hand, if the initial distribution of cars is as described at the outset, then a merely redistributive policy which would simply give A's third car to D, so that D would then have two cars rather than one, may well be better than an economic growth policy which would crete a fourth car for the already well-to-do A. For D's second car may well have more use value than A's *third and fourth cars combined.*

Whether or not D's second car has more use value than A's third and fourth cars combined depends on the mathematical *rate* at which additional or marginal goods decline in use value compared with goods which already exist. If a second car is worth half as much as a first car, a third car half as much as a second, and a fourth car half as much as a third, then someone's second car will indeed be worth more than someone else's third and fourth cars combined. But if each additional car is worth, say, 90% of the use value of the previous car, then D's second car is *not worth as much* as A's third and fourth cars combined. For, if the value of additional cars declines at this rate, rather than at the 50% rate assumed above, then a third car has 90% of the use value of a second car, and a fourth car has 81% of the use value of a second car; thus A's third and fourth cars combined have 171% of the use value of D's second car.

The question, then, is whether the use value of newly created goods (or 'marginal utilities') declines arithmetically, algebraically, or perhaps exponentially, or in some more complex pattern, as compared with previously existing goods.

But now consider an additional question which might shed some further light on this one. Suppose a Rawlsian reflector in the original position asks herself which of the above outcomes she would prefer. The basis for the decision will be a risk analysis in which she will consider the *probability* of being benefited or harmed and the *amount* of benefit or harm, with the loss or gain of *necessary* goods weighing more heavily in the analysis than *less-necessary* goods, and with the probability of benefit or harm determined by the *number of people* in the total society, combined with the *extent* to which each one is benefited or harmed. In the case where we assumed that each car is worth *half* the value of that family's previous car, the person in the original position will calculate that a growth policy which would produce an additional car for the already well-to-do A would give the person in the original position a 25% chance of ending up with *four* cars (if she turns out to be A), but also a 25% chance of having only *one* car (if she turns out to be D); whereas the merely redistributive policy which would simply give A's third car to D would lead to everyone's having two cars, so that the person in the original position could count on a 100% chance of enjoying exactly 1.5 units of use value (defining the first car as one unit). By contrast, the growth policy just described, resulting in a fourth car for the already well-to-do A, would offer, from the standpoint of the original position, a 25% chance of enjoying 1.87 units, a 50% chance of 1.5 units, and a 25% chance of only 1.0 unit. Now it would seem to be irrational to incur a 25% chance of gaining .37 unit in exchange for a 25% chance of losing .50 unit. In this case, then, the Rawlsian reflector apparently would recommend the same policy as would the use-value utilitarian. Note that the distinction between necessary and non-necessary goods has already been taken into consideration when we determined that D's second car had more use value than A's third and fourth cars combined; thus there is no need for the rational reflector to re-introduce this distinction after the use values have been assigned. If two goods have equal *use* values (as opposed to exchange values), there is no reason for a Rawlsian reflector to prefer the one over the other.

On the other hand, how would a Rawlsian reflector assess the same set of options if the use value of additional goods diminishes at a *small arithmetic rate* rather than algebraically or geometrically? E.g., suppose a second car is worth 90% as much as a first car, a third car is worth 90% as much as a second, etc. Then to reassign A's third car to D is to increase the amount of use value by the difference between .81 (the car's value as A's third car) and .90 (the same car's value as D's second car)---a net increase of only .09. But a policy which would let everyone keep all the cars they have, but create one additional car, to be assigned to the already-well-to-do A as her fourth car, would increase the total amount of use value by .73 (the value of anyone's fourth car). This policy, then, would increase the total amount of use value more than would the redistributive policy mentioned above, even though it does not benefit the least advantaged (D) at all. The question is: How would the Rawlsian rational reflector assess these options? By insisting that the rational reflector would necessarily use 'maximin' rather than some other decision principle, Rawls assumes that the use value of additional (less-necessary) goods diminishes algebraically or exponentially rather than at the small arithmetic rate this last example assumed. *If*, on the other hand, it *were* to be granted that the use value of additional goods increases only at a small arithmetic rate, *then the rational reflector would not use 'maximin'*. Instead, she would often prefer policies which benefit the privileged classes even though they do not benefit the least advantaged at all, or conceivably even demand a small sacrifice from the least advantaged.

It must be admitted that Rawls' only reason for assuming that the rational reflector would use 'maximin' is the way the distinction between necessary and non-necessary goods affects risk taking.[12] His essential point is that no rational person would risk necessary goods for the chance of gaining non-necessary ones. But if the distinction between necessary and non-necessary is a matter of degree rather than a rigid either-or, then this gradual distinction can be mathematicized in terms of what we have called use value. When Rawls insists on 'maximin', what he is saying is that the value of additional goods always diminishes very exponentially, so that it would never be rational to risk goods which are as necessary as those owned by the least advantaged person for the sake of gaining *any amount* of goods which are non-necessary enough to be added to those which most people already possess. This represents a *very* exponentially-diminishing value indeed for additional goods. But then, 'maximin' is a *very* conservative risk principle.

For our purposes here, the important points to be drawn from this analysis are the following: (1) Rawls' system is equivalent to a use-value utilitarianism with a very exponentially diminishing use value for additional goods. (2) Whether the use value for additional goods diminishes exponentially, algebraically, arithmetically, or in some other pattern is neither a *normative* nor a *logical* question. It is a *factual, empirical* question. To be more precise, it is a question to be answered by means of phenomenological reflection on the emotional and motivational dimension of consciousness. We must simply ask ourselves, as honestly as possible, to what extent we experience marginal goods as less-and-less valuable as we acquire more. If we experience their value as diminishing to such-and-such an extent, this experience must be accepted as an empirical fact for both Rawls and use-value utilitarianism. (3) When Rawls asks which decision principle would be used by the rational reflector in the original position, he is asking essentially the same question that the use-value utilitarian is asking when she asks whether the use value of additional goods decreases arithmetically, algebraically, exponentially, or in some other pattern.

Thus use-value utilitarianism, contrary to traditional utilitarianisms, does entail a principle of distributive justice. And at the same time, systems of distributive justice of the Rawlsian type are merely particular types of use-value utilitarianisms.

It is important to notice, however, that Rawls' assumptions are not sufficient to establish his conclusion. If the person in the original position realizes that necessary goods are fundamentally more important than non-necessary ones, and therefore should not be risked as readily, it does not follow that she must choose 'maximin' as her principle of risk-taking.[13] Nor, therefore, does it follow that she would never choose any policy which would be at all harmful to the least advantaged person. In order to make this conclusion follow, it is necessary that the readers of Rawls bring with us an unconscious intuition: We must intuit at the very beginning of *A Theory of Justice* precisely what Rawls warns us not to assume---that those policies which best promote fairness as Rawls defines it are the ones that ought to be used; in short, that fairness has intrinsic value, and that Rawls' system is meant, not to prove this value judgment, but to clarify what it means.[14] But it is precisely the fundamental intuition that fairness has intrinsic value, and that whatever would be preferred by the person in the original position corresponds with what *is* fair, that *appears* to distinguish Rawls' system from a use-value utilitarianism and to make it instead into a type of deontic system whose purpose is not merely to maximize the amount of use value that there is, but also to distribute this use value as fairly as possible.

It is true that Rawls does provide a reason for this initial assumption. Rawls' entire system is built on the assumption that its purpose is to define the properties of a fair (i.e., legitimate) *social contract*, which is the one that a rational person would choose to agree to under conditions of equal bargaining power. It is the assumption that a social contract is to be set up that justifies the intuition that the contract ought to be a fair one, and that the preferences of the person in the original position are decisive in defining what is a 'fair' contract.

But we saw in the last chapter that the assumption of a social contract leads to the conclusion that the society prima facie ought to distribute goods exactly in proportion to the need of its individuals, tending ultimately to distribute all goods exactly equally. The value of this distribution then conflicts with the result of the use-value-utilitarian calculation of the *maximization* of use value. But the calculation of the person in the original position, far from relying on 'maximin' (as we have seen), instead approximates the reasoning that a use-value utilitarian would use if she believed that the use value of additional goods diminishes exponentially rather than merely arithmetically. Rawls' system is therefore not at all an attempt to elucidate the genuinely deontic concept of fairness. Instead, it is an attempt to resolve the conflict between the use-value-utilitarian concept of fairness and the use-value-utilitarian advocacy of creating additional use values even if at the expense of use-value-utilitarian 'fairness'. As such, Rawls' system is really a purely use-value-utilitarian one and does nothing toward resolving the conflict between the maximization of use value and the intrinsic value of genuinely deontic fairness. But because Rawls does not see himself as a use-value utilitarian, he chooses a decision rule, 'maximin', which the rational reflector in the original position really would not choose. What decision principle the rational reflector *would* choose is, as indicated above, an empirical and phenomenological question. But we have seen that it would not favor the least advantaged position as heavily as Rawls thinks it would. However, what decision principle the person in the original position would choose is really irrelevant to what is fair in the genuinely deontic sense anyway. Fairness in the deontic sense is much simpler than Rawls' decision theory would lead us to believe. It corresponds simply to the prima facie aggregate value of an *exactly equal* distribution of goods. It is only after the value of this deontic fairness is balanced against the outcome of a use-value-utilitarian decision that we end up with the conclusion that what ought to be done is to allow somewhat unequal distribution, though not too unequal.

One might at first be tempted to think that a use-value utilitarianism does not have exactly the same implications as a Rawlsian system---that, in a use-value utilitarian system, for example, it might conceivably be legitimate to force an individual to suffer an amount of hardship that a rational person in the original position would not be willing to contract for. The reason for this supposed difference is that, in the Rawlsian system, the person in the original position must compare one person's risks of losing certain goods with one person's chance of gaining certain goods. By contrast, use-value utilitarianism compares the amount of use value lost by one person with the amount of use value gained, not by one other person, but by the society as a whole. But it must be remembered that the Rawlsian rational reflector would also have to measure her *risk* of undergoing each possible outcome. And this risk corresponds to the *number of people* who will end up undergoing each outcome. To ascertain whether a Rawlsian risk analysis yields any different outcome from a use-value utilitarian decision, we must therefore note that, in both cases, the comparative value of any proposed policy is a function of (1) the amount of benefit or harm to each person, (2) the necessity of the goods gained and lost by each person, and (3) the number of people who will gain or lose as a result of the policy. It then becomes apparent that the 'number of people' criterion does not in the least distinguish Rawls' system from use-value utilitarianism. Rawls' system is rather one particular *type* of use-value utilitarianism, and each of the numerous interpretations and reinterpretations of the Rawlsian system is still another specific type of use-value utilitarianism.

It is very instructive to notice a certain source of incompleteness which causes incoherence in the Rawlsians type of system, and which for the same reason will cause incoherence in use-value utilitarian systems generally. Suppose we grant the Rawlsian assumption that the person in the original position would allow unequal distribution only in instances where the least advantaged person's condition is improved to some extent, however slight. There is a major problem with this kind of solution. Suppose, at the beginning of mankind, everyone was very bad off. In the next generation, the majority's condition was improved exponentially while improving a minority's condition only negligibly. In the third generation the same thing happened again, until finally we ended up with a very well-to-do majority and a minority which is negligibly better off than in cave-man days. Now, certainly, if we measure value in terms of use value, we ought to redistribute goods so that those who need certain goods worst would have them, i.e., distribute them more fairly. But the less-fair distribution just described is justifiable in terms of Rawls' theory. Thus Rawls' theory justifies doing what we ought not to do.

A defender of Rawls could protest that, according to Rawls, if at any given point in history it would benefit the least advantaged person more to redistribute the existing wealth than to generate more wealth, then the former is what ought to be done at that point. But there is a problem with this defense. It is almost always the case that, *in the short run*, redistribution of goods would benefit the least advantaged more than would any available scheme for producing a larger quantity of goods, at least if this redistribution could be accomplished without such traumatic upheavals as to destroy the system of production itself (as often happens just after violent revolutions). On the other hand, it is also true that, *in the long run*, the least advantaged person may be benefited more by increased productivity than by redistribution. The essential problem is this: The least advantaged person who is expected to sacrifice *now* may not be numerically *the same individual* as the least advantaged person at some future time who is expected to benefit as a result of his least-advantaged ancestor's sacrifice. If we count the interests of the members of all past, present and future generations as on an equal footing, then it would be unfair by Rawls' own standard to force the least advantaged member of one generation to benefit less than she might otherwise benefit, in order that the least advantaged member of a later generation might benefit more. For the least advantaged member of the earlier generation is, *ex hypothesi* in this case, less advantaged than the least advantaged member of the later generation. Therefore, by Rawls' own standards, the interests of the earlier least-advantaged person ought to take priority over the later one. So, if we were to apply this standard at any given point in history, we would simply redistribute all goods equally (or at least as equally as feasible) throughout the population and let it go at that. And in this case, the capitalist system of production and exchange---which even Marx admits was historically necessary in order to raise the general standard of living above what we would now consider abject poverty---never would have been allowable. This kind of interpretation of Rawls' system, then, would give absolute priority to equality at the expense of the general welfare. This cannot be a tenable position, because we have already seen that both equitable distribution of existing goods *and* increasing the absolute amount of use value have intrinsic value, and thus that the correct moral system must find some correct balance between the two, not simply sacrifice one completely for the sake of the other.

A basically similar problem detracts from the completeness, and thus from the coherence, of use-value utilitarian systems generally. If we force the least advantaged of one generation to forego a redistributive policy at any given moment in history in order to increase productivity, then when the fruits of the increased productivity are reaped, at least some of those who have sacrificed will be dead and thus will not be present for the eventual redistribution-to-increase-use-value to come. If the injunction 'Maximize use value!' means to maximize the total amount of use value to be summed up only *at the end of history,* then goods will never be redistributed (except insofar as doing so does not conflict with maximizing productivity), and therefore the value of producing additional use value must take absolute priority over the value of redistribution in all instances. On the other hand, if 'Maximize use value!' is interpreted to mean that we should maximize the amount of use value that can be enjoyed at some or any particular moment *in* history, then redistributive policies will at that point take absolute priority over increasing productivity in every conceivable instance. However, the further into the future we plan, the less accurate will be the predictions on which our plans are based; thus there must be some correct balance between the extremes so that neither of the conflicting principles can take absolute priority over the other. We must both maximize use value now (thus redistributing goods) *and* maximize it later (thus increasing productivity at the expense of optimal redistribution), and there can be no unique and definitive mathematical resolution for the conflict. Moreover, any attempt to resolve it also presupposes a resolution of the fourth of the fundamental conflicts listed above---the conflict between the value of existing conscious beings and of future possible conscious beings. But we shall see presently that there is no unique and definitive mathematical resolution for that conflict either. In principle, the uncertainty resulting from the failure to accurately predict the future is a factual rather than a normative one; but the uncertainty resulting from failure to assess the value of future possible conscious beings as compared with present ones is essentially a normative uncertainty, and can be even approximately and probabilistically resolved only after we have confronted that problem directly.

Thus, although it is difficult to discuss the problem of future possible people without first having considered the relative importance of genuinely deontic fairness, it will be best to go ahead and consider the problem of future people at this point. For such a discussion is needed in order to appreciate the extent to which the resolution of even the conflict within use-value utilitarianism is susceptible only to a probabilistic coherence resolution, not a unique and definitive one.

3. The Problem of the Value of Future Possible Conscious Beings

The conflict between optimizing the consciousness and well-being of present conscious beings and maximizing the number of future possible conscious beings is a normative conflict which is susceptible only to a comparatively coherent (not a mathematically unique and definitive) resolution. Clearly, the principle of fairness---whether the genuinely deontic fairness principle, or only the use-value-utilitarian one--- demands that the interests of each conscious being who is going to exist in the future be considered just as important as the interests of each presently existing being. But the real problem is deeper and more difficult than the question of whether and to what extent we ought to promote the interests of those who are *going to* exist in the future.

The problem is to decide how many of such beings we ought to try to *bring into* existence, given the possibility that the endeavor to increase the number of future conscious beings may sometimes conflict with the interests of those who already exist. Since consciousness definitely has prima facie value, it would seem to follow that we ought to facilitate the future existence of conscious beings. But what *amount* of value does each of these *merely possible* future people have compared with the value of an *actual* person who already exists?

It cannot be denied that possible future people have some value, because their existence is necessary in order for there to be any future value whatever. In fact, the existence of an optimal number of people will be likely to facilitate a maximum amount of value, both because the existence of these conscious beings will be intrinsically valuable (to the extent that such beings are conscious), and because their existence will facilitate other values besides the mere *existence* of conscious beings. I.e., it will facilitate, in many instances, the attainment of goals and purposes which these beings will choose to set for themselves (such as, for example, the actualization in each person of a greater degree of consciousness). I say the existence of these future people will be *likely* to facilitate value, not that it will be certain to do so, because it is conceivable that the existence of some conscious beings will lead to more negative than positive value, although, under normal circumstances, at least in our experience so far, conscious beings bring about more positive than negative value (as evidenced, for example, by the fact that most people do not choose to commit suicide).

Furthermore, it is obvious that actual people and possible future people have exactly the same value as far as their being necessary to there being any value at all is concerned. The existence of each future being is as necessary to there being a given quantity of value in the future as a present being is necessary to there being that same quantity of value at present. However, there are certain differences between the amount of value which, at present, has been brought into being by actual people and the amount that has been brought into being by possible future beings. For example, at present, it makes a difference to each actual being whether her actually existing hunger, which she actually feels, is satisfied. Not to satisfy the hunger brings about negative value which must be subtracted from the total of positive value in that person's life, as well as from the total of positive value which exists generally. By contrast, future possible people have not yet begun to care about whether they get something to eat. To illustrate the difference this makes, suppose we are confronted with the option as to whether we should (a) feed 100 people who now exist at the expense of sacrificing the existence of 100 future people, or (b) allow the 100 actual people to starve so that the existence of the 100 additional future people would be facilitated. It is inescapable, under normal conditions, that feeding the actual people has greater net intrinsic value, because the pain and anguish actually experienced by the actual people and their friends and relatives must be taken into account and subtracted to obtain the net total of value; we must consider the negative value of all the wasted effort that has already been devoted to the achievement of goals which now will be thwarted just as they are almost within the person's grasp. Analogously, it is worse to have the completed manuscript of a book destroyed than to lose the mere outline of a projected book. In the same way, it is worse to destroy an actual person, whose actualization has already consumed a great deal of striving, effort and suffering, than to merely prevent the existence of a future possible person whose actualization has not yet consumed any striving, effort or suffering. This logic is essentially similar to the basis of James Rachels' notion of 'having a life.'[15] What it means to 'have a life' is to be engaged in ongoing projects whose realization involves an unfolding series of stories or plot developments, many of which would be cut off in mid-course if the person were to die.[16] For these kinds of reasons, according to Rachels, it is more tragic for a mature adult to be struck down in the flowering of his self-actualization than for an infant to die in childbirth, although the latter is also of course a bad thing. For the same reason, the death of an infant in childbirth, who already 'has a life' to some extent in that it wants to exist and wants to have its hunger, thirst and other needs gratified, is worse than the mere failure of a possible future person to come into being in the first place.

Of course, there may be special circumstances in which future possible people have more value, all things considered, than actual people. These instances are the ones in which the future possible people have *extrin-*

value in addition to their intrinsic value. For example, if the 100 future possible people are the *only* 100 people who will exist at that time, then their existence is necessary in order for there to be any value at all at that time. Not only is it better that there be some value than that there be no value, but the value of there-being-some-value as opposed to no-value is a more *necessary* value than any other on the scale from very-necessary to very-non-necessary values. Also, these 100 people, if they are the only 100 who exist at that time, are necessary if humankind is to reproduce itself so that there can be an indefinite number of future generations of people, each one of which will have value. But all of these considerations apply only to the *extrinsic* value of the 100 future possible people in question. As far as intrinsic value is concerned, the actual present people still have more value than those who do not yet exist, for the reasons mentioned above.

There are many specific normative problems in the working out of the problem of our duties and supererogatory oughts toward future generations which we cannot take the time to go into here.[17] For example, it might seem that another important point that affects the comparative value of actual and future people is that we (who now exist) are members of the same society with actually existing people to a greater extent than the extent to which we constitute a society with future possible people. However, it is not at all clear that an ideal, hypothetical social contract (which is the one that we ought to try to implement, insofar as possible) could not include people from different generations as parties to it, and that the veil of ignorance could not then include ignorance as to which generation one will belong to. If so, then, even though it is better to preserve the existence of an actual person than to facilitate the existence of a future possible person, it might still very well be the case that, once it has been established that a future person is going to exist, her needs and interests should count the same as those of any presently existing person, both with respect to use-value utilitarian calculations and with respect to deontic fairness.

Given that an actual person has more value than the bringing into existence of a merely possible future person, on what basis can we determine *how much* more value the actual person has? The reasons for saying that the actual person has more value, we must remember, are that (1) in addition to the value of the mere existence of the person we must add the value of the particular goals the person has set for herself and the value of avoiding the waste of all the effort and struggle which has gone into the achievement of the person's goals and the actualization of her consciousness; and (2) there is the deontic-fairness value in terms of which any actually existing person's life ought to be protected, insofar as possible and reasonable (i.e., as correctly balanced against other values), by the society in which she lives. It might be argued that the correct balance between the values at issue in argument (1) can be resolved in non-normative terms. Obviously, a person would prefer, all else being equal, to exist and to set and accomplish some goals than to exist while setting and accomplishing no goals. Perhaps the relative value of mere existence and existence-plus-setting-and-accomplishing-goals, or existence-plus-having-a-life in some sense, can be resolved through phenomenological reflection to reveal how an informed and authentic person would feel toward these values. But (2) cannot be resolved on any such basis, and thus constitutes a genuinely normative conflict. That is, the relative value of society's deontic obligation to protect the lives and well-being of actual people as compared with its deontic obligation to increase the number of future people who can be brought into being (if indeed there is any such obligation) is a normative question.

If the question of the correct balance between use value maximization and deontic fairness had been settled at this point, then it would be possible in principle to determine the correct balance between the value of the existence and welfare of present people and the value of facilitating the existence of future people; this could be done, in fact, without making any further *normative* assumptions. And if the comparative value of actual and possible people's existence and well-being had been settled, then the conflict within use-value utilitarianism could also be given a mathematical resolution, again without making any further normative assumptions. (For we saw at the end of the last section that the essential *normative* uncertainty there hinged on the question of the relative importance of the intrinsic value of each additional future possible person.)

The absolutely crucial normative conflict, therefore, is *par excellence* the conflict between use value maximization and deontic fairness. If this one conflict would be resolved, then it would be possible, at least in principle, to resolve all the others without making any additional normative assumptions. Therefore, let's now consider this final and most crucial type of conflict, to see how definitive a resolution is likely to be applicable to it.

4. *The Mathematical Commensurability of the Values of Use Value Maximization and Deontic Fairness*

We should begin by noticing that the principle of deontic fairness does not require, even prima facie, that the society should promote equality of distribution by taking goods away from some when doing so will fail to contribute to anyone's well-being or self-actualization. Increased equality, of course, even if it is achieved by taking certain goods away from the privileged without giving anything tangible to the underprivileged, may often have a certain tendency to increase people's well-being and self-actualization. For example, Alexander the Great's voluntary insistence on suffering any hardships that his men had to endure might superficially appear to be a decision to deprive one person (himself) without thereby increasing anyone else's well-being. But, on closer inspection, one realizes that the increased empathy thus established between Alexander and his men did benefit both himself and them, both by more fully actualizing their potential for certain meaningful states of consciousness, and by facilitating the achievement of goals through the promotion of group solidarity and mutual respect.

Nonetheless, in principle it remains true that, if there are any instances in which subtracting from the well-being of the advantaged does not thereby benefit the disadvantaged in any way, then the principle of deontic fairness does not require that this be done. For example, deontic fairness does not require that those who are fully conscious be reduced to a state of virtual unconsciousness so that they will be exactly equal in consciousness to those who suffer from degenerative brain diseases. Nor does it require that those who are not severely arthritic should be forced to suffer an amount of pain equal to that suffered by severe arthritics. Deontic fairness requires only that the society *distribute* those goods whose distribution is within its power as equally as possible, not that it destroy some goods in order to make the well-off more similar to the bad-off. For the society has an equally binding quasi-contractual obligation toward each individual in which the society assumes the responsibility to promote that individual's well-being. And, to the extent that the actually-existing society does not approximate the conditions of a legitimate social contract, it ought to rearrange things (including the possession of goods) in such a way as to approximate those conditions as closely as possible. But this duty does not imply taking goods from the well-off if doing so will not promote the well-being of the bad-off. (Here again, 'well-off' means not only or even primarily *materially* well-off, but rather well-off in the total condition of one's conscious life, and 'goods' are defined as any conditions which tend to promote well-being in the broadest possible sense, which includes opportunities for self-actualization.) Deontic fairness thus may require that goods be taken from the well-off in order to benefit the bad-off, but not that goods be taken from the well-off and simply destroyed merely in order to make them more equal to the bad-off. This, in fact, should *not* be done, not so much because such a policy would be deontically unfair, but because it would reduce the total amount of use value.

There are many instances in which the rights which result from the principle of deontic fairness conflict with each other. One person's right to freedom of speech---say, when she wishes to shout 'fire' in a crowded theatre---conflicts with other people's right not to be killed as a result of this person's negligent behavior, etc. Genuinely deontic rights also sometimes conflict with the general welfare, as is now well established, even if the general welfare is measured in terms of use value rather than exchange value. To show that such conflicts can exist, suppose there is some good whose use value does not depend on the amount of other goods the user already possesses. There may not be any such goods, but let's suppose hypothetically that there are, just in order to understand in a very simple case what the resulting value relationships would be. Suppose, for example, that classical music concerts have the same use value for everyone because, although the well-to-do need additional benefits less than do the poor, this fact is exactly counterbalanced by the fact that the well-to-do have more cultivated tastes in classical music than the poor, on the average, and therefore can use the classical music more effectively (i.e., they benefit more from it, in terms of use value, than would poor people). And suppose further that there is no way anyone is going to deter the musicians from playing classical music; they are absolutely resolved to do so. Thus there is no hope of re-channeling resources away from the creation of classical music and toward the creation of some good that would have greater use value for the poor (such as televised football games). Suppose, in sum, that, all things considered, a well-to-do person on average will derive the same *use* value from attending the concert as would a poor person. And, finally, suppose that attending a first concert so cultivates one's tastes that one values the second concert even more, so that, unlike in the earlier example involving a family's second or third car, attending a second concert has exactly the same use-value as attending the first, once the effect of the diminishing use value of additional goods is compensated for in this way. How, then, should the tickets be distributed? Does it make a difference whether Smith gets tickets for two concerts while Jones gets tickets to none, or whether both Jones and Smith get one ticket each?

It would seem that a use-value utilitarian would have no grounds for preferring the one distribution over the other, since not only the amount of exchange value, but also the amount of use value promoted by the two options is exactly the same. On the other hand, a theorist who intrinsically values fair distribution regardless of the total amount of individual use value promoted might well say that Smith and Jones ought to get one ticket each. Her reasoning, given that the use values involved are not a relevant variable, must inevitably run something like this: If the use values of the tickets are the same for Smith and Jones, then Jones ought to have the tickets to the same extent that Smith ought to have them. If Jones and Smith constitute a society which approximates the conditions of a social contract as defined above, then the society ought to promote value for Jones to the same extent that it ought to promote value for Smith, as we saw in the last chapter. This means that, to the extent that Smith and Jones constitute a society, they have rights and duties toward each other such that each is obligated to do what she ought to do in relation to the other as well as in relation to herself; i.e., each is obligated to try to see to it that value is promoted in relation to the other, and if anyone does not do what she is obligated to do in this respect, the society ought to encourage or force than to do so, all else being equal. Thus the society ought to encourage or force people to act in such ways that, all else being equal, and to the extent that individuals constitute societies with each other, value will be optimized to the same extent for all individuals, and thus goods will be distributed equally.

Since the concept of 'social contract' is important here, it requires a little further clarification. We have spoken so far as though the existence of a social contract (or the approximation to one) implied only the prima facie value of absolutely equal distribution. While it is true that the existence of a social contract has this implication, it also implies another prima facie value which conflicts with this one. The reason for this implication stems from consideration of a type of problem posed by Nozick[18] for which a conractualist resolution is required. Suppose we distribute goods in the most fair way, whereupon one of the people, because of a (predetermined, we now know) defect in her character, throws her goods into the sea and then demands more. We again redistribute the goods so that she has a fair share, and again she throws hers into the sea and again demands more. At this point, we realize that, if we continue redistributing the goods in this way, there will soon be a negligible amount left to distribute.

We might attempt a communitarian solution to this problem: I.e., we might devise more effective ways to organize the society in such ways that few people with defective character are produced. But, although we try diligently and do achieve some modest success in this endeavor, there still end up being a few individuals who continue throwing away their goods and then demanding more.

We cannot solve the problem as Nozick does, by simply denying that we ought to continue trying to provide the person with the goods she needs. In the first place, Nozick's assertion here calls for a direct moral intuition, and we saw in Chapter One that intuitionism is not an adequate basis for ethical beliefs. In the second place, we saw in Chapter Four that, because of determinism, it would be incorrect to say that a morally bad person is any less *deserving* of goods than anyone else.

We might then attempt to solve the problem by saying that, if the person is not *using* the goods we give her, then we ought not to give her any more, since the principle of distribution according to use value requires that we allot goods to those who have the most use for them. But suppose that, instead of throwing all her goods into the sea, she merely uses them so ineffectually that, say, 90% of them go to waste. For example, suppose she spends her money on outlandishly expensive foods, so that she never has quite enough to be adequately nourished.

There is no easy Rawlsian solution to this problem either. In Rawlsian terms, the person who throws away her goods becomes at that point the least advantaged person in the society. Thus nothing ought to be done at that point unless it benefits her to some extent. Of course, a true Rawlsian would have to consider fairness at the *macro* level, i.e., calculating the disadvantages to all other members of the society of such a continually wasteful redistribution. But if 'maximin' is the principle used, it seems that the goods should continue to be redistributed, and if 'maximin' is not the rule used, then Rawls' system becomes a use-value utilitarianism which is prepared to benefit the majority at the expense of the misguided wastrel's (undeserved, because of determinism) suffering.

It seems that any coherent resolution for this kind of problem must make room for the idea that we sometimes ought to *force* a person to do her duty---'we' meaning any society of which the person is a part. Clearly, there are instances in which a person's doing her duty would also promote value. Thus we ought to do so. Furthermore, we have a right to do so because the society of which we are members ought not to prevent us from doing so.

It is at this point that a concept of the 'social contract' must come into play. Sometimes it is necessary to force people to do their duty by offering them negative and positive incentives to do so. A social contract is, among other things, a system according to which the society forces someone to do his duty. Such a system does not require, per se, that the person has committed herself to respect the terms of the contract, either tacitly or otherwise. However, I think anyone will admit that it would be better, all else being equal, if the person has as much choice with respect to the terms of the contract as possible. So, all else being equal, the society ought to offer her as much choice as possible in this respect. Thus a contract which a person, if well-informed and authentic, would *choose* to enter, if she were given a choice, is a better contract than one which such a person, if given a choice, would not choose to enter. Now if a society imposes on people a contract which is worse than the best possible contract it could impose on them, such a society is acting contrary to the way it ought to act (for it ought to use the best possible contract that can be devised). In this sense, a contract which falls short of the best contract that *could* have been chosen, under the circumstances, is just to this extent an 'illegitimate' social contract, and ought to be converted to the best possible contract which that society could choose under those circumstances. But it is not necessary that every actual individual in the society would have preferred just this specific contract over any other possible one in order for it to be the case that the contract ought to be enforced. Different people, in fact, might have preferred somewhat different risk principles in the original position. A contract, if it is to be legitimate, must of course have given each person's preferences equal weight and must have been preferable in each person's opinion to the lack of any contract; in addition, it should achieve the best possible balance between deontic fairness and the general welfare. But the justification for enforcing the terms of such a contract has nothing to do with the far-fetched hypothesis that individuals have 'tacitly agreed' to obey it, nor even that they *would have* agreed to just that exact contract under ideal conditions. The justification for enforcing the terms of the contract is that it is better to enforce them than not to enforce them, and that it is better to enforce the terms of this contract than any other available contract. 'Best', of course, does not mean 'productive of the maximum sum total of individual values,' but rather the correct or proper balance between this value and the value of fairness, which has as yet to be resolved. It is also important to remember, when choosing whether to enforce a contract, and which contract to enforce, that (as in all other cases) use value rather than exchange value should be the standard of measurement for individual value.

If there is to be any concept of a social contract, without untenably justifying its enforcement with reference to 'tacit agreements' which in reality were never consented to, then it must be admitted that, in some instances, the enforcement of the contract is good only because the general good is sometimes more important than whether a particular person is treated fairly in the deontic sense. Given determinism, it is less fair to punish a person for having a morally evil character or doing morally evil things than it would be not to punish the person. After all, she does not *deserve* punishment, and to administer punishment is to distribute goods unequally. Moreover, anyone who has universal empathy and realizes that determinism is true must have utmost sympathy and compassion for someone who has the misfortune to have a morally evil character and consequently be punished by her society. Such a person often seems to qualify as the 'least advantaged' member of society in the Rawlsian sense. But this does not mean that the entire general welfare ought to be sacrificed for the sake of that person's welfare. On the other hand, fairness also has value and must not be completely sacrificed to the general welfare. The correct social contract must achieve the correct balance between fairness in the deontic sense and the general welfare in the use-value-utilitarian sense. The problem of establishing this correct balance is what we must now consider.

Given that there are genuine conflicts between deontic fairness and use-value maximization, yet both have value, we need a way to determine the proper balance between the two in various instances. And, in order to make such comparisons, we need a way to measure the relative importance of any given instance of fairness, as compared with other instances of fairness and as compared with instances of the importance of promoting use value.

If deontic fairness is ever to be sacrificed for the sake of some instance of the general welfare (i.e., maximization of use value), yet is not *always* to be sacrificed whenever it conflicts with the general welfare, it follows that it would make more sense to sacrifice a given amount of it for the sake of that which has *more* use value than for the sake of that which has *less* use value. Since the use value of a given good is proportional to its degree of necessity, it also follows that, if deontic fairness is ever to be sacrificed at all, it makes more sense to sacrifice it for the sake of necessary goods than for the sake of non-necessary goods. And by the same reasoning, the *extent* to which the creation of additional goods is important enough to outweigh the importance of deontic fairness is proportional to the *extent* to which the goods being created are *necessary* goods. For example, it might make a good deal of sense to sacrifice some deontic fairness in the distribution of computer games in order to facilitate the production of enough cars so that each family can have a car. It would make much less sense to sacrifice deontic fairness in the distribution of cars (in a society whose transportation is dependent on cars) in order to facilitate the production of enough computer games so that each family can have a computer game. There can be trivial and important instances of deontic fairness just as there can be large and small amounts of use-value-utilitarian goods. To sacrifice a huge amount of use-value-utilitarian goods for the sake of a trivial instance of deontic fairness can just as well be an untenable way to resolve the conflict as to sacrifice an important instance of deontic fairness for the sake of a small amount of use-value-utilitarian goods.

The quantification of deontic fairness can therefore in principle be accomplished in the following way: Deontic fairness in the distribution of more necessary goods must always be considered more important than deontic fairness in the distribution of less necessary goods. I.e., the value of a given instance of deontic fairness is proportional to the quantity of use-value to be distributed in the instance in question. Deontic fairness in the distribution of cars is more important (i.e., has more 'aggregate value') than deontic fairness in the distribution of computer games. We thus have an unambiguous way to compare the value of different instances of fairness with each other.

We must remember, of course, that not only the comparative importance of the type of unfairness involved must be considered, but also the *amount* of unfairness of that particular type that is involved. I.e., not only is fairness in the distribution of cars more important than fairness in the distribution of computer games, but a great deal of unfairness in the distribution of cars is worse than a slight unfairness in the distribution of cars. The question then arises whether a great deal of unfairness in the distribution of computer games might be more important than a slight unfairness in the distribution of cars. It seems that the importance of any instance of distributive fairness depends on both the average amount of use value affected for each person involved and the degree of inequality that would be engendered by each available option. And, just as there was a conflict within use-value utilitarianism, we are now finding that it is difficult to resolve this conflict within the theory of deontic fairness. The negative value of any given unfair policy is proportional to both the *amount of inequality* it engenders (as measured by the proportion of goods consequently enjoyed by those who benefit and by those who are harmed by the policy) *and* the degree of necessity of the goods in question. But which of these two factors weighs more heavily in the determination, and how much more heavily, has as yet to be resolved.

In principle, however, this question can be resolved phenomenologically. We simply ask ourselves: Would I prefer to be in the position to be victimized by *this* instance of unfairness, or *that* one? For example, would I prefer to be victimized by *gross* unfairness in the distribution of computer games, or by *mild* unfairness in the distribution of cars (in a society in which cars are necessary for transportation)? Mathematically expressed, *how* severe an unfairness in the distribution of computer games would I be willing to risk suffering in order to avoid that same risk of victimization by a given amount of unfairness in the distribution of cars? The answer to this question would be mathematically unique in theory (though not easily resolved in practice) except for the individual differences between people as regards their perception of the degree of 'necessity' of cars and computer games. But we are assuming that the degree of necessity of the goods in question is known in advance and accounted for in the way the problem is posed to begin with. So, in principle, the solution is available to an authentic and well-informed phenomenological reflection, and any remaining disagreement is thus factual (i.e., pertains only to what the results of the reflection in fact *are*) rather than normative.

In principle, then, we have a way to compare the importance of different instances of fairness or unfairness, designating some as relatively trivial compared with others. However, the problem that remains is that we need a way to compare the importance of a certain 'amount' of unfairness relative to a certain 'amount' of general welfare (as measured in use value). But these two scales of measurement have not yet been made commensurable with each other. The 'amount' of value that one instance of fairness has is meaningful only *compared with* the 'amount' of value that another instance of fairness has.

One might be tempted to think at first that this conflict also can be resolved phenomenologically. I simply ask myself how much of a risk I would be willing to assume of being victimized by a given unfair policy in exchange for the chance of gain which the same policy would offer. But at this point we are faced with many (if not all) of the same problems which Rawls faces with his original position argument. The worst of the problems is that some people are more daring risk-takers than others, so the decision principle that would be chosen by the person in the original position just depends on her emotional constitution. And, if we insist that the person's emotional constitution be part of the information that is unavailable within the 'veil of ignorance,' then, as we have seen, the person simply *would not know* how much of a risk she would be willing to take, and therefore would not know which decision principle to choose.

Although I can see no unique and definitive resolution for this conflict (perhaps someone will correct me on this point by discovering one), it would seem that there can be a solution that is more coherent than any other. Given what has been said so far, we should be able to assess how much risk *people on the average* in a given society would choose to assume if completely authentic, well-informed, and not biased by bad habits which they should not have cultivated in the first place. The way to determine this quantity is to imagine what would happen if each actual person in the society were to perform a complete phenomenological reduction, thus becoming completely authentic, in addition to having the complete knowledge of natural and social science described by Rawls for the person in the original position, and lacking knowledge of her particular position in the society, and having completed the ideal Aristotelian training school so that she is as uninfluenced as possible by bad habits. After all these actual people have completed this 'reduction', we then determine how much risk each would be willing to assume in exchange for a given chance of attaining a given quantity of use value, and arithmetically average the results. The result of this arithmetic average, applied to all questions of conflict between use value maximization and deontic fairness, will come as close as any calculation can to establishing the answer to the question: How unimportant must a given instance of fairness be in order for a person to be willing to incur the risk of victimization by it in exchange for her probable share of a given amount of general welfare? The solution just described, in effect, is to interpret 'a person' to mean the average actual person, unbiased by the knowledge of her particular station in life, phenomenologically reduced, with ideal knowledge of the sciences and devoid of bad habits that would tend to distort her judgment.

The reason this solution seems to be the most coherent one available at this point is as follows. If there were some reason to believe that the judgment of the more *daring* risk-taker, under authentic and well-informed conditions, is more correct than that of the less daring one, then we would skew the relative importance of possible benefit and possible harm accordingly, and vice versa. But, given that there is no rational reason to prefer the attitude toward risk of one authentic and well-informed risk taker over another, it follows that we should weight them all equally, so as to devise a policy which comes closer than any other policy possibly could to approximating the degree of risk preferred by each individual. And this procedure is tantamount to arithmetically averaging them all. In this way, we come as close as is mathematically possible to optimizing the balance between deontic fairness and use value maximization for all actual individuals in the society.

Let's consider a concrete example of the way such a balance between deontic fairness and use value maximization might work out in practice. It was often supposed that Ronald Reagan took positions on various issues which presupposed ethical-theoretical stances which contradicted each other. For instance, in 1982, certain types of social security benefits such as Social Supplemental Income (SSI) were illegally terminated for many eligible recipients, but were finally reinstated as the result of work by the Legal Services Corporation, the federally-funded network of Legal Aid Societies in the U.S. which handle such cases for people who are too poor to hire their own attorneys.[19] Many empirical studies, including one conducted by the U.S. Office of Management and Budget, have shown overwhelmingly that private legal firms cannot be relied upon to take such cases; thus the Legal Services Corporation's work is vital if the poor are to have equal protection of the law.[20] Yet in 1982 the Reagan administration, presumably with his knowledge and approval, persuaded Congress to approve a budget which cut the Legal Services Corporation by 25%---for no other official reason than to save money for the government ---and immediately began working to persuade Congress to eliminate the Legal Services Corporation altogether, despite the well-established fact that without its work many poor people would not have access to equal protection, especially in certain important types of cases where private attorneys could not profit by taking the cases on a percentage-fee basis. Apparently, in this example, Reagan believed that maximizing the general welfare, which he believed could be done by saving the money involved, sometimes should take priority over deontic fairness.

Yet in other cases, Reagan championed fairness at any cost to the general welfare. For example, the World Health Organization in 1981 conducted a study which showed that one million infant lives could be saved per year in the third world if certain American food companies could be stopped from inducing mothers in these countries to unwisely use infant formulas produced by those companies.[21] The use of the formulas, which were often mixed with impure drinking water or used in insufficient quantities because of cash flow problems, resulted in the death of infants either through disease from the impure water or from malnutrition. All countries represented in the U.N. then voted for a resolution to attempt to stop the marketing of the formulas in these countries---all, that is, except for the U.S. When questioned as to why the U.S. government supported the food companies as against the million lives per year, Reagan did not question the validity of the W.H.O. study, but insisted that to interfere would be an unfair infringement of the right of free trade. Clearly, in this case, Reagan relies on the assumption that fairness does take priority over a quite substantial amount of general welfare.

The interesting point for our purposes, however, is that those who say that Reagan assumes mutually contradictory ethical-theoretical stances on these two issues, yet also (like the present author) want to disagree with Reagan's positions on both issues, must answer the following question: Are *we* not therefore contradicting ourselves as well? If we say that the general welfare should take priority over fairness in the infant formula case, can we consistently deny that the general welfare should take priority over fairness in the case of the Legal Services Corporation?

But the answer is that, no, we are not contradicting ourselves. For what we are asserting is that fairness should take priority over the general welfare in instances where the amount of difference our decision will make to the general welfare involves small amounts of relatively non-necessary goods, whereas the fairness issue involved concerns the distribution or redistribution of fairly large amounts of extremely necessary goods. By contrast, in the infant formula situation, the amount of general welfare, measured in use value, is huge, because it affects the most necessary possible goods for millions of people, whereas in this case the instance of fairness involved is very trivial because it involves the distribution or redistribution of only small amounts of extremely non-necessary goods. And the average well-informed and authentic subject will obviously assess the relative importance of these instances of fairness and general welfare as falling within the same priority ranking that we have just given them, regardless of her attitude toward risk, assuming that she does not subscribe to some incorrect moral theory according to the foregoing analyses. There will, of course, be other examples in which the amounts and degree of necessity of the relevant goods are much closer, and therefore in which one's attitude toward risk will be crucial in determining whether one decides in favor of fairness (i.e., genuinely deontic fairness) or the general welfare (i.e., use-value maximization). It is in these cases that the answer is not so definitive, and requires us to average people's attitudes toward risk in order to arrive at the solution which, based on the best available evidence, is most likely to be most nearly correct. It is therefore merely a coherent solution, but is the most coherent solution available. For this reason, it is more likely to be correct than any other available solution and, what is perhaps more important, it is likely to be the least-wrong of all available solutions if it is wrong. By relying on it, we therefore maximize our chances of promoting as much value and as little disvalue as possible, where 'value' includes both deontic fairness and use-value maximization.

5. *The Theoretical Incompleteness of the System*

The above reasoning is incomplete in a way that is very simple but at the same time very important. While we may believe that we have now established definitively that both use value maximization and deontic fairness have intrinsic value, there is nothing about that reasoning that would imply that these two values, under the conceptualizations of them used in our arguments here, are necessarily the *only* intrinsic values. It is therefore possible that moral philosophers will in the future demonstrate the truth of other value beliefs which neither fit into the above categories, nor are excluded by means of conflict either with our principles or with the factual considerations we have discussed.

Several points therefore need to be made about all such future moral discoveries. First, they must not *contradict* the two basic principles we have demonstrated here. For a true statement cannot contradict another true statement. Secondly, they must not contradict the factual considerations we have discussed (unless someone can show that we have gotten the facts wrong). Third, they must be at least minimally supportable by means of some sort of evidence or argument; that is, they must be somewhat more likely to be true than their own contradictories.

If additional moral discoveries can meet these conditions, then some of them may well affect our assessment of the correct balance between use value maximization and deontic fairness. In fact, some such discoveries may consist precisely of new arguments pertaining to the correct decision about the relative importance of use value maximization and deontic fairness, either in general or as applied to specific types of situations. If so, then the above resolution of this conflict would have to be altered accordingly. Until such arguments are discovered, however, we ought to continue using the most coherent balance currently available to us, since it is the one that is most likely to be correct. And, of course, if other possible balances also have some degree of probability of being correct, then we should also take them into consideration, but only to the extent that the strength of their probability requires our doing so (see Chapter Two, section 2(b)).

If some future moral discovery is demonstrated to be absolutely certain, then the demands of such a moral principle must be given equal weight with the principles we have so far discovered. On the other hand, if (as seems at this point much more likely) future moral discoveries are only demonstrated to be more likely to be true than rival positions, and therefore to have in each case only a certain probability of being true, then the relative weight of the demands of such principles, as we have seen, must be considered proportional to the probability of their truth.

There is, however, still another impediment to the completeness of the principles we have discussed which can and must be resolved if these principles are to be applicable to any individual's personal decision-making. We have spoken so far about the way value decisions ought to be made at the level of whole societies. However, societies consist of constellations of individuals, and social decisions result ultimately from the decisions of individuals. But the system of ethics as we have understood it so far is difficult to apply at the level of individual decision-making, because it does not specify how an individual is to decide *to what extent* she is obligated to promote value, and to what extent she *ought* to promote value, as opposed to simply doing what she wants to do, at any given moment. This problem is so serious that, when I listed the most important questions with which any metaethical inquiry must concern itself, this problem was listed as the fourth and last of those general questions. It is now time to address this problem.

6. *Quantitative Questions About Duties and Oughts*

At the beginning of Chapter Five, we divided the important fundamental questions of ethics into four broad types. The fourth type, which we have still to consider, are the quantitative questions about duties and oughts:

(a) To what extent ought people to channel their resources into promoting value? (b) To what extent are people *obligated* to channel their resources into promoting value? (c) To what extent ought one, and to what extent is one obligated, to give non-egoistic (in the narrow sense) values priority over egoistic ones?

The distinction between sub-questions (a) and (b) hinges on the distinction between mere oughts and obligatory oughts, which has already been clarified. I am obligated to do what I ought to do in relation to others in any given respect to the extent that some 'society' (in the broad sense defined above) ought to require me either formally or informally to do what I ought in this respect, i.e., to the extent that the society ought to protect others' rights to have me behave in this way. (Whether the society *actually does* what it ought is not the issue here; if, all things considered, it *ought if possible* to require me to behave in a given way, then I am morally, though not legally, obligated to behave in that way.) The real question about obligation, then, is what the society ought to require me to do. (In the case of each smaller 'society' within the larger society, such as a family or personal relationship, the same question arises, although the requirements that these smaller societies ought to make will usually be informal rather than formal.) And the answer to this question seems to follow from the definitions of the terms. The society, like any other entity, ought by definition to do, insofar as possible, what it is 'aggregately best' for it to do according to the principles outlined above. What is 'aggregately best,' of course, is a certain balance which recognizes the value of both use value maximization and deontic fairness.

The really difficult problem arises when we try to become more specific about what each individual, in fact, ought to do. The increased specificity which is needed revolves around the following type of dilemma: It is always possible that I could promote more value than I am actually promoting. Even the most devoted priest or social worker could promote more value than they actually do. Even if someone devotes her life to the service of the poor and disadvantaged, working many hours of overtime without pay, she *could* still work *even more* overtime. She could spend her paycheck itself on the needs of the poor, relegating herself to true abject poverty and self-denial. The problem this poses is that it would therefore seem vague, indefinite, and overly severe to tell people that they ought to promote 'as much aggregate value as possible.' How much value, then, should any given individual endeavor to promote?

Of course, it hardly seems questionable that each individual *prima facie* ought, as a minimum, to do what is her absolute *duty,* i.e., what the society ought to require of her. But there are two major problems with this answer: (1) There are many other things which one *ought* to do beyond one's mere *duty.* And (2) the rule that one ought to do one's duty is circular; for, in order to determine what is one's duty, i.e., what the society ought to require people to do, we need first to know what the individuals in the society ought to do in relation to each other, and how much of their time and energy they should devote to promoting aggregate value as opposed to simply doing whatever they want to do.

Problem (2) can perhaps be resolved easily enough in theory (though not easily in practice). If the society ought to decide what obligations to impose on people on the basis of which particular combination of obligations will maximize aggregate value on the whole---recognizing personal freedom as one of the things that have value to people---then, as soon as we ascertain this particular combination of obligations, we will have determined how much the society should require of people in the way of moral obligations. (Note that personal freedom here is merely one among many goods, though it does enjoy a certain priority for the reasons explained in Chapter Five, section 3.)

Problem (1) is more difficult, however, not just in practice but in theory as well. How do we know how much I ought to do above and beyond my absolute duty? In particular, how do we know how much of my own egoistic good I ought to sacrifice, where necessary, in order to promote more and more aggregate good? Is it enough to give 10% of my income to charities, or should I give 20%? Is it enough to go out of my way to save a drowning person, or should I volunteer as a full-time lifeguard?

An extra complication to this problem is that, if I am living in a society where most people do not promote much aggregate value beyond their minimal duties, but instead devote their remaining energy to egoistic concerns, then if I go far beyond my mere duty, not only do I put myself at a competitive disadvantage (where competitive situations exist), but it can be argued that I even create a certain amount of injustice: I create a redistributive process in which more goods flow habitually away from myself than toward myself; thus, if I am in an average position as far as my general (not just material) welfare is concerned, I may increase the amount of injustice, all else being equal, by making these supererogatory sacrifices. Moreover, if I am one of a small number of people who habitually volunteer to get certain types of work done, I may be discouraging the lazy ones from volunteering as near to a 'fair' percentage of the time as they otherwise would, since they will perceive that others will do their share for them. Anyone who has served on a college committee at whose meetings attendance is not mandatory knows all too well how this latter dynamic can operate.

Part of the problem posed here seems to arise from the difficulty of answering the following type of question: Assuming that someone has ascertained the correct principles of ethics, and has deduced the specific applications of these principles to real-life situations that occur in the realm of that person's normal, day-to-day business affairs, what sacrifices is it reasonable and fair to expect her to make---in terms of the profits of her business firm, for example---in order to abide by moral principles which her competitors are under no compulsion to follow? Is it reasonable and fair to expect such ethical practice in the context of a situation where the agent knows full well that some of her competitors are not going to follow the same rules; and that this unscrupulousness on their part, subject to no formal sanctions whatever, is going to work tremendously to their advantage?

For example, suppose it has been ascertained as following from the correct ethical system that it is morally wrong for chemical companies to purposely suppress information about the harmful effects of chemicals that this company markets. Is it realistically within the power of company A to reveal the harmfulness of its products, when company B is busily suppressing all information about the harmfulness of *its* produces? Ultimately, to say that A has the power to do this is to say that A has the power to lose its stockholders to company B (whose profits will be slightly higher because of the resulting competitive advantage), and in the extreme case to end up closing its doors. Worse still, the effect of this outcome would by no means be morally desirable, because the field would then be left entirely to unscrupulous company B which, due to the consequent lack of competition, would now have even more opportunities to engage in immoral practices.

Now, of course, there are instances where it is easily within the power of businessmen to act morally. These instances are confined primarily to contexts in which the moral action in question does not affect the profits and prospects of the firm very much. For example, companies sometimes can and do hire the handicapped as a gesture of good will, without being under any external compulsion to do so. In some instances, this may be done even though it involves some slight expense or sacrifice which, let us suppose for the sake of argument, is not altogether compensated by the positive public relations effect of the good deed. Nonetheless, the existence of such isolated good deeds does not erase the fact that in many instances---perhaps in most instances---to expect a business firm voluntarily to act morally when doing so conflicts with its economic interest is to expect that which at best is unreasonable or unfair to expect, and at worst may be impossible.

The problem is no mere academic one, but one which concerns everyone. When trapped between that which I ought but am not obligated to do, and that which is necessary for survival within the system as it exists (and is not likely to change much anytime soon), what am I to do? How can I act morally? The problem is complicated, furthermore, by the fact that individual human beings historically are becoming less and less accountable for the actions of groups such as business firms. The stockholder, while she may be willing to sacrifice a little profit in the interest of investing only in morally reputable firms, is not going to sacrifice much, and in most cases is not even likely to know much about the morality or lack thereof in the firm's practices. Moreover, her alternative is frequently simply to invest in other firms which are equally unscrupulous, since they, too, are competing for profits in the same system. The executive who, for moral or any other reasons, acts contrary to the economic interest of her firm is likely to find herself out of a job. In short, the businessman can well say to the moralist---and apparently with a certain validity---'When everyone else is hitting below the belt, it is absurd for you to ask me unilaterally to refrain from doing so.' This is a bleak picture, but we must remember that an essential step in solving any problem is to understand just how serious the problem is. We cannot solve it by wishing it did not exist.

Part of the solution might to be transfer some carefully selected oughts from the realm of supererogatory to obligatory ones. To see how this could work, consider an analogous example from the realm of sports. Imagine a neighborhood basketball game in which, as is usually the custom, there is no referee. Nonetheless, there are rules to the game, and the players can be observed, for the most part, to follow these rules. Why do they? Because a system of enforcement is operative, commonly called 'street rules.' The principle of street rules is essentially that, if you foul me in a certain way, then at the next opportunity I will foul you in the same way (but perhaps a little more forcefully). Therefore, you had better not foul me. Our next questions, then, is: If street rules work so smoothly, then why does anyone ever use a referee? Why do college basketball teams, for example, never play by street rules?

The answer seems obvious. It is to everyone's advantage, or almost everyone's, for certain very concrete reasons, to use a referee. In the first place, although it may be in the interest of a specific player in a specific situation to commit a foul, it is even more in the interest of this same player as a general rule to have a consistent set of rules which reliably prevents other players from fouling her. And, given a choice, almost any player would prefer to have a referee than not to have one, assuming that the fairness of the referee is more reliable than the fairness which would result from the somewhat more chaotic and unpredictable process of enforcing street rules in the informal way. Fairness is in most people's interest in general, even though it may not be in a particular individual's interest in a particular situation. Of course, there are a few isolated individuals who, given a choice, would prefer street rules over the referee system. There are always those big bullies who feel that they could get away with unreciprocated fouls under street rules because the opponent would be afraid to foul them back. But for this very reason, it is still more in the interest of all the other players to prefer the referee system. Certainly, in such a case, a moral system consisting of the correct balance between deontic fairness and use-value utilitarianism would prescribe that the referee system is preferable.

The point is that, although rules can be enforced by means of the street rules system, it is better to use a referee. The analogue of this point in terms of business practices is that, if the situation is such that most people would like to be more moral than they dare be, for fear that others will not follow the same rules, then what we need is a referee to enforce these rules. In this way, we remove the competitive disadvantage associated with following ethical business practices. In concrete terms, in a competitive economic system, it is often unfair, or at least unrealistic, to expect people to abide by counter-competitive moral principles unless these principles have tangible teeth---unless they are legal rules rather than mere moral rules. Barry Goldwater's dictum that 'You can't legislate morality' has been disproven by the history of the civil rights struggle over the past thirty years. Obviously, there are some cases in which morality not only can but must be legislated. If the moral principle that murder is wrong were not legislated, chaos would reign. The question is to what extent the complexity of urban-industrial and 'post-industrial' economic, political and social life is also an example of the type of situation in which more moral oughts ought to be legislated. The answer seems increasingly, in our contemporary system, to be affirmative. The street rules have broken down.

There are, of course, some objections to the conversion of too many oughts into strict legal duties. Some may object that the increasing regulation of the business life of the community is harmful because it decreases profits in absolute terms, which in turn decreases capital investment. And it is well understood that if capital investment cannot be maintained as a constant percentage of total production, so that economic growth remains exponential, the economic growth cannot keep up with exponential population growth.[22] But this is merely an empirical question which must be taken into account when we decide how much regulation is best on the whole. It does not affect the question as to whether regulation should be increased once we have determined that it is best on the whole to do so. Nor does it concern the 'fairness' of the regulation. 'Fairness' as we have conceived it must be applied at the 'macro' level, whether it is deontic fairness or only use-value utilitarian fairness that is at issue. What seems 'unfair' to businesses at the 'micro' level may be what is best and most fair for everyone, all things considered.

There is, however, a far more serious problem which remains unresolved by such regulatory policies. Such regulation transfers certain mere oughts from the status of mere oughts to the status of obligatory oughts. It does nothing to solve the problem which will always remain to some extent, of what to do about those oughts which *still do* have the status of non-obligatory oughts. And this category will always constitute a significant proportion of the oughts.

What each of us therefore still needs to know is how much of our time and energy to put into oughts which are not required of us as moral duties. It is true by definition, of course, to say that I ought to do as much of what I ought to do as possible. Or, if the question is posed in the form, 'How much ought I to do,' the answer to this question also seems technically to follow from the tautologous answer just given. The answer seems to be that I ought to do as much as I can to promote aggregate value (which, of course, includes promoting value for myself).

But how does such an answer translate into practicable terms for conducting an individual life? Does it really mean that I ought to work overtime as a voluntary social worker until all my time and energy are used up, or to work full time as a volunteer lifeguard?

There are really two problems embedded in this question. The first is that, if everyone devoted all her time and energy to the service of others, then everyone would probably be miserable. The second is that, as mentioned above, if I do what I ought to do while others do not, then I may well be creating injustice and encouraging their moral slackness. These two problems are distinguishable but interrelated.

The solution to the first problem seems deceptively simple. We only need to calculate the percentage of time and energy that it would be best, on the whole, for all individuals to devote to their own enjoyment of life and self-improvement, and the percentage that it would be best for all individuals to devote to promoting the aggregate good. But the reason this solution is not as simple as it deceptively appears is that if, say, we find that it is best on the whole for everyone to devote 10% of her time and energy to non-obligatory oughts, we know very well that many people will fall short of this percentage. So how can it be rational for me to act as if everyone were going to contribute their 10% when I know full well that many will not? On the one hand, more than 10% may be needed from those of us who are conscientious, in order to compensate for the irresponsibility of the slackers. And on the other hand, we may be creating injustice and encouraging further laziness in the slackers if we carry their load for them. Some variation on this problem can be found in or posed against almost any moral system. It usually runs something like this: Can it really be reasonable to act in the way that it would be best for everyone to act if I know that everyone is *not* going to act that way?

The solution to the first problem thus exacerbates the second, which for this reason turns out to be the real crux of the issue: Given that many if not most others are *not* going to do what they ought, should I act just as I would if everyone did; or should I try to do more in order to pick up the slack; or should I do less in an effort to even out the workload?

It is possible in principle (though not easily in practice) to mathematically compute the correct balance among these various prima facie demands. First, the prima facie value of personal freedom requires that an overwhelming number of oughts ought not to be converted into obligations unless some really important purpose is served by doing so. Secondly, in the interest of fairness in the distribution of both positive value and negative value (e.g., non-egoistically-motivated work), I prima facie ought to avoid doing too much more than an equal share of work---not in comparison with what others ought to do, but in comparison with what they actually do. Third, I prima facie ought to do more than the slackers do in order to set an example for them. And, fourth, I prima facie ought to do *considerably* more than an equal share so that more good in effect will actually get done---bearing in mind that it is sometimes more efficient to produce a given amount of good for myself than to produce it for others.

Although such a balance in principle can be translated into mathematical terms, in practice it seems that the best we can do is to estimate. In general terms, I should contribute more to the well-being of those who are less fortunate than I am than they do to me, since this policy will increase both fairness and use value. But I should not contribute *too much* more than do those who are better off than I, since this policy would both promote unfairness in my status vis a vis theirs *and* encourage further slacking on their part by making them feel that there will always be some cheerful volunteer who will do their work for them. However, to the extent that I can afford to do so, I *should* contribute *somewhat* more than do the slackers who are at least as well off as I, as long as there continue to be slackers (i.e., those who contribute less than they ought), both in order to increase the total quantity of use value by helping the least advantaged, and in order to set an example for the slackers. One must, at almost any cost, avoid setting off a 'slacking war' in which each person tries to do less than the next.

Before determining *how much* more I should contribute than the slackers do, however, there is another important factor which must be taken into consideration. I have spoken so far in this section as if contributing to the well-being of others necessarily subtracts from my own well-being. In some instances, of course, there simply is no sugar-coating the fact that it does. But in many instances, the effort that is expended in helping others also promotes value for myself. For we have seen that the altruistic motivation to help others is also 'technically egoistic in the broad sense.' by engaging in moral action, I concretely symbolize and therefore increase my feeling of universal empathy with conscious beings per se. This universal empathy in turn facilitates the symbolization of my own consciousness, which in turn promotes the optimal degree of consciousness and the pattern of conscious progressions ('self-actualization') which, to the extent that I am a conscious being to begin with, I am authentically motivated to seek. Thus it is possible that some individuals may be so fortunately endowed with altruistic motivation, or may have developed it to such an extent through rigorous Aristotelian training programs to which they have been fortunate enough to have been motivated to submit themselves, that they genuinely want to devote their lives to the service of the poor and disadvantaged or to the betterment of mankind in general, insofar as possible. And those who are so motivated should by all means do so, since such activity can do no harm, other than the comparatively slight harm of possibly further encouraging the moral laziness of slackers---a negligible sacrifice in exchange for the amount of good that can be accomplished by a truly motivated moral worker. This encouragement of moral slackness, moreover, will be at least partly compensated for by the contrary effect that the example of a diligent worker may have. Other ways can also be devised to discourage moral slackness. Moreover, since our desires and motives are largely matters of habit, we all ought to continually be engaged in Aristotelian training to cause ourselves to become the kinds of people who are more and more altruistically motivated and thus will naturally want to perform more and more supererogatory oughts. This Aristotelian training, in fact, as we saw in Chapter Three, is really the one thing that is more in our 'self-interest' (in the broad sense) than anything else is.

To engage in an Aristotelian training program is really analogous to re-investing a constant percentage of the productivity of industry into more and more secondary capital---plant equipment, etc., which increases future productivity. If we continue engaging in such training, it will not be long before we are motivated to perform more than the minimum amount of non-obligatory moral action that we determined above everyone ought to perform (though some inevitably will not). Once we have reached this point, we will then *want* to continue participating in the Aristotelian training, and therefore will continually *want* to perform more and more non-obligatory oughts. Thus, beyond the minimum amount of non-obligatory action that everyone ought to perform, we ought also to perform the amount of non-obligatory moral action that, at that particular point in the training course, we *want* to perform, provided that this amount at least exceeds the minimum amount of non-obligatory moral action that everyone ought to perform as computed informally above. This minimum amount of non-obligatory moral action, in turn, exceeds the amount of moral action which it is people's *duty* to perform, i.e., which the society ought to require them to perform.

Conclusion

The Strait of Messina has been a somewhat circuitous one. We saw initially that, if we were to demonstrate the truth of moral statements even with some degree of probability---so that we could answer Scylla's question, 'But why should I believe your proposed moral principles (and thus believe that I should obey them)?'---it was necessary to develop a broad coherence strategy for verification. But we found that such a coherence strategy could not work unless there were at least one value statement on which all minimally coherent normative systems must necessarily agree. We then discovered that there is such a statement, i.e., the statement that consciousness has prima facie value. This statement served as an anchor which could be used through the rest of our treacherous journey to prevent us from being sucked into the whirlpools of emotivism on the one hand, or of groundless intuitionisms on the other. For the Scylla of egoism devours all emotivist vessels, and the combined efforts of this Scylla with the Charybdis of psychological determinism (in the modified sense that we ended up developing) are sufficient to rip apart all intuitionist ones. It was also necessary to show that, while there must be a motivation to be moral, if morality is to avoid being pointless and a waste of time, this motivation to be moral must not dictate *what is* moral. It must only motivate us to find out, and then to do, whatever turns out to be moral. These excursions into moral psychology had to be taken in order to ground an adequate epistemology, because one of the primary ways to eliminate untenable theories within our broad 'comparative coherence' strategy was to show that certain theories are inconsistent with certain factual statements, and psychological statements are factual (i.e., empirical and/or ontological) statements.

As soon as we saw that people are motivated to be moral, yet without this motivation's dictating *what is* moral, it became obvious that there are at least some 'realist' (as opposed to emotivist or cultural-relativist) truths about ethics, and that these truths are of a genuinely normative nature. I.e., they do not simply describe psychological facts, but rather state that certain kinds of things and actions really do have more value than others. For example, a universe containing some conscious beings has more value than a universe containing no conscious beings. We also noticed in the course of the discussion of motivation that the value of consciousness entails certain other values, such as the value of the 'self-actualization' of consciousness in each conscious being (which has intrinsic value) and the value of certain forms of human activity and human relationships which promote this self-actualization (and therefore have extrinsic value). This discovery, however, did not commit us to a form of quasi-utilitarianism which would merely substitute 'self-actualization of the consciousness of conscious beings' in place of the more traditional 'happiness of conscious beings,' because we could not at that point close the question as to whether the maximization of opportunities for self-actualization has greater aggregate value than fairness in the distribution of these opportunities. Retributive concepts of fairness were nonetheless excluded because they conflicted with the type of psychological determinism we had found to be true. Rule-bound concepts were also excluded because those rule-bound concepts which are not essentially distributive in their ultimate foundation lack any epistemological foundation altogether. We sometimes erroneously feel that we 'intuit' that some sort of proportion between 'welfare and well-doing' has *intrinsic* value only because of the overwhelming frequency with which such proportions do in fact have great *extrinsic* value

At this point in the inquiry, the range of possible value systems other than use-value quasi-utilitarianism (i.e., one which would distribute opportunities for self-actualization according to a utilitarian-style calculus, using use value rather than exchange value as the unit of measurement) had been narrowed to include only distributive systems which intrinsically value distributive fairness in addition to intrinsically valuing the use-value maximization of that which is to be distributed. The crucial point at which it became obvious that distributive fairness, in the genuinely deontic sense (as opposed to the merely use-value utilitarian sense), does have such intrinsic value occurred when we defined the notion of a 'society'. A society, in this sense, is simply a relationship between conscious beings, and may exist to greater or lesser extents. But as soon as a society in this sense exists, it is possible to say that the society ought to do certain things in relation to its members, insofar as possible. I.e., it would be good, all things considered, if the society were to do these things, insofar as possible. One of the things that the society ought to do prima facie (though of course not without attenuation by conflicting values) is to distribute goods so as to promote what we called 'genuinely deontic fairness' (i.e., exact equality in the distribution of 'goods' or opportunities for both self-actualization and happiness). Societies also ought to promote use-value maximization and use-value 'fairness'. And they ought, insofar as possible, to require individuals to do certain things.

It is precisely because societies ought if possible to require individuals to do certain things that individuals have moral duties. It is not necessary, in order for an individual to have a moral duty, that the society *does in fact* require such actions---only that it *ought if possible* to require such actions. Sometimes, even though there is no way possible that a society could require people to do a certain thing, it remains true to say that, *if it were* possible for the society to require such action, then it ought to. It might, of course, remain an open question at this point whether one *ought* to do one's 'duty' in this sense, except that, if the society ought to require me to do X (i.e., if it would be good if the society were to require me to do X), then it is also true that I ought to do X (i.e., it would be good if I were to do X).

It is always true, then, that I ought to do my duty. But there are also other things that I ought to do besides my duty, and not all of these are simply supererogatory. We saw in the last section that it is possible to establish quantitatively a minimum amount of value that I ought to promote beyond my duty. (Some people might use the notation 'duty' to denote this concept rather than using this notation to denote the meaning I have assigned to it; but, as shown earlier, this difference in the usage of words does not imply any difference in what is actually being said.) Finally, if some of us *want* not only to go beyond what is *legally* required, and beyond our *duty* in the moral sense, and beyond the *minimal non-obligatory oughts* that apply to us, in order to promote *still more* value, then we should. And if we can succeed in wanting this, then we should want it. But if not, then at least no one can say that there are things that we ought to do that we are not doing as long as we are discharging both our moral duties *and* our minimal non-obligatory oughts. On the other hand, even if we *cannot* succeed in wanting to do our duties and our minimal non-obligatory oughts (because we have been predetermined to be evil people), it remains true that we ought to. Thus, if others have the opportunity to get us to do what we ought to, then they ought to.

NOTES

[1] John Hodson, *The Ethics of Legal Coercion* (Dordrecht: D. Reidel, 1983), does a good job of facing up to this kind of conflict in working out the normative implications of the principle of 'respect for persons,' though he admittedly makes no attempt to *ground* this principle.

[2] R. D. Ellis, "Toward a Reconciliation of Liberalism and Communitarianism," *Journal of Value Inquiry* 25 (1991), 55-64.

[3] Amy Gutman, "Communitarian Critics of Liberalism," *Philosophy and Public Affairs* 15 (1986), 308-22.

[4] Moore, *Principia Ethica*.

[5] E.g., see the reports on the administration of welfare programs in *Journal of Human Services Abstracts*, April 1982.

[6] See Kaye, cited above.

[7] Discussed in Ellis, "Reconciliation of Liberalism and Communitarianism."

[8] It is discussed in the books by May, Gendlin and Ellis cited above, as well as Abraham Maslow, *Motivation and Personality* (New York: Harper and Row, 1954).

[9] Edward Cornish, *The Study of the Future* (Washington: The World Future Society, 1977).

[10] As dramatically demonstrated by such futurists as Dennis Meadows, *The Limits to Growth* (New York: Universe Books, 1974).

[11] George Gamow, *One, Two, Three...Infinity* (New York: Viking, 1979).

[12] Rawls, *A Theory of Justice*.

[13] Kaye, cited above, addresses this point very incisively.

[14] Rawls, *A Theory of Justice*, 35ff.

[15] See James Rachels, *The Elements of Moral Philosophy* (New York: Random House, 1986) and other recent works by Rachels.

[16] MacIntyre, *After Virtue*.

[17] See notes 9 and 10.

[18] Robert Nozick, *Anarchy, State, and Utopia* (New York: Basic Books, 1974).

[19] Carl Wellman, *Welfare Rights* (Totowa, N.J.: Rowman and Littlefield, 1982); David Lyons, "Utility as a Possible Ground of Rights," *Nous* 14 (1980), 17-28; Nan Aron, *Financing Public Interest Advocacy* (Washington: Center for Responsive Governance, 1980).

[20] Marshall Breger, "Legal Aid for the Poor: A Conceptual Analysis," *North Carolina Law Review* 60 (1982), 282-337.

[21] Atlanta Constitution, May 22, 1981, 10-B.

[22] Meadows.

APPENDIX

DEFENSE OF A REVISED VERSION OF VAN INWAGEN'S INCOMPATIBILISM

Consider the way van Inwagen uses the word 'can' throughout his argument for incompatibilism. The argument runs as follows: Suppose a judge, J, at time T, will prevent an execution if he raises his hand, but he chooses not to do so. And suppose 'T_0' stands for some instant of time prior to J's birth; 'P_0' is a proposition describing the total state of the universe at T_0; 'L' is a proposition expressing all the laws of physics; and 'P' is the total state of the universe at T. Then, according to van Inwagen,

(1) If determinism is true, then the conjunction of P_0 and L entails P.

(2) It is not possible that J have raised his hand at T and P be true.

(3) If (2) is true, then if J could have raised his hand at T, J could have rendered P false.

(4) If J could have rendered P false, and if the conjunction of P_0 and L entails P, then J could have rendered the conjunction of P_0 and L false.

(5) If J could have rendered the conjunction of P_0 and L false, then J could have rendered L false.

(6) J could not have rendered L false.

(7) Therefore, if determinism is true, J could not have raised his hand at T.[1]

Critics have challenged statement (5) on the grounds that the question whether J *'can'* do something such that, if he did it, P_0 would have to have been false, is the very question at hand, is controversial, and depends on the meaning of the word 'can'.[2] For this reason and others which will soon become obvious, the argument is easier to defend if we slightly alter statement (5) so that it retains van Inwagen's essential meaning, but becomes analytically true:

(5a) If J could have rendered the conjunction of P_0 and L false, then J could have rendered *either* P_0 *or* L false.

To preserve the validity of the overall argument, we must then alter (6) to read:

(6a) J could not have rendered L false, and could not have rendered P_0 false.

232   COHERENCE AND VERIFICATION

The purpose of these changes is only to incorporate the claim that J could not have rendered P_0 false explicitly into the argument.

Now suppose van Inwagen defines 'S can render P false' to mean (paraphrasing his more recent definition,[3] which is a revision of his earlier one)[4]

It is within S's power to arrange his present environment so that this rearrangement, and P, and the previous history of the universe cannot all be true at the same time.

If our (5a) and (6a) are substituted for (5) and (6), and this clarification of van Inwagen's definition is assumed, the argument becomes invulnerable to the objections recently advanced by its critics; for the argument, stated in this way, simply is deductively valid. (5a) is true by definition, given van Inwagen's usage of 'can' and our interpretation of his 'render false' (i.e., S 'can' render P false only if he is able to rearrange his present environment so that this rearrangement, and P, and the previous history of the universe cannot all be true at the same time). If it were within J's power to rearrange his present environment so that this rearrangement, and (P_0 & L), and the previous history of the universe cannot all be true at the same time, then it would be within J's power to rearrange his present environment so that either this rearrangement and P_0 and the previous history of the universe cannot all be true, or so that this arrangement and L and the previous history of the universe cannot all be true. For if we let PHU stand for the previous history of the universe, and RE stand for the proposed rearrangement of the environment, then if J could rearrange things so that

(i) -(RE & [P_0 & L] & PHU)

then he could also rearrange things to match what is entailed by this formula, namely,

(ii) -RE or -P_0 or -L or -PHU

and therefore so that

(iii) -(P_0 & RE & PHU) or -(L & RE & PHU)

By van Inwagen's definition, if J could make (iii) obtain, then he could render either P_0 or L false. Thus (5a) is true by definition. (Later we must consider whether this truth is trivial.)

The first part of (6a) is also true by definition if we use the clarification of van Inwagen's definition. J cannot render L false because it is not within J's power to rearrange his present environment so that this rearrangement, and L, and the previous history of the universe cannot all possibly be true at the same time. If we assume that the previous history of the universe has already occurred and cannot be changed, and that L is true, then to rearrange the present environment so that L and PHU and this rearrangement cannot all be true would be to rearrange the present environment so that this same rearrangement cannot be true. For, given any X, to arrange things so that L and PHU and X cannot all be true, while it is assumed that L and PHU *are* true, would be to arrange things so that X is not true. Thus, to rearrange things so that this rearrangement and L and PHU are not all true would be to rearrange things so that this rearrangement is not true, which is self-contradictory.

In the same way, the second part of (6a) is also true by definition. J cannot render P_0 false because it is not within J's power to rearrange his present environment so that this rearrangement, and P_0, and the previous history of the universe cannot all be true at the same time. If we assume that the previous history of the universe has already occurred and cannot be changed, and that P_0 has already occurred and cannot be changed, then to rearrange the present environment so that P_0 and PHU and this rearrangement cannot all be true would be to rearrange the present environment so that this same rearrangement cannot be true. For, given any X, to arrange things so that P_0 and PHU and X cannot all be true, while it is assumed that P_0 and PHU *are* true, would be to rearrange things so that this rearrangement is not true, which is self-contradictory.

Thus, if we modify van Inwagen's argument in the way indicated, and use his more recent definition of 'S can render P false,' (which packs most of the brunt of his definition into the word 'can', yet without making his argument trivially true, as we have seen), then both (5a) and (6a) are true by definition. So determinism is incompatible with 'J could have raised his hand at T' in the situation van Inwagen describes.

NOTES

[1]Van Inwagen, "The Incompatibility of Free Will and Determinism."

[2]See Chapter Four, note 33.

[3]The one used in *An Essay on Free Will.*

[4]See note 1.

INDEX

Aggregate good 156-7, 174-82
Altruism 92-105
Aristippus 81-2
Authenticity 100-101, 183
Ayer, A. J. 1, 9, 13-17
Bloom, A. 1
Brandt, R. 149
Business ethics 221-4
Categorical imperative 165
Coherence, as criterion for meaning 11-12
Coherence, as verification method 33-58
Communitarianism 183-89
Compatibilism 122-39, 231-3
Conflict resolution 188-195
Contingency management 88-9
Contractualism 137-8, 210-13
Cost-benefit analysis 175
Counterfactuals and compatibilism 125-6
Deconstructionism 154
Deontic fairness 179-81, 214
DePaul, M. 33
Desert 130-5
Determinism Chapter 4
Diminishing marginal utility 175
Duty 65, 158-9
Egoism Chapter 3
Emotivism 10
Empathy 92-105
Epiphenomenalism 95
Fairness 161
Frankena, W. 170
Freedom, political 184
Free will 167-8, Chapter 4
Freud, S. 97-8
Future 205-8
Game theory 190
Gewirth, A. 7, 59-71
Good 155
Hare, R. M. 1
Hartmann, N. 20-23
Hedonism 79-80 and passim
Hempel, C. G. 9, 14-15
Horgan, T. 125-6
Hudson, W. D. 8, 59
Husserl, E. 18-19
Hypothetical imperative 165

Imaginative variation 17
Intentionality 20
Interactionism 95
Intrinsic value 64
Intuitionism 2-3, 21-2, 53-4, 147
Kant, I. 4-5, 7, 164-173
Legal rights 158-9
Logical positivism 1, 5
Mathematicization of value 196-204
Merleau-Ponty, M. 23, 118
Mill, J S. 6, 8, 146
Mind-body problem 93ff.
Moore, G E. 6, 53-4, 146-52
Moral intuition 2-3, 21-2, 53-4, 147
Mothershead, J. 150
Natural attitude 18
Naturalistic fallacy 148
Necessary goods 176, 198-9
Nielsen, K. 7
Nihilism 53
Nowell-Smith 129-30
Nozick, R. 211-12
Obligation 65, 158-9
Open question argument 148
Ostensive definitions 146, 154
Ought, definition of 157
'Ought implies can' 127-30
Perry, R. B. 149
Phenomenological reduction 17, 183
Phenomenology 13, 17
Pierce, C. S. 110
Positive reinforcement 85
Prima facie oughts 161
Prima facie value 56-7, 64
Prudential value 52, 165-6
Putative rightness 48
Rawls, J. 164, 190, 198, 200-204
Reagan, R. 216
Reflective equilibrium 2
Relativism 182
Responsibility 135-8
Retributive systems 163
Rights, moral vs. legal 158-9
Rights, positive ve. negative 158
Ross, W. D. 22
Sayre-McCord, G. 34-58
Scheler, M. 24ff.
Searle, J. 8, 110
Sharp, F. C. 149

Slavery 6
Smart, J. J. C. 3
Society, definition of 158
Supererogatory oughts, 159
Symbolization, need for in
 consciousness 101-2
Talbott, T. 112-13
Urmson, J O. 149
Use value 175-6, 208
Use-value utilitarianism 177-9
Van Inwagen, P. 122-39, 231-3